THE
PECCARIES

THE
PECCARIES

Lyle K. Sowls

The University of Arizona Press
Tucson, Arizona

About the Author

LYLE K. SOWLS became interested in peccaries in the early 1950s when he and some graduate students began a long series of research projects on the collared peccary at the University of Arizona in Tucson. He later traveled to Latin America to see the other two living species of peccaries. Besides his work in Brazil, Guatemala, Peru, and Paraguay, Sowls spent a year in Zimbabwe on a Fulbright Scholarship where he carried out research on bushpigs and warthogs. The author received his doctorate from the University of Wisconsin and conducted waterfowl research in Canada before becoming leader of the Arizona Cooperative Wildlife Research Unit at the University of Arizona. His book, *Prairie Ducks*, received The Wildlife Society's Terrestrial Publication award in 1956. He has been a member of the Pigs and Peccaries Committee of the Species Survival Commission of the International Union for the Conservation of Nature.

THE UNIVERSITY OF ARIZONA PRESS

Copyright © 1984
The Arizona Board of Regents
All Rights Reserved

This book was set in 10/11 Alphatype CRS Uranus
Manufactured in the U.S.A.

Library of Congress Cataloging in Publication Data

Sowls, Lyle K.
    The peccaries.

    Bibliography: p.
    Includes index.
    1. Peccaries.   I. Title.
QL737.U58S68 1984   599.73'4   84-8619

ISBN 0-8165-0822-4

45,231

To

Senhor Olavo Amaral Ferraz

Conservationist, Humanitarian, Planter

Who, when he arrived in western Brazil by horsecart in 1927 to clear land for coffee, left one-third of it in primeval forest for the wildlife. This relict of the original forest is known today as "reserva dos caitetus," the reserve of the peccaries, and is under the protective custody of The Instituto Florestal of the state of São Paulo.

Contents

FIGURES

TABLES

A Word From
the Author

The family Tayassuidae, or peccaries, consists of only three living members, the collared peccary, *Tayassu tajacu* (L.), the white-lipped peccary, *Tayassu pecari* (Link), and the Chacoan peccary, *Catagonus wagneri* (Rusconi). Of the three species, the collared peccary has the largest latitudinal range, surpassed among the New World ungulates only by the white-tailed deer *(Odocoileus virginianus)*; consequently it has come into closer contact with European man than have the other two species.

The white-lipped peccary lives in such dense jungle or remote scrub forest that only the indigenous people who live in the same land have had close contact with it. Consequently, only a few biological studies of this interesting species have been written.

For the Chacoan peccary, the explanation of its obscurity is different. Not until 1972, when Dr. Ralph M. Wetzel of the University of Connecticut found it in Paraguay, was its existence known to European man. Before that it was known only to science as a fossil from Rusconi's (1930) description. It was thought to be extinct.

My own interest in peccaries began in 1955 when two graduate students and I began the first research projects on the collared peccary at the University of Arizona in Tucson. We quickly realized the dangers of handling these animals because of their powerful jaws, long sharp teeth, and quick defense reactions. Thus, we concentrated on developing techniques of handling and studying them. Our second study concerned methods determining their age, followed by research on behavior, populations, reproduction, and nutrition. The results of much of this research is contained in this book or cited here.

My work with the collared peccary in Arizona aroused my interest in finding out about the other two members of this family. To gain

more information on the white-lipped peccary and to understand the
collared peccary in more of its diverse range I traveled to Guatemala,
Brazil, Peru, and Paraguay. In 1975 and 1976 I visited Senhor Olavo
Ferraz's Fazenda Paraiso in the state of São Paulo, Brazil, where I
observed a large herd of white-lipped peccaries at a bait station in a
virgin forest. In 1976 I accompanied Dr. Ralph Wetzel to the Chaco of
northwestern Paraguay to observe firsthand herds of the Chacoan
peccary as well as the white-lipped and collared. In 1977, 1979, and
1981 I revisited the same area to view the Chacoan peccary.

The purpose of this book is to bring together in one place most of
the existing information on the family *Tayassuidae*, scant though some
of it may be. I include descriptions of the three species, where they
live, what they eat, how they die, their behavior, and their interactions
with humans. Although this book deals mostly with the collared peccary, I also present the meager information available on the white-
lipped and Chacoan peccaries. Of all my experiences with peccaries,
the most interesting has been to see all three species and compare
them. Despite similarities in their structure and behavior, in many
subtle ways they are different, with different management and habitat
needs.

ACKNOWLEDGMENTS

This work is a contribution from the Arizona Cooperative Wildlife
Research Unit, a research department in the School of Renewable
Natural Resources of the College of Agriculture of the University of
Arizona in Tucson. It is jointly sponsored by the University of Arizona,
the Arizona Game and Fish Department, the U.S. Fish and Wildlife
Service, and The Wildlife Management Institute.

During the period of this study and the preparation of the manu-
script I received valuable help from many people. I want to thank
especially the students who helped me care for captive animals and
assisted in gathering data on them: W. J. Bigler, J. B. Carrol, Jr., S. J.
Dobrott, T. A. Eddy, R. Hernbrode, H. D. Irby, W. C. Jolly, R. D.
Kirkpatrick, T. B. Knopp, J. P. McCraren, L. P. McCraren, T. J. McMichael,
S. J. Miller, P. S. Minnamon, B. J. Neal, G. L. Richardson, R. W. Rigby, R.
E. Schweinsburg, A. G. Shaw, J. C. Truett, and J. M. Welch.

My thanks go to the following members of the University of
Arizona faculty: W. H. Brown, R. Fossland, V. R. Smith, R. S. Swingle, J.
W. Stull, T. N. Wegner, and F. M. Whiting who assisted in the analyses
of stomach samples for volatile fatty acids and nutrients in peccary
milk. I want to thank A. R. Kemmerer, W. F. McCaughey, M. G. Vavich of
the Agricultural Biochemistry Department for analyzing wild plants
for nutrient contents; my appreciation goes to R. A. Reed, D.V.M., P. P.
Frailey, D.V.M., and S. Kaluzniacki, D.V.M., of the Veterinary Science

Department for performing surgery on captive peccaries (vasectomies and scent gland removal); I want to thank R. B. Chiasson, R. Trautman, J. N. Shively, J. J. Sheldon, T. H. Noon, and R. E. Watts of that department for assisting in the autopsy of animals and diagnosis of cause of death.

I want to thank C. R. Hungerford, P. R. Krausman, and N. S. Smith, wildlife biologists, who helped many ways in gathering and analyzing data. I want to thank W. R. Ferris and M. J. Wolford of the Department of Cellular and Molecular Biology for sectioning tissues and analyzing them as part of the reproduction studies. Thanks are due B. A. Maurer of the Statistical Support Unit for advice on statistical analysis, and Kathy Groschupf for her work in recording the vocalizations of the collared and white-lipped peccaries.

I wish to acknowledge the help of the following employees of the Arizona Game and Fish Department: G. H. Blaser, D. Brown, G. I. Day, W. R. Hernbrode, R. Hernbrode, R. A. Jantzen, C. Jordan, A. Kester, R. J. Kirkpatrick, T. Knipe, R. Olding, L. Packard, R. J. Reed, J. Stair, and V. Supplee. I would like to thank J. J. Pratt, K. Brown, and F. V. Buciarelli of the Ft. Huachuca Wildlife Management staff for assistance in obtaining information on the peccaries killed on the Ft. Huachuca army grounds.

Several people, specialists in certain fields of study, helped me by reading certain chapters of the manuscript. I would like to thank S. M. Zervanos of the Pennsylvania State University Biology Department; R. M. Wetzel of the University of Connecticut Biology Department; E. H. Lindsay, University of Arizona Department of Geosciences; W. H. Brown, University of Arizona Department of Animal Science; and P. Langer, Department Institute of Anatomy and Cytobiology, Justus Liebig University, Germany; T. N. Wegner of the University of Arizona Department of Animal Science; P. R. Krausman of the School of Renewable Natural Resources of the University of Arizona; R. E. Reed of the University of Arizona Animal Pathology Department; G. I. Day and V. Supplee of the Arizona Game and Fish Department; and B. L. Fontana and E. Basso of the University of Arizona Department of Anthropology.

I would like to thank the National Science Foundation and the American Philosophical Society for funding parts of the research with captive animals; the University of Arizona (institutional grants) for funding the chemical analysis of foods and the study of vocalizations in the collared peccary; the National Geographic Society for funding two trips to South America; and Safari International for assisting in funding one trip to South America.

I would like to thank the Zoological Society of London for permission to republish a modified version of a paper entitled "Reproduction in the Collared Peccary," which I first presented to a symposium of the society in 1964 in London. I would also like to acknowledge permission from the International Union for the Conservation of Nature for permission to republish a revised version of my paper entitled "Social

Behavior of the Collared Peccary," presented at the International Symposium on the Behavior of Ungulates and Its Relation to Management held at Calgary, Alberta, Canada in 1971. My thanks go to the National Geographic Society for use of the climatographs for areas occupied by peccaries, to be published in National Geographic Society Research Reports. Thanks also go to the Carnegie Museum of Pittsburgh for the drawings by C. L. Ripper in Part I and to the American Museum of Natural History for use of the drawing by C. R. Knight.

Several artists made drawings for this work. I would like to express my thanks to the following: J. Jokerst, D. McDonnell, H. D. Irby. G. Sowls drew the behavorial sketches that appear in Chapter 8.

My deep appreciation goes to the following people who assisted me either in the field or otherwise on my trips to South America: P. S. Martin of the University of Arizona Department of Geosciences, who furnished information on where to study peccaries in Brazil; P. E. Vanzolini and H. F. A. Camargo of the Museo de Zoología de Universidade de São Paulo; Paulo Nogueira-Neto, Secretário do Meio Ambiente do Brasil, and Olavo Amaral Ferraz for help while I was studying peccaries in Brazil.

I would like to thank R. M. Wetzel of the University of Connecticut, who first invited me to join him for a trip to the Chaco; P. Hazelton, who accompanied me in the Chaco in 1976 and 1977; B. Spicer, who accompanied me in the Chaco in 1979 and 1981. I would also like to thank J. J. Mayer; P. N. Brandt; E. Fidalski; Clotilde Cenoski; P. Meyers; and Sr. Hilario Moreno, Jefe, Departamento de Manejo de Bosques, Parques Nacional, Ministerio de Agricultura y Ganaderia, Government of Paraguay, who obtained necessary permits and arranged for housing in Enciso for us. I wish also to thank the following officials in Sr. Moreno's department for their help: C. Bogado, J. A. Colman, and F. Pintos. Peace Corps volunteers who assisted in the field were R. Anderson and M. Ludlow.

I would like to thank the following people for the use of unpublished material on peccaries: D. Hanson, R. A. Mittermeier, H. A. Reichert, S. Russell, J. Stair, P. E. Vanzolini, and B. Villa R.

Finally I would like to thank the following secretaries for the many hours spent typing drafts of this manuscript: V. Catt, J. Davenport, and B. Hunt.

LYLE K. SOWLS

An Introduction to Peccaries

WHEN ONE TRAVELS WITHIN THE RANGE of the peccaries, one hears references to "wild pigs" or "wild hogs." In Spanish-speaking countries these are "los puercos," "los cerdos," or "los cochinos" while in Portuguese-speaking countries the country people talk of "porcos." German settlers in South America refer to "the schwein." All of these names have been given to peccaries by people who first knew domestic hogs and equated them with peccaries in the New World.

Another group of names, however, was applied to peccaries before people knew European imported livestock. Traveling through the ranges of the three species of peccaries, one hears many different names given to them by indigenous people of the New World, depending on what tribal language is spoken. These names appear in explorers' reports, anthropologists' studies, and naturalists' diaries. The accompanying table lists some names for the collared and white-lipped peccaries. The Chacoan peccary, which has never inhabited a large range, has fewer names. Wetzel (1977, 1981b) gives only four local names for the Chacoan peccary: taguá, paguá, curé-buro and quimilero.

According to Seton (1929), the word *Pecari*, for many years the accepted generic name for the white-lipped peccary and now the accepted species name, is of Brazilian Tupi Indian origin meaning "an animal which makes many paths through the woods." The word *Tayassu*, the generic name for both collared and white-lipped peccaries, is also of Indian origin. Its meaning, according to Cabrera and Yepes (1940), is "the gnawer of roots."

TAXONOMY

The position of peccaries in relation to other animals in the Class Mammalia and Order Artiodactyla (even-toed hoofed mammals) is:

1

Local Names for Peccaries

Local Names	Locality	Authority
	Collared Peccary	
Ots-il-aiye	Arizona (Apache Indian) New Mexico	Keith Basso (personal communication)
Javelina	Arizona, New Mexico, Texas	Personal observation
Caitetu	Brazil	Personal observation
Angro	Brazil (Suya Indians)	Seeger (1981)
Cateto	Brazil	Santos (1945)
Catete	Brazil	Santos (1945)
Taitetu	Brazil	Santos (1945)
Caleira-branca	Brazil	Santos (1945)
Canela-ruiva	Brazil	Santos (1945)
Chancos de monte	Brazil	Walker et al. (1975)
Porco do monte	Brazil	Ihering (1968)
Taicu-canigoara	Brazil (Tupí Indian)	Ihering (1968)
Tayasú coagara	Brazil	De la Tour (1949)
Jabali	Mexico	Leopold (1959)
Candangas	Mexico	De la Tour (1949)
Sainos	Mexico	Restrepo (1960)
Quitam	Mexico (State of Yucatán)	Gaumer (1917)
Coche de monte	Mexico (State of Chiapis)	Alvarez del Toro (1952)
Pecari de collar	Mexico	Gaumer (1917)
Pecari de collar	Guatemala	Ibarra (1959)
Citam	Guatemala (Maya)	Ibarra (1959)
Kenken	Guatemala (Maya)	Ibarra (1959)
Cuyam	Guatemala (Kekchí)	Ibarra (1959)
Cuy	Guatemala (Kekchí)	Ibarra (1959)
Ak	Guatemala (Kekchí)	Ibarra (1959)
Pakki, Yankipi	Amazonian (Jívaro)	Karsten (1935)
Chancho rosillo	Guaycuru	De la Tour (1949)
Patira	The Guayanas	De la Tour (1949)
Tayasú Taitetú	Argentina, Paraguay (Guaraní)	De la Tour (1949)
Saíno	Panama	Mendez (1970)
Bidó	Panama	Mendez (1970)
Bidove	Panama	Mendez (1970)
Pidove	Panama (Chocó)	Mendez (1970)
Gutarra	Panama	Mendez (1970)
Huédar	Panama (Cuna)	Bennett (1962) Mendez (1970)
Shtokó	Panama (Teribe)	Mendez (1970)
Tatabra	N.E. Ecuador	Acosta-Solis (1966)
Lomocuchi	E. Ecuador	Acosta-Solis (1966)

Other names, areas not specified:
Báquira de collar, chácharo, chancho de monte, pecari de coleira, puerco silvaje, quank, quenk, nabelschivein, and navelzwyn (Mendez 1970).

Family: Suidae — pigs or hogs
Family: Tayassuidae — the peccaries
Family: Hippopotamidae — hippopotamuses

In the family Tayassuidae are the three living species of peccaries: the collared peccary, *Tayassu tajacu*; the white-lipped peccary, *Tayassu pecari*; and the Chacoan peccary, *Catagonus wagneri*.

In the past there has been considerable disagreement over the number of subspecies of the collared peccary. Miller and Kellogg (1955) recognized ten separate subspecies in North America, two of

Local Names for Peccaries
(continued)

Local Names	Locality	Authority
Hungana	Ecuador, N. Peru	De la Tour (1949)
Zaino	Colombia	Borrero (1967)
Taitetú	Paraguay	Wetzel and Lovett (1974)
Chácharo	Venezuela	Röhl (1959)
La Báquira de collar	Venezuela	Röhl (1959)
Ondo	Peru (Sharanahua)	Siskind (1973)
White-lipped Peccary		
Angro-Mbedi	Brazil (Suya Indians)	Seeger (1981)
Queixada	Brazil	Santos (1945); personal observation; Ihering (1968)
Queixada-ruiva	Brazil	Santos (1945)
Tiririca	Brazil	Santos (1945)
Taiacu-tiragua	Brazil (Tupí)	Santos (1945)
Taiteteu-taiacu	Brazil (Guaraní)	Santos (1945)
Sáino	Ecuador	Acosta-Solis (1966)
Guangaro	Ecuador	Acosta-Solis (1966)
Senso	Mexico	Alvarez del Toro (1952)
Marina	Mexico	Leopold (1959)
Cehnikax	Mexico (Yucatán)	Gaumer (1917)
Warree	Guatemala	Murie (1935)
Keken	Belize	Handley (1950)
Ukeken il kaax	Guatemala, Belize	Murie (1935)
Cafuche	Colombia	Borrero (1967)
Bidó	Panama (Chocó)	Mendez (1970)
Zagino or Zajino	Panama	Enders (1930)
Yanu	Panama (Cuna)	Bennett (1962)
Puerco de monte	Panama	Mendez (1970)
Vaquira	Paraguay	Seton (1929)
Tayasú tanyika-ti	Argentina and Paraguay (Guaraní)	De la Tour (1949)
Tanicati or Toñihca-tî	Guaraní, Argentina, Paraguay	Hunter (1838); Wetzel and Lovett (1974)
Pecari de quijada blanca	Argentina	De la Tour (1949)
El Coche de monte	Guatemala	Ibarra (1959)
Báquira labiada	Venezuela	Röhl (1959)
Pinque	Venezuela	Röhl (1959)
Unta pákki	Amazonia (Jívaro)	Karsten (1935)
Yawa	Peru (Sharanahua)	Siskind (1973)
Peccary	Carib root	Simpson (1941)
Pinque	Surinam	Mittermeier and Reichert (Personal communication 1981); Husson (1978)

Other names, area not specified:
Pecari labiado, pecari de quijada blanca, tiragua, carbilanco, pátria (De la Tour 1949), chancho de monte, tatabra, báquira cachete blanco (Mendez 1970).

which occur in the United States. Hall (1981) recognized ten separate subspecies of the collared peccary and two separate subspecies for the white-lipped peccary. These divisions primarily are based on size and color, northern animals tending to be lighter and heavier than animals living in the tropics.

Some authors have divided the white-lipped peccary and the collared peccary into separate genera. Woodburne (1968) referred to the collared peccary as *Dicotyles tajacu* (Linnaeus 1758) and the white-lipped as *Tayassu pecari* (Fisher 1814). These were the first names given to them when they were discovered by European man. Hall (1981) follows the system used by Woodburne, dividing the collared and white-lipped peccaries into two separate genera. Walker et al. (1975), however, recognized the two species as one genera — *Tayassu* — and Wetzel (1977) has followed suit. This is the system I will follow here. For a complete account of the various names given to these species and the changes, the reader should see Woodburne (1968, 1969) and Wetzel (1977).

DISTRIBUTION

Detailed descriptions of the habitats in which the three species of peccaries live will be described separately. However, since species overlap in many places, distribution of all three species is shown graphically here. Over much of this vast area the collared peccary and the white-lipped peccary exist together in a sympatric relationship. Throughout most parts of the range of the Chacoan peccary, all three species live sympatrically.

ORIGIN

Most writers agree that peccaries originated in the Western Hemisphere (Scott 1913; Simpson 1950, 1980; Woodburne 1968, 1969a, 1969b; Colbert 1980) and that the true pigs, members of the Suidae family, developed in the Eastern Hemisphere. Colbert (1980) says: "The first pigs and peccaries were of early Oligocene age, the former appearing in the Old World, the latter in North America. Throughout their phylogenetic histories these artiodactyls, although clearly related to each other, retained separate ranges in the Old and New Worlds and thus had parallel histories." Fossil peccaries belonging to a different subfamily than the New World peccaries have been recorded from Europe (Pearson 1927), Asia (Colbert 1933), and more recently southern Africa (Hendey 1976).

Compared to the amount of fossil material found in the Western Hemisphere, the isolated examples in the Old World are very few. Hendey (1976) suggests that since no Eurasian peccaries are known from later than the Miocene, it is unlikely that peccaries of America have any direct phyletic relationships to those of the Old World.

Scott (1913) gives North America as the place of origin of the peccaries and says that they are recent immigrants to South America. Simpson (1950) and Colbert (1980) also place the origin of the peccary family in North America along with a large number of other mammals which invaded South America late in the Cenozoic following the rise of the Central American land bridge. Woodburne (1968, 1969a, 1969b) gives evidence that the collared peccary, as a single species, evolved in South America. He says (1969b): "To the best of my knowledge there are no pre-recent records of the collared peccary in North America,

Distribution of the three peccary species

notwithstanding the referral of various Tertiary fossil species of that continent to *Dicotyles*. The data summarized here increase the probability that the lineage leading toward the collared peccary underwent most, if not all, of its evolution in South America."

Since the peccaries first evolved during the Oligocene, many forms have appeared and have become extinct. Some of the extinct species are poorly known because of a scarcity of fossil material. In all the references to extinct peccaries, as would be expected, representatives from the Pleistocene are the most common. Of the early peccaries, more information exists on the genus *Platygonus* than any other form because it was one of the most recent of the now-extinct forms and more fossil material has been found for examination. Other extinct genera also are represented in the material from North America. The remains of extinct peccaries, principally of *Platygonus*, have been found in most parts of the United States and parts of Central and South America (Simpson 1980). Remains of *Platygonus* from Kentucky were reported by Leidy (1889) and Guilday, et al. (1971). Hay (1923) reported remains from Florida, Illinois, Indiana, Maryland, Michigan, New York, Ohio, Pennsylvania, Tennessee, Virginia, West Virginia, and Wisconsin. Webb (1974) also found remains of *Platygonus* in Florida. Colbert (1938) reported the same from California, Oregon, and Nevada. Hibbard (1941) reported remains from Kansas. *Platygonus* remains have been reported from Arizona by Skinner (1942) and Lindsay and

Artist's impression of *Platygonus*, an extinct peccary genus (Courtesy of the American Museum of Natural History, Negative No. 35811, Photograph by Van Altena)

Tessman (1974). Simpson (1949) reported remains from Missouri. Slaughter (1966), and Lundelius (1967) reported *Platygonus* remains from Texas. Ray et al. (1970) reported remains from Pennsylvania. Lewis (1970) found remains of *Platygonus* in Colorado. Eshelman et al. (1972) and Holman (1975) report remains of *Platygonus* from Michigan. The farthest north that a specimen of *Platygonus compressus* has been found has been Yukon Territory, Canada (Beebe 1980). Thus there is abundant evidence that *Platygonus* inhabited a large area of North America.

Restoration of the skeletons of *Platygonus* has shown that it was a considerably larger animal with proportionally longer legs than modern peccaries. Above figure is an artist's conception of what this peccary looked like, while the second compares it with one other primitive, now-extinct peccary *(Mylohyus)* and the three living forms. Radiocarbon dating of remains has given valuable information on the date that this peccary was last alive. Radiocarbon dates of specimens

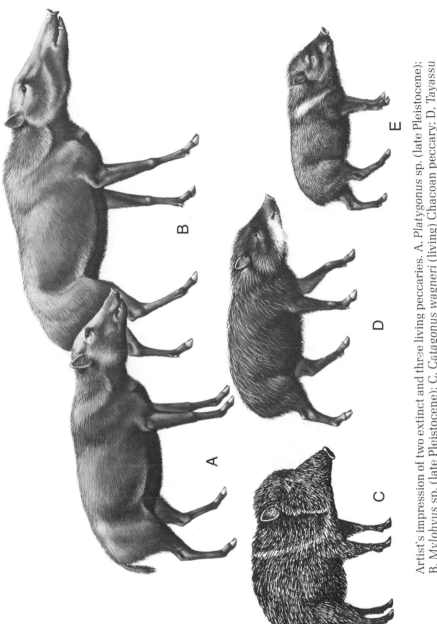

Artist's impression of two extinct and three living peccaries. A. *Platygonus* sp. (late Pleistocene); B, *Mylohyus* sp. (late Pleistocene); C. *Catagonus wagneri* (living) Chacoan peccary; D. *Tayassu pecari* (living) white-lipped peccary; E. *Tayassu tajacu* (living) collared peccary. (Courtesy of the Carnegie Museum, Painting by Charles L. Ripper; Drawing of *Catagonus* by Deboragh McDonnell)

from Pennsylvania were given by Ray et al. (1970). They obtained a minimum date of 11,900 ± 750 years B.P. from rib fragments of a skeleton but warned that their figures should be used with caution. Guilday et al. (1971) gave a radiocarbon date of 12,950 ± 550 years B. P. for *Platygonus* material from Kentucky. In Michigan Eshelman et al. (1972) obtained a radiocarbon date of 10,790 ± 150 years B. P.

Some writers have speculated on the type of climate and vegetation that existed in the Western Hemisphere when *Platygonus* inhabited such a large part of the continents. Webb (1974) believed that *Platygonus* inhabited grasslands and savannas so its presence was taken as an indicator of a drier climate. Martin and Webb (1974) believed that "the extinct peccaries, armadillos, and ground sloths are forms that probably lived under climatic regimes similar to their living relatives."

DIFFERENCES BETWEEN PIGS AND PECCARIES

Confusion between peccaries and pigs is natural. Superficially peccaries and true pigs look alike, and they have many similar habits. To understand the ecological and evolutionary place of the peccaries, we must consider their origin, where they evolved, how they differ from hogs and how they are similar, and what exists today. The morphological and anatomical differences and similarities between peccaries and true pigs are convenient clues to the relationship between the two groups. For the answers to the real relationship, however, we must turn to the paleontologist and the evolutionist. These scientists tell us where the peccaries originated and describe the evolutionary sequence, with its development of new forms, their eventual extinction, and the new species that followed. Luckily, these explorers into the past have found the peccary and its kin interesting subjects. Many times they have had to obtain their impressions of what the early ancestors were like from only tiny bits of jaws or other bones. Consequently, the information is sketchy and there are disagreements on many issues, such as the relationship between the various forms.

The Suidae of the Old World and the Tayassuidae of the Western Hemisphere have developed along similar lines. They have evolved over evolutionary time into animals that appear alike — the disclike snout, the general shape of the head and body, and general features. A comparison of their differences and similarities is given in the table below.

SOME CHARACTERISTICS OF PECCARIES

Early writers noticed some of the peccaries' most unusual characteristics — namely the scent gland and the unusual chambered stomach. All three species have a scent gland on the middle of the back about a quarter of the way from the base of the tail. This gland, in particular, drew the attention of early explorers and naturalists. In 1681 Lionel

**Morphological and Anatomical Comparisons
Between Living Peccaries and Old World Swine**

Character	Peccary	True Swine	Authority
Feet	Median metacarpals and metatarsals fused into cannon bones	Not fused	Alston (1879)
Legs	Ulna and radius co-ossified	Not fused	Scott (1913)
	Has no more than 3 toes on hind foot*	Has 4 toes on hind foot	Walker et al. (1975)
Teeth	All species have 38 teeth; dental formula different from all hogs	Number of teeth either 34 or 44. None has 38 teeth	Walker et al. (1975)
	Upper canines relatively small, straight with vertical direction	Upper canine tusks curved upward and out	Simpson (1946)
	Posterior grinding teeth not enlarged	Posterior grinding teeth much enlarged	Simpson (1946)
	All species have 3 premolars on each side, above and below	Premolars vary between species from 2-4 top and bottom both sides	Walker et al. (1975)
Scent Gland	Present at mid-dorsal line about 6 inches ahead of base of tail	Absent	
Stomach	Complex	Simple	Tyson (1683)
Gall Bladder	No gall bladder	Gall bladder present	Tyson (1683)
Tail	Diminutive, abortive	Usually long	
Liver, hepatic lobules, and large hepatic arteries	Absent	Present	Steiner and Ratcliffe (1968)

*The collared and white-lipped peccaries have only 3 toes on the hind foot. The Chacoan peccary usually has only 2 toes on the hind foot (see text).

Wafer (Restrepo 1960) described the collared peccary in Panama, referring to the gland as a navel:

> The Country has of its own a kind of Hog, which is called *Pecary*, not much unlike a Virginia Hog. 'Tis black, and has little short Legs, yet is pretty nimble. It has one thing very strange that the Navel is not upon the Belly, but the Back: And what is more still, if upon killing a Pecary the Navel be not cut away from the Carcass within 3 or 4 hours after at farthest, 'twill so taint all the flesh, as not only to render it unfit to be eaten, but make it stink insufferably. Else 'twill keep fresh several days, and is very good wholesome Meat, nourishing and well tasted.

Like many other explorers, Wafer incorrectly described the scent gland as a navel. A few early writers correctly described it. Most notable of these was an English medical doctor named Edward Tyson, who in 1683 called it a scent gland and completely described it. He also described most of the other features, including the several-chambered stomach, the skeleton, and the leg bone.

Azara, writing from 1783 to 1796, described both the collared and white-lipped peccaries:

> They have, moreover, upon the back, and above the buttocks, what in this country is called *catinga*, that is, a gland whence flows a liquor like thick serum, which has a disagreeable smell in the first species *(T. pecari)*, although I found it agreeable and like sweet musk in the second *(P. angulatus)*. (Hunter 1838)

In a book published in 1795, Father Ignaz Pfefferkorn described the peccary from Sonora, Mexico:

> In Sonora the musk hog is called *sayno* (seno), or more commonly *javalie* (Jabali). Although not so large as the European wild hog, it is just as savage, and it resembles the European wild animal in all respects except its back. The back of the Sonoran hog is much higher than that of the common wild hog. In the middle of its back is a navel-shaped hole from which is exuded a heavy odor of musk, which spreads throughout the flesh and makes it distasteful. For this reason, almost all the Spaniards have an aversion to it. (Treutlein 1949).

Although not all early writers agreed with Pfefferkorn's appraisal of the palatability of peccary flesh, many noted that the scent tainted the meat. A writer in 1849 commented:

> It is said, and I believe it; that their flesh is good, but not so fat as that of the hog; when killed, however, the glandular orifice between the haunches must be removed, since, if this is not done, the flesh acquires a bad odor and taste. Nevertheless the Indians eat it without this precaution. (Anon 1849).

After experience with all three species, I would award the white-lipped the prize for smelling the strongest. While staying in a land-clearer's camp in the Chaco, I noticed that the German Mennonites sought the Chacoan and collared peccary for camp meat and shunned the more locally abundant white-lipped peccary. When I asked the camp cook why, he answered simply "sie stinken."

The pungent odor serves the animals well, however; all three species live in a world of scent and sound and find their way around and stay together in social groups by means of smell.

Contrary to the usual rule that forest-dwelling animals live in small groups and open-country animals move in large groups, the white-lipped peccary travels through some of the world's thickest forests in groups equal to or surpassing the size of herds of African plains animals. This seems to be accomplished by a highly developed scent system and an excellent repertoire of vocalizations which guides and holds the herd together, protecting them from danger.

RESEARCH, MANAGEMENT, AND CONSERVATION

Of all large game mammals the peccaries have been the last to receive the attention of wildlife biologists. In many places they have been considered "vermin" or pests to livestock owners. While dozens of studies were being done on deer, elk, and antelope, scarely any attention was being given to the peccaries.

In the last thirty years, however, interest in these species has increased markedly. Most of the studies have been on the collared peccary in Arizona, Texas, and New Mexico. The first of these to appear was the work of Jennings and Harris in 1953, followed by Knipe in 1957. Since then, numerous studies have been completed or are in progress, and publications have appeared on almost all phases of the biology of the collared peccary. The reader will find most of these publications referred to in this book.

Besides the many studies that have been done in the United States, work is being done farther south as well. Hanson's work in Honduras (pers. comm.), Vaughan's work in Costa Rica (pers. comm.), and Castellanos's (1981) work in Venezuela are examples of studies being done in the tropical habitats of the collared peccary.

The white-lipped peccary has not received much attention. Kiltie's (1980, 1981a, 1981b) excellent papers are the only studies that have been available on this animal except for anthropologists' notes on animal use scattered through articles on Indian subsistence. I refer to these studies in Chapter 11.

Inasmuch as the Chacoan peccary was not known to European man until 1972, it is natural that little has been published on this species. All papers published about this animal to date are referred to in Chapter 10.

From a position of "vermin" the collared peccary has moved to respected big game animal status in the three states that it occupies north of Mexico. Careful counts and careful harvests have insured its survival in these places, if habitats can be preserved.

From the U.S.–Mexico boundary to the end of the peccary ranges in Argentina, peccaries are sought year-round for meat and hides. This persistent hunting would not greatly damage the population of these three species if the habitats could be preserved. Everywhere, however, the landscape is giving way to the axe, the plow, the chainsaw, and the bulldozer. The future for these interesting animals does not look bright. Areas of unspoiled habitat need to be set aside to insure their future existence.

Collared
Peccaries

Description, Weights, and Measurements

1

THE COLLARED PECCARY IS A SMALL, WILD, piglike animal with a large head in comparison to the rest of its body. In general appearance, the size and conformation of the collared peccary resembles a small domestic hog of one of the more rangy, thin breeds. The legs are fine and slender for an animal of its size and height. The tail is abortive, measuring only about one-half inch in length. Several writers have given descriptions, weights, and measurements of peccaries, including Mearns (1907), Ligon (1927), Seton (1929), Baily (1931), Jennings and Harris (1953), Knipe (1957), Neal (1959), Leopold (1959), and Low (1970). These records are primarily for animals taken in Texas, New Mexico, and Arizona, although a few figures are from Mexico.

Early explorers and writers, upon encountering the collared peccary, naturally compared it to domestic hogs and its European and Asian ancestors. It is for this reason that special reference in these writings was often made to two of the most striking anatomical differences between the peccary and the common pig: the presence of a scent gland in the peccary and the absence of the inner dewclaws on the hind feet.

During the early days of biological exploration investigators tended to recognize numerous species and subspecies rather than grouping the local variations as one. The peccaries, like so many other animals, did not escape this treatment. Thus Elliott (1905) recognized three separate species of collared peccaries and separated these into seven separate subspecies to which he applied subspecific names. Mearns (1907) recognized only one species in the United States but separated the species into two subspecies.

PELAGE

The color of the hairs is generally black with whitish annulations. There is an erectile mane which tends to be blacker than the long hairs

15

on the sides and belly. The mane extends from the occiput to the scent gland on the rump. The collar of whitish hair crosses the hind part of the neck and extends obliquely upward and backward from in front of the shoulder to the black mane on the back. Individual hairs have a series of black and white bands of annulations. An adult animal with a winter coat has hairs on the back up to 8 inches in length.

Details on the hair length and the percentage of the hair that is white have been given by Zervanos (1972). When studying seasonal changes, he found that the highest density of hairs per square centimeter was along the mane and that the density decreased in summer because of loss of hairs. Animals appear lighter in color during the summer than in the winter months. Zervanos pointed out that the reason is that the hairs are a lighter color near the body, and when they break off they appear whiter.

DENTITION

Figure 1.1 shows the skull and normal dentition in the adult collared peccary. The other two species have the same dental formula. A normal adult peccary has the following dental formula:

$$\text{Incisors } \frac{2\text{-}2}{3\text{-}3}, \text{ Premolars } \frac{3\text{-}3}{3\text{-}3}, \text{ Canines } \frac{1\text{-}1}{1\text{-}1}, \text{ Molars } \frac{3\text{-}3}{3\text{-}3}.$$

Total number of teeth is 38.

In all our studies we have numbered the teeth as shown in Figure 1.1. The top third incisor and P 1/1 are considered absent. For this reason, the first existing premolars are labeled P 2/2. The two sides of the jaw are symmetrical, and no apparent differences were noted between the eruption of the teeth on the two sides.

As pointed out by Kirkpatrick and Sowls (1962), the collared peccary has all four temporary canine teeth and two lower incisors (I /3 on each side) at birth. No variation from this was noted in 16 young examined during the first few days of life. The first teeth to erupt after the animal is born are the third premolars (P 3/3) which are soon followed by the first lower incisors (I /1) and then the second premolars (P 2/2). These are followed by the fourth premolars (P 4/4) and the top first incisors (I 1/), which are followed closely by the second incisors (I 2/2). This completes the temporary dentition.

The first permanent teeth to erupt are the first molars (M 1/1) at 21 weeks. The canines are then replaced before the second molars (M 2/2) appear between 29 and 41 weeks. The third lower incisor (I /1) is replaced at about the same time that the second molar appears at 37 to 47 weeks. Following the eruption of the second molar, the remaining incisors are replaced before the eruption of the permanent premolars. The last teeth to erupt are the third molars (M 3/3) at 74 to 94 weeks. With their appearance, the permanent dentition is complete. Temporary canine teeth persist for varying periods, and young animals

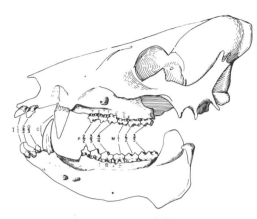

Figure 1.1. Skull of a collared peccary showing tooth labeling system. (Drawing by James Jokerst)

commonly have these extra canines. The adult canine teeth grow in width for a considerable, but variable, period after the appearance of all adult teeth.

The temporary canines differ materially in appearance and size from the permanent teeth, and the two can be easily distinguished. They are nearly round in cross section, whereas the permanent canines, even when small, have a more triangular cross section. Furthermore, the angle of protrusion of the temporary canines changes greatly as the jaws grow and elongate. From a position at birth of being nearly vertical to the axis of the jaw, the angle of protrusion becomes more nearly horizontal to the axis as the jaw matures. The permanent canines come in forward of the temporary canines in a more perpendicular position with respect to the long axis of the jaw. They retain this relative position permanently.

Temporary premolars can be easily distinguished from permanent premolars. Like the molars, they are of the bunodont type. The temporary premolars show considerable wear before they are replaced. They are noticeably smaller than the permanent premolars, and the fourth lower premolar has three transverse ridges forming six indistinct cusps; the permanent fourth premolars, both upper and lower, have only four cusps. Both the first and second molars have four cusps. This is the same in the upper and lower jaws. Considerable variation seems to occur in the third molar. These teeth may have four, five, or six cusps. When five are present, the fifth cusp is centered along a line extending from a point between the forward cusps of these teeth.

Dental Irregularities

Dental anomalies among mammals are common, and many have been described in the literature. Given the number of opportunities to observe the dentition of some species of mammals, however, it appears likely that anomalies are far more frequent in some species. The dentition of deer has probably been observed more often than in any other North American mammal because of the now common practice of collecting and studying jaws for aging purposes. Cowan (1946) regarded variations in numbers of teeth in deer (*Odocoileus*) as rare.

Robinette (1958), from wide experience, reported eight instances of an abnormal number of teeth in the mule deer. Benson (1957) reported four instances of abnormal dentition in the eastern white-tailed deer.

When collared peccary skulls and jaws were first gathered in Arizona for aging purposes, several dental abnormalities were found. One highly unusual development of a canine tooth from these collections was reported by Neal and Kirkpatrick (1957). As the sample size increased through expanded checking station activities, it was apparent that the presence of dental anomalies in this species could be examined on large series of individuals.

Table 1.1 summarizes these anomalies. Nine percent of 581 specimens closely examined showed some dental anomalies.

The Canine Tooth

Few noncarnivorous mammals possess as large and as sharp canine teeth as do the three species of peccaries. Although the collared peccary is much smaller than the other two species, its canines are nearly the same size. The peccaries' upper canine teeth are directed

Table 1.1. Frequency of Various Tooth Irregularities in 581 Hunter-killed Collared Peccaries in Arizona

	1957	1958	1959	1960	Totals
Total Sample	249	122	175	35	581
TYPE OF IRREGULARITY					
Extra teeth					
Incisors					
Upper No. 1					
No. 2	1	3	4		8
Lower No. 1					
No. 2	1				1
No. 3		1			1
Premolars No. 2		1	1		2
No. 3	5	2	2	1	10
No. 4					
Molars No. 1	1				1
No. 2					
No. 3			1		1
Indented teeth					
Upper molars			1		1
Lower molars			1		1
Upper premolars		1	4		5
Lower premolars			2		2
Premolars outside of line	3	2	1		6
Irregular tooth row	1	3	1		5
Juvenile canines persisting			1		1
Upper	1				1
Lower	1		1		2
Indistinct molars	1				1
Total Irregularities	15	13	20	1	49

straight down, and the lower canine teeth are directed straight up. Canine teeth of all peccaries have been so located throughout their long evolutionary history. The lower and bottom teeth work against each other, which results in razor-sharp edges.

Of what value are these long, sharp teeth in a mammal that does not need them to kill its prey or tear flesh? From observation it is clear that the canine teeth are of little value for eating. They are, however, definitely useful to the peccary as a defense mechanism against enemies. Geist (1966) has described the role of the canine teeth among the true pigs (Suidae) as display organs in interspecific interactions. Although the teeth of the peccaries are not conspicuous in small animals with the mouth closed, as they are in the true pigs, they could serve as display organs during "squabbles" between herd members. At these times the mouth is often open in threat positions. Among captive animals, we have observed considerable fighting with injuries inflicted with the sharp canine teeth. However, among wild free-roving animals there is little evidence that serious injuries result from such fights. The canine tooth serves one other important function — it is an acoustic instrument to generate loud clacking sounds of chatter as warning threats to enemies and also in intraspecific situations.

Data on the length of the lower permanent tooth in known-age wild animals killed in Arizona are given in Table 1.2. With fewer measurements of the upper canine tooth the same tendency, shortening with age and becoming more pointed at the base, is seen.

The sharpness of the canine teeth is ensured, because they continue to grow until the animals are about four years old, about two years beyond the time when all the permanent teeth are in. Data on the amount and rate of growth in length of the lower canine tooth for some captive collared peccaries are in Table 1.3. From these data it is evident that the growth is most rapid during the first year or two after all the permanent teeth are in, but growth continues until at least 46 months in some animals. On one captive male animal with a malocclusion, the left lower canine protruded through the upper lip at the age of 36 months. When the canine tooth stops growing, the wear becomes more noticeable. The sharp edges gradually become dull. As

Table 1.2. Length (mm) of Lower Canine Teeth of Collared Peccaries in Different Age Groups

	Exposed Portion			Root Portion		
Age (yrs.)	No. in Sample	Range	Avg.	No. in Sample	Range	Avg.
2–3	12	31–45	36.6	11	31–47	37.8
3–5	44	29–44	36.0	46	29–49	37.6
5–7	33	34–46	38.5	38	30–44	38.1
Over 7	53	27–43	35.7	53	34–46	39.5

Table 1.3. Rate of Growth of the Lower Canine Tooth
of Some Captive Collared Peccaries

				Rate — mm per month	
Animal	Sex	Age During Growth Period in Months		Lower Right	Lower Left
953	F	10.5	17.5	2.35	—
746	F	12	18.5	2.92	2.77
942	F	15	27	.66	—
737	F	17	20	2.3	1.67
964	F	20	29	—	.77
922	F	21	30	.66	—
941	M	22.5	32.5	1.25	1.58
921	M	30	47	—	1.06
923	M	36	58	—	.89
20	F	46	70	—	.46

the blood supply stops and nerves to the canine tooth cease to function, the open cavity at the end of the root becomes closed and the root becomes pointed-at the end. The root closure is gradual, and after closure the root continues to become more pointed.

ADULT BODY WEIGHTS

In Texas, Jennings and Harris (1953) collected 52 adult peccaries that averaged 36.5 pounds. They found that one pregnant sow weighed 50 pounds and the heaviest male weighed 49 pounds. In Arizona Knipe (1957) gave the field-dressed average weight of 130 peccaries considered to be full grown as 31.0 pounds. Among 65 boars, the average weight was 32.5 pounds, and for 65 sows it was 30.0 pounds.

Since the Arizona Cooperative Wildlife Research Unit first began its studies in 1956, a vast amount of data on weights has been obtained. Some of these data are useful in comparing physical conditions between animals in different years, whereas other data could reveal relative vigor of populations in different habitat types.

One way to obtain quickly a large number of weights is at hunter-checking stations where hunters bring dead, field-dressed animals to be weighed and examined. The field-dressed weights can be translated into complete body weights within reasonable limits if the dressing percentage is known. Table 1.4 summarizes the available data on the percentage of weight lost by the animal when it is "hog dressed." Animals are said to be "hog dressed" when head and hide are still on but all internal organs are removed. This is the most common procedure followed by hunters in the field, and consequently the largest number of available weights for most game species are of this type. The percentage of loss from field dressing varies with the size and condition of the animal. Weights of animals obtained in this manner can be useful in comparing the physical condition of animals during different years or between different areas. Fat animals and large animals tend to lose less weight when field dressed than do small or thin animals.

Because of such important variables as stomach contents, which can vary greatly, there is no point in attempting an exact figure on weight loss. During most years in Arizona, very few, if any, fat animals were killed by hunters, but in some years, as in 1973 following good winter rainfall and abundant food, most animals were fat.

Figure 1.2 shows graphically the distribution of weights for 450 (50 percent males and 50 percent females) randomly taken from checking station records. These figures are the calculated whole weights of the animals as determined by adding 27.6 percent to the field-dressed weights as determined by Table 1.4.

In all these weight tables the wide range of weights among adult animals is apparent — from about 25 to almost 70 pounds. This wide variation is from a variety of factors. The first and most important, of course, is the quantity and quality of food that the animal can obtain. The influence of high quality diets can be seen with captive animals. In our pens, animals weighing more than 70 pounds were common when they were fat. The heaviest collared peccary I have seen was a captive male that weighed 78 pounds; he did not appear to be excessively fat. There seems to be tremendous variation in the general body conformation which makes some animals much heavier than others. Some large, well-fed captives weighed more than 70 pounds, while many weighed less than 50 pounds.

Males vs. Females

Practically no sexual dimorphism exists between male and female collared peccaries. With the exception of the appearance of the scrotum on males when observed at close range (Fig. 1.4), an observer cannot distinguish between the sexes on a live specimen. To determine if a statistically significant difference existed in the weights of males and females, I analyzed the data used for Figure 1.3. In this

Table 1.4. Weights of Adult Wild Arizona Collared Peccaries Before and After Field-dressing

Specimen	Date	Sex	Whole Weight Kg (Lbs.)	Dressed Weight Kg (Lbs.)	Percentage Loss
477	2/23/55	F	22.7 (50)	15.8 (35)	30.0
—	2/23/55	M	23.1 (51)	16.8 (37)	27.5
62–58	2/15/58	M	23.1 (51)	15.8 (35)	31.4
—	4/11/58	F	14.0 (31)	9.5 (21)	32.0
32–59	2/07/59	F	23.1 (51)	18.1 (40)	21.6
33–59	2/07/59	M	14.0 (31)	9.5 (21)	32.3
58–59	2/08/59	M	24.9 (55)	18.6 (41)	25.5
83–60	2/13/60	F	21.7 (48)	15.8 (35)	25.1
84–60	2/13/60	F	23.6 (52)	16.8 (37)	28.8
85–60	2/13/60	F	22.2 (49)	15.8 (35)	28.6
86–60	2/13/60	F	20.8 (46)	15.8 (35)	23.9
76–61	3/05/61	F	24.0 (53)	17.2 (38)	29.0
86–61	3/09/61	F	23.6 (52)	22.2 (49)	23.1
48–65	2/28/65	F	24.5 (54)	17.7 (39)	28.0
				Average	27.6

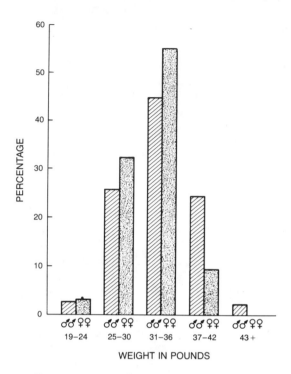

Figure 1.2. Distribution of weights of 450 collared peccaries killed by hunters in Arizona

sample 225 males had a mean weight of 42.5 pounds, S.D. 5.89. The females showed a mean weight of 40.7 pounds, S.D. 5.30. Males in this sample were significantly heavier than females (t=3.25, significant at .001 level). The same tendency for males to be heavier than females shows in Figure 1.3.

GEOGRAPHIC SIZE VARIATION

Most size data on the collared peccary are from the northern part of its range. To those who have seen it in more southernly places, however, the northern animals (Arizona, New Mexico, Texas) appear larger. There is a lack of information on the weights and body measurements of collared peccaries from Central and South America. I compared the available information from 10 animals (6 from Costa Rica, [Vaughan pers. comm.] 3 from Surinam [Husson 1978] and 1 from Paraguay [Ludlow pers. comm.]); with similar data on 104 animals from Arizona. Applying a student's "t" test to these data, I found that the Arizona animals were significantly larger than the Central/South American animals except for the neck measurements where the Central/South American sample was only 6 animals (Table 1.5).

Another means of comparing the size of animals is that commonly used by archaeologists who have unearthed large amounts of bones but

Figure 1.3. Male peccaries can be distinguished from females when the scrotum is visible. (Photograph by Lyle K. Sowls)

no other parts. Hamblin (1980) noted that the bones of collared peccaries found in excavations at Mayan sites on Cozumel Island were considerably smaller than modern reference material from Arizona. This is a small island in the Atlantic Ocean near the coast of Yucatán, Mexico. She measured parts of skulls from 28 specimens from Cozumel and compared these measurements with similar data from 43 skulls from Arizona. Six different mandibular and maxillary measurements were taken according to standard techniques described by Driesch (1976). She found that the jawbones of peccaries from these sites were significantly smaller (P<.01) than those from modern peccaries in Arizona.

I compared the Cozumel data with similar data from Ecuador from skulls obtained by Dr. Rollin Baker of Michigan State University. Dr. Baker furnished these data for comparisons. Multiple range tests showed a significant difference between the Arizona and the Cozumel data, a significant difference between the Ecuador and Cozumel data, but no significant differences between the Arizona and Ecuador data.

Table 1.5. Comparisons of Measurements of Collared Peccaries From Arizona and Central/South America

| | Arizona | | | | Central/South America | | | |
Measurement	N	Range	$\overline{X}$	S.D.	N	Range	$\overline{X}$	S.D.	Sign (t-test)
Weights	104	28.0–54.0	42.8	5.67	9	29.0–48.4	39.7	6.54	*
Head and body	57	32.5–41.5	37.58	2.096	10	31.5–36.2	33.96	1.431	*
Hind foot	84	7.5– 8.5	7.72	.263	9	6.7– 7.9	7.24	.456	*
Ear	83	3.5– 4.0	3.66	.140	10	2.8– 3.3	3.11	.173	*
Neck	82	14.5–21.0	17.62	1.784	6	14.8–21.6	17.26	2.45	NS

NS = Not significant.
* = ‹ .01

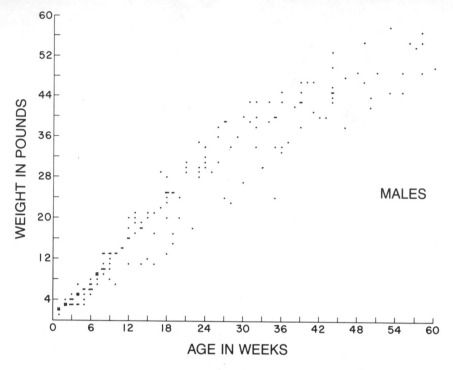

Figure 1.4. Weight increases of male pen-reared collared peccaries

Little doubt exists that significant differences in the sizes of collared peccaries from different parts of their range do exist. Additional data from scattered parts of the range are needed before such a complete analysis can be made.

GROWTH RATE

Because growth of wild peccaries is difficult to determine directly, inferences from other sources must be made. One source of this information is to obtain regularly scheduled weights and measurements from growing captive animals. Such information sets an optimum base for comparison. Even this optimum possibly could be and probably is reached by some wild herds where food is abundant. For most wild herds in Arizona, however, we know that the rate of growth could not equal that normally obtained in captivity.

Certain rough measurements of growth besides weight can be obtained, including total length, height, hind foot, and ear. Total length and height were not precise measurements because the posture of the animals varied and was difficult to control. The inside measurements of the ear and the hind foot, however, were accurate and similar to measurements obtained for taxonomic purposes on dead specimens. Figure 1.4 illustrates the rate in weight gain of males born in captivity or raised in captivity from a few days of age. Figure 1.5 gives the weight gain of females. Both males and females attained adult weight at about

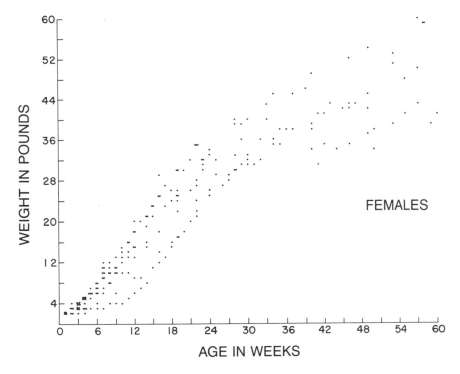

Figure 1.5. Weight increases of female pen-reared collared peccaries

40 weeks. Weights exceeding those reached in about 40 weeks were generally due to excess fat.

Figures 1.6 and 1.7 show the rate of increase in total length of body and hind foot of males and females respectively. The measurements of the hind foot are considered as accurate as similar measurements taken on dead animals. Like the weight figures, these tend to show maturity when the animal is about 40 weeks of age; in some cases, when animals are kept on good quality diets, they continue to grow slowly until about one year of age. Figures 1.8 and 1.9 depict the growth changes in height and ear of captive animals measured periodically. Height, like length, is not a uniformaly accurate measurement because of the difficulty of always obtaining the same posture. Height is measured at the shoulder when an animal is standing in a normal position with head down. The growth rate curve for height measurement of both males and females tends to flatten out at about 40 weeks of age. Of all measurements, those of the ear show earliest maturity. Very little change in the growth curve of the ear occurs after about 30 weeks of age.

CHROMOSOME NUMBERS

Wetzel (1981, from Hsu and Benirschke, 1969:Folio 132) gives the karotype of the collared peccary as 2 n = 30, 16 metacentrics, submetacentrics and subtelocentrics, 12 acrocentrics, X medium-sized metacentric, Y small submetacentric.

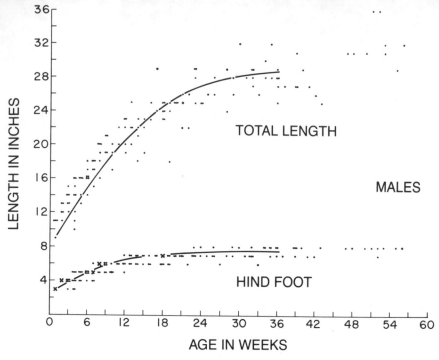

Figure 1.6. Increase in total length and hind foot measurements for male pen-reared collared peccaries

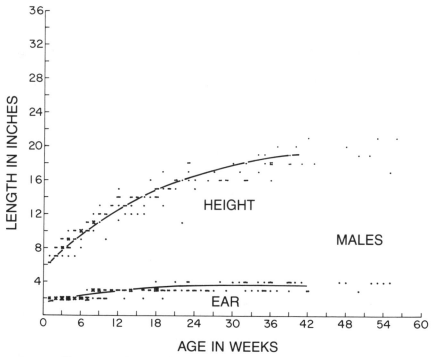

Figure 1.8. Increase in measurements of height and ear of male pen-reared collared peccaries

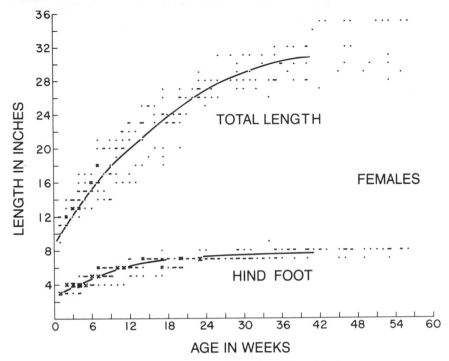

Figure 1.7. Increase in total length and hind foot measurements for female pen-reared collared peccaries

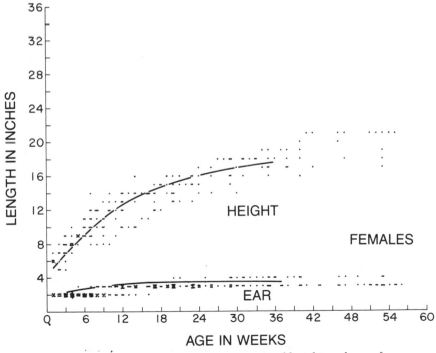

Figure 1.9. Increase in measurements of height and ear of female pen-reared collared peccaries

27

Distribution, Habitats, and Adaptability

GEOGRAPHICALLY THE COLLARED PECCARY HAS one of the largest ranges of any living wild ungulate. Within this area it inhabits a wide variety of vegetative types and adapts itself to many climatic conditions. In its vast range, the species is not consistently distributed; there are many areas where it does not occur. The characteristics of the country it inhabits vary greatly and much of the land is not suitable for its existence. In other areas the remoteness and absence of outside travelers makes its status unknown to the outside world. In some places, man has eliminated collared peccaries from their former range. Thus, it is not possible to draw accurate distribution maps of the species in many areas. While the map in the introduction showed the approximate range of the collared peccary and compared it to the range of the other two species, Figure 2.1 is a more detailed map showing the approximate range of the collared peccary in the United States and northern Mexico.

The collared peccary does not inhabit the islands of the Caribbean Sea with the exception of those close to the mainland such as Cozumel near the coast of Mexico (Hamblin 1980; Varona 1973) and Trinidad off the northern coast of South America (Joseph 1970). Some introductions have been made into these areas, however. Varona says that both collared and white-lipped peccaries have been released in the extreme western part of the state of Pinar del Río and in the Sierra Cristal in the province of Oriente, Cuba. These releases were made in 1930 with animals from Mexico.

FORMER AND PRESENT DISTRIBUTION

Like many native American mammals, the original range of the collared peccary has been reduced since European man's arrival in the New World. At the same time, it has moved into new areas at the

28

Figure 2.1. Approximate distribution of the collared peccary in the United States and northern Mexico

northern fringe of its range. Evidence of its early distribution in Arizona and Texas shows that it is a recent immigrant into some of this country. Inglis (1964), in an exhaustive study of early explorers' records, found numerous references to buffalo, deer, antelope, wild cattle, and mustangs in Texas. However, he found little reference to the peccary in areas where today it is common to abundant. Ellisor and Harwell (1979), while commenting on the overall reduction of the range of the collared peccary in Texas, described the recent extension of its range into the Edwards Plateau.

In Arizona also evidence is abundant that the collared peccary is a recent immigrant. Knipe (1957) describes the spread of the collared peccary from the mesquite bosques along the alluvial valleys to the surrounding areas, an extension that occurred simultaneously with the spread of mesquite over what was originally grassland. It has also extended its range in Arizona into the edge of the higher country above the Mogollon Rim, an escarpment running across the state. According to Knipe, this extension has occurred since 1929 when the peccary legally became a game animal in Arizona. This, however, does not represent a very great extension of range because in 1907 Mearns found them as far north as Pine and Fossil creeks in central Arizona, just under the Mogollon Rim. In an exhaustive survey of the early literature in Arizona, Davis (1982) found few references to peccary in early explorer records. Other evidence that collared peccary may be recent in Arizona is that the Papago and Pima Indians of southern Arizona have no word in their languages for peccary. Although peccaries are present today on their reservations, the people apply the Spanish word "coche" or "Kohji" when they speak of it. Carmony and Brown (see Davis 1982) give an excellent summary:

> Remarkably few encounters with javelina were reported by the early explorers of Arizona. James Ohio Pattie found them on the lower San Pedro River in 1825. Emory reported wild hogs along the Gila River in Safford Valley in 1846, and C.B.R. Kennerly mentions this animal in San Bernardino Valley in 1855. Dr. B.J.D. Irwin reported "peccary" or "Mexican hog" to be present in the general vicinity of Fort Buchanan. No other reports of javelina were uncovered by this study. John Bartlett, who traveled extensively in southeastern Arizona, does not include the javelina in his lengthy list of animals of the region. Likewise, Coues does not mention javelina as occurring in Arizona.

> Today, javelina are common animals and second only to deer as big game species. Javelina are found throughout the southeast quadrant of the state, south of the White Mountains and Mogollon Rim, southwestward to the Bradshaw and Ajo Mountains. They now occur in the Verde Valley and in the upper Agua Fria River drainage only a few miles southeast of Coues' former headquarters at Fort Whipple.

> Some of the best javelina populations in Arizona are presently found in the scrub-invaded grassland and evergreen oak woodland in the mountain foothills along the International border within a 50-mile radius of the city of Nogales. This area was much traveled, hunted, and described by the American pioneers, and only Irwin mentions javelina as being present. In 1855, C.B.R. Kennerly made an extensive collection of mammals in the vicinity of Nogales but found no javelina. There can be little doubt that javelina are now much more widespread and numerous in Arizona than in the mid-1800's.

> Why javelina should be more abundant in modern Arizona than in presettlement times is a matter for some contemplation. Vegetation changes during the last century certainly have favored this species. However, we may be observing a northward expansion of the range of javelina that began before American involvement in the Southwest.

Concerning their spread into some of the mountain ranges in western Arizona, Brown (pers. comm. 1982) says, "There is no question but that javelina are expanding their range to the northwest. Javelina are now present in the Hieroglyphic, Harquahala, and Weaver Mountains — areas where they were not present prior to the 1950s.

Long-time residents and ranchers have remarked on the 'invasion,' and many believe that the Arizona Game & Fish Department released javelina in these ranges. This was not the case, and the animals are the result of natural range expansion."

Similar extensions of the range of the collared peccary have been reported in New Mexico by Donaldson (1967) and by Findley et al. (1975). They report that while populations in the extreme southeastern corner of that state have been exterminated, the collared peccary has spread through Hidalgo County and into the Tres Hermanas in Luna County and north into the Gila and San Francisco drainages.

HABITAT TYPES

Habitats occupied by the collared peccary in the northern part of its range have been intensively studied. Thus most of the research and written accounts that have come to the attention of English-speaking people have originated in Arizona, New Mexico, and Texas. This undoubtedly has given the impression that the collared peccary is a desert or semi-desert animal. Most research reports on the collared peccary have described its habitat as dry hillsides and brushy valleys with agave, yucca, and prickly pear. However, the habitat occupied in these areas is far different from many areas that make up a major part of the animal's range and which have received little study.

An inspection of reports from various parts of its range illustrates the diversity of the collared peccary's habitat. Goodwin (1946) described its habitat in Panama and Costa Rica as being both the coastal lowlands and the central plateau to 8,000 feet above sea level. In Guatemala, Handley (1950) described its habitat as the lowlands of both coasts and the forests and brushlands up to an altitude of 6,000 feet above sea level. In these coastal forests of Central America and many other vast areas, the collared peccary inhabits dense tropical forests with practically no openings or clearings. Leopold (1959) describes collared peccaries in Mexico as very adaptable animals. He states that they occur in the tropical coastal thickets, cut-over rain forests, pine-oak uplands and manzanita and scrub oak woodlands. Baker and Greer (1962) reported that the collared peccary in the state of Durango, Mexico, inhabited both areas of tropical vegetation and higher oak woodlands. In Colombia, Borrero (1967) says that the collared peccary is an animal of both the desert and jungle in tropical and semi-tropical lands.

Descriptions of the habitat in Arizona have been given by Elder (1953, 1956), Neal (1957, 1959), Minnamon (1962), Bigler (1964), and Schweinsburg (1969). These authors gave detailed descriptions of mountainous areas of the Sonoran Desert where collared peccaries inhabit the canyons and bajadas. Knipe (1957) describes habitats in the Sonoran Desert in Arizona and in chaparral, oak woodland, and yellow pine forests above 6,500 feet. Eddy (1959, 1961) gave detailed descriptions of peccary habitats in the Sonoran Desert of Arizona and the desert grassland or "semi-desert" subtype at about 2,900 to 3,500 feet elevation. He also described the oak woodland where the collared peccary are found up to about 6,000 feet elevation.

The habitat occupied by the collared peccary in Texas has been described in detail by Jennings and Harris (1953), Low (1970), Bissonette (1976), and Ellisor and Harwell (1979). In that state, which has over 100,000 square miles of land occupied by the collared peccary, rainfall varies from 16 inches a year in the west to 27 to 30 inches per year in the east (Jennings and Harris 1953). The resulting vegetation varies greatly from dry desert in the west to lush chaparral and deciduous brushland in the east.

The wide variation in the types of country inhabited by the collared peccary can best be illustrated with photographs. One type of habitat occupied by the collared peccary in Arizona is the saguaro cactus-palo verde type shown in Figure 2.2. In this type ocotillo, cholla, and acacia are also common. Similar habitat occupied by the peccary can be found in Texas, New Mexico, and parts of Mexico. In this same geographic area peccaries also inhabit more open grassland (Fig. 2.3) where species such as *Agave palmeri* are the principal food plants. This type of country would probably not be inhabitable by the peccary without brushy valleys and some timbered slopes for protective cover. Still another type of habitat where the peccary thrives is the heavy mesquite thickets of southern Texas (described by Ellisor 1979), Arizona, New Mexico and Mexico (Fig. 2.4). Even in the more arid places, the dense timber growth in these valleys is the home of the peccary. These bosques often border agricultural lands where the peccary eats corn, melons, sorghum, and other cultivated crops.

In sharp contrast to the dry open areas found in the northern part of the range, vast areas of the collared peccaries' range are humid and heavily forested. An example of this type of country in southern Brazil is shown in Figure 2.5. The heavy cover in this type of forest allows little light to penetrate. In such undisturbed forest the collared peccary is sympatric with the white-lipped peccary. Within the heavily forested tropical and subtropical habitats where the two peccaries live, there is a great deal of variation in plant species. Beneath the dense canopy is an under-growth of many shade-tolerant species. This is in marked contrast to the open mesquite grasslands of Arizona, Mexico, New Mexico, and Texas where the sun beats down on the bare soil between the sparse desert plants.

CLIMATIC TOLERANCES

One commonly accepted way to compare the climates of different areas is by the use of the climatograph. The vertical axis of the graph represents the average monthly temperature and the horizontal axis represents the average monthly precipitation. Figure 2.6 shows climatographs from various parts of the range of the collared peccary. Areas were selected at widely scattered parts of the range. Weather

Figure 2.2. Lower Sonoran Desert vegetation type occupied by the collared peccary. (Photograph by Lyle K. Sowls)

Figure 2.3. Desert grassland in southeastern Arizona, habitat of the collared peccary. *Agave palmeri* in foreground is principal food. (Photograph by Lyle K. Sowls)

Figure 2.4. Mesquite bosques, favorite shelter areas for collared peccaries in Arizona, New Mexico, Texas, and northern Mexico. (Photograph by Lyle K. Sowls)

Figure 2.5. A herd of collared peccaries in semi-tropical forest, favored habitat in Brazil. (Photograph by Lyle K. Sowls)

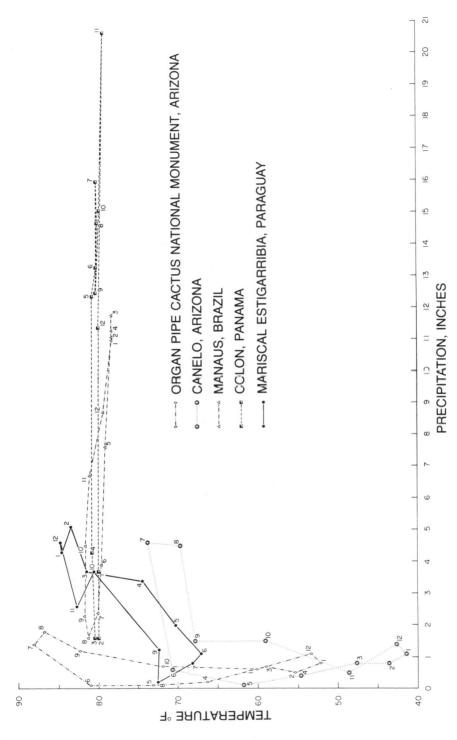

Figure 2.6. Climatograph for five locations within the range of the collared peccary

stations selected were at a location where the collared peccary is known to occur naturally. Points include Mariscal Estigarribia, Paraguay; Colon, Panama; Manaus, Brazil; Canelo, Arizona; and Organ Pipe Cactus National Monument, Arizona. An inspection of these figures illustrated the wide range of suitable climates for the collared peccary. Rainfall within its range varies from as low as 9.17 inches per year at the Organ Pipe Cactus National Monument (Sellers and Hill 1974) to as high as 127 inches per year (Reed 1941) at Colon, Panama. The pattern of rainfall is not always conducive to maximum production of vegetation as at Organ Pipe in Arizona, where over 50 percent of the annual precipitation falls as summer rains in July, August, and September (Sellers and Hill 1974). The key to the survival of the peccaries in these areas is the adaptability of staple alternate food plants to this pattern of rainfall. Annual plants often grow in considerable quantity in the moister microclimates, and succulent cactus plants store water and thus remain palatable and are able to provide alternate food during dry periods. This will be more thoroughly discussed in Chapter 3.

ADAPTATIONS

Physiological

Few large mammals inhabit such a wide variety of habitats with so many variations in temperature as does the collared peccary. Because of this, one might expect them to possess some extraordinary means to cool themselves in summer, to keep warm in winter, and to prevent dehydration during periods of high temperatures and low humidity in arid regions.

Zervanos (1972, 1975), Zervanos and Hadley (1973), and Zervanos and Day (1977) reported on detailed studies of the collared peccary in Arizona. They studied the animal's thermoregulation, water relations, and energy requirements under changing environmental conditions. They found the daily body core temperature to vary from 37.5°C (99.5° F) to approximately 49.0°C (120.2° F) during all seasons; skin temperatures always exceeded surrounding air temperatures. They also found that the pelage had a poor insulative value and that in summer the outer dark portion of the bristles broke off, exposing the lighter bristles nearer the body. Because of this, the pelage became lighter in color and had a less dense bristle coat in summer over certain parts of the body. They pointed out that this change results in increased reflectance of high-energy, short-wave radiation and decreased absorbance, an advantage during hot summer weather. The longer, dark pelage of winter is advantageous during cold weather when absorption of solar radiation helps to keep the animal warm. Zervanos found a significantly higher basal metabolic rate (20.7 percent) in winter than in summer. This increased rate helps compensate for the peccary's poor insulation. With this higher winter metabolic rate, food consumption is higher.

Zervanos (1972, 1975) also found that the captive peccaries had a narrow thermal neutral zone with a lower critical temperature of 24.9°C (77°F) in winter and 29.5°C (85°F) in summer and an upper critical temperature of 28.5°C (83°F) in winter and 35°C (95°F) in summer. Critical temperature here means the environmental temperature at which the animal's insulation is inadequate to maintain body temperature without an increase in metabolism. The thermal neutral zone is the environmental temperature range within which the animal is able to maintain its body temperature using basal metabolic heat production. Because of the animal's ability to acclimatize itself to seasonal temperatures, the critical temperature values are higher in summer than in winter. The research on thermoregulation by Zervanos has demonstrated that the collared peccary cannot prevent increased body temperature when directly exposed to summer sun if the air temperature is greater than 30°C (86°F) and the wind velocity is greater than 197 ft per sec. He believed that a temperature of 45°C (113°F) could probably be tolerated in partial shade conditions if there was concurrently maximum evaporation, minimum metabolism, and a maximum body temperature. Thus in parts of its range where desert conditions exist, the collared peccary lives in an environment which, from the standpoint of thermoregulation and water balance, must be considered adverse.

Zervanos has pointed out that the critical temperature ranges which he found for the collared peccary correspond to the temperature range found for tropical mammals by Scholander et al. (1950). The data on the collared peccary that Zervanos has reported indicate some physiological adaptation to cold and heat but probably not enough to allow it to live in much of the country it presently occupies. To understand how this tropical animal survives in some of the colder parts of its range and in areas of high desert heat, we must also look to its behavioral adaptations.

Behavioral

Several authors have reported on the activity patterns of the collared peccary in Arizona and Texas. Jennings and Harris (1953) in Texas observed that herds moved out of the bedding areas at daylight and fed in early morning and bedded down during the heat of the day. Elder (1956) showed peaks of daily visits to waterholes in southern Arizona and concluded that the visitation at waterholes in June and July, the hottest and driest months, was greatest from sunset to sunrise. Bigler (1964, 1974) also found that in the hot summer months most feeding and watering took place at night.

In Arizona Eddy (1961) followed herds closely to gather feeding information. He observed that they usually began feeding in early morning and sought shade during the daylight hours. Feeding stopped when the temperature reached 31–33°C (88–92°F). Bigler (1974), Eddy (1959, 1961), and Schweinsburg (1969) have all commented on the fact that herds feed later in the day as the weather becomes colder. Schweinsburg observed that they bedded down in the summer when the temperature approached 26.5° C (80° F). Bissonette (1978) studied the onset and cessation of activity and found that their activities can be largely controlled by ambient temperatures alone. In the Big Bend country of Texas he found that in the summer the peccaries spend eight to 10 hours in their bed during the day and in the winter only two to four of the daylight hours in their bed. Day (1977b) used radio transmitters on a number of herds in Arizona to obtain detailed information on their movements and found that night feeding was common during the hottest periods of summer.

Phelps (1971) studied the role of behavior in thermoregulation in the collared peccary. He found that it could not maintain a normal body temperature when exposed to full environmental radiation during a clear summer day in southern Arizona. The animal was unable to lose enough moisture through panting to survive and so it resorted to a behavorial pattern which made full use of cool microclimates during the hot part of the day.

Just as they avoid the heat by selecting the cooler places in their environment in summer, they are able to select the warmest parts of their environment in winter. Eddy (1959), Neal (1959), and Schweinsburg (1969) observed herds in the Tucson Mountains of Arizona using caves and tunnels to escape the cold winter. In addition, they sleep and rest in huddled groups to prevent excess heat loss (see Contact Behavior, Chap. 8). Basking in the sun during early morning hours in winter is also common.

TOLERANCE OF HUMANS

The collared peccary has not only shown great adaptability to various climates and vegetative types, but it also has shown an ability to adapt to changes in habitat brought by man. Though it thrives in primeval forest, it can also thrive in cut-over land and agricultural areas (Leopold 1959, 1966); it is able to live in areas of second-growth and subclimax timber. In agricultural land it thrives on crops as long as suitable cover is available for hiding. I have seen such situations not only in the irrigated fields of Arizona and Texas but also in the rich coffee country of southern Brazil and other areas of agricultural land that were once forest. In parts of southern Arizona only a small area of natural vegetation is necessary for its survival if agricultural crop land is nearby.

3 | Diet and Nutrition

THE ANATOMY OF THE PECCARIES' TEETH, jaws, and digestive system indicates the types of foods they eat. Like their relatives, the hogs, they have a well developed snout used to root out bulbs, roots, and tubers. Unlike the hogs, peccaries cannot move their mandibles sideways and thus chew their food. All three species of peccaries possess long, interlocking canine teeth which greatly reduce the transverse movement of the mandible in chewing motions. Thus, the only extensive chewing of food that can occur is an up and down movement which crushes the food (Herring 1972; Langer 1978). The incisors, however, are well adapted to cropping the vegetation, which is swallowed after a minimum of chewing.

One of the characteristics of the digestive system in all three species is the presence of an unusual stomach. It consists of a voluminous gastric pouch with two blindsacs and a glandular stomach. This peculiar stomach was first described in 1683 by an English surgeon named Tyson, seventy-five years before Linnaeus gave the collared peccary its first scientific name. The stomach has since been studied by Stewart (1964) and in greater detail by Langer (1973, 1974, 1979). Stomachs of the other two species have not been studied thoroughly, but superficially they show the same pouches as does the collared peccary (see Figs. 3.1, 3.2, and 3.3).

FOODS EATEN

Because of the wide range of the collared peccary and the many different types of habitat in which it lives, a list of food items would be long. From published observations, however, it is possible to conclude what types of foods are eaten and thus determine what plants may be

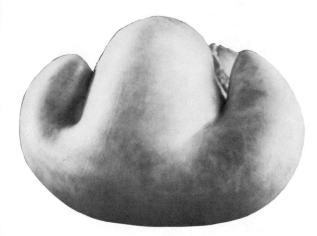

Figure 3.1. Stomach of the collared peccary. (Photograph by Lyle K. Sowls)

Figure 3.2. Stomach of the white-lipped peccary. (Photograph by Lyle K. Sowls)

Figure 3.3. Stomach of the Chacoan peccary. (Photograph by Lyle K. Sowls)

Figure 3.4. Cladophylls and fruits of prickly pear, eaten by peccaries. (Photograph by Thomas A. Eddy)

taken in any one area. Therefore, in any particular place, certain plants can be considered staple items — fruits, underground tubers, rhizomes and bulbs, acorns, green grass, green shoots of annual plants, fruits and cladophylls (stems) of prickly pear cactus, and the growing point of succulent agaves.

Jennings and Harris (1953) examined the stomach contents of 107 peccaries collected in southern Texas. They concluded that prickly pear cladophylls (Fig. 3.4) were the main staple of the peccary in that area and that seasonal foods such as grass, mesquite and ebony beans (*Pithecellobium* sp.), and a great variety of other plants also made up substantial parts of the diet. In two stomachs collected in the Trans-Pecos region of Texas, lechuguilla (*Agave lechuguilla*) made up more than half the contents. These same writers believed that acorns were important in the diet of the peccary at certain times.

Knipe (1957) concluded that in Arizona prickly pear was the preferred food of the peccary, but he also found tubers, bulbs, and rhizomes to be important, chiefly the roots of *Cucurbita foetidissima* and *C. digitata* and the roots of *Ipomoea* sp. and *Rumex* sp. He also lists the root of *Abronia* sp. as a favorite food.

Leopold (1959) studied the animal over a large part of Mexico and concluded that: "A wide variety of fruits, roots, bulbs, and greens contribute to the normal fare. Acorns (*Quercus* sp.), pine nuts (*Pinus* sp.), and manzanita berries (*Arctostaphylos* sp.) are favorite foods in the pine-oak uplands. Cactus fruits (*Opuntia* sp.) and the beans of mesquite (*Prosopis* sp.), catclaw (*Acacia* sp.), and juniper (*Juniperus* sp.) are other common items of diet in the uplands."

Eddy (1961) studied the foods eaten by peccaries in three different vegetation zones, including the palo verde-bursage-cactus vegetative type; the semi-desert subtype where the dominant vegetation was cactus, burroweed, and mimosa; and a foothill subtype where the dominant vegetation was live-oak, manzanita, and century plant (*Agave* sp.), reaching altitudes of up to 5,000 feet. By the study of stomach contents and droppings and by intensive systematic field observations in which feeding periods of individuals were timed, the role of various plants was determined. Although different groups of plants grew in each area, the number of species of plants that peccaries ate in each habitat type was nearly the same — 15, 17, and 19, respectively.

Of all foods eaten, the prickly pear cactus was the most common. It was eaten on 56.4 percent of the observed feedings in the desert study area where it was abundant, and on 52.3 percent of the observations in the intermediate area. Where it was uncommon in the higher areas, it was eaten on less than 1 percent of the observations. In this area two plants, the century plant and *Ipomoea* sp., were taken most frequently; they made up 70.7 percent of all the feeding observations in the foothills area.

Low (1970) examined 73 stomachs from peccaries in Texas and found that they contained an average of 63 percent prickly pear, 18 percent grass species and 7 percent forbs and small parts of animal matter and unidentified plant fibers. He found great seasonal variation in the composition. Besides the cladophylls, he found that flowers and fruit of prickly pear also were heavily taken when available. Low found that a high percentage of the diet consisted of grass: 25 percent in spring, 14 percent in summer and 10 percent in the fall. He also found that forbs were taken in preference to other plants whenever they were available. Dominguez et al. (1972) said that in the state of Chihuahua, Mexico, the collared peccary lives on roots, acorns, manzanita berries, and tubers. The peccaries also fed on small mammals and reptiles. Bissonette (1976) found prickly pear the dominant food throughout the year in Big Bend National Park in Texas. Everitt et al. (1981) found that in the south Texas rangelands prickly pear cactus made up 81.5 percent and 74.7 percent of the diet on two study areas where it was abundant; on a third study area where it had a low density, it made up 32.5 percent, with forbs making up 48.5 percent of the diet. Other foods listed were prickly pear fruit and mesquite pods, woody plants, and a small percentage of grasses.

Although the foods eaten by the collared peccary in the drier northern parts of its range are well understood, little accurate information is available for the moist rain forest and other areas farther south. In Yucatán Gaumer (1917) observed the collared peccary eating fruits of various trees, such as the palm, as well as roots, snakes, grubs, and caterpillars. Cabrera and Yepes (1940) reported that the collared peccary in South America ate roots, fruits, tubers, and tender stems from all classes of plants. They mentioned particularly the bulbs of the various Araceae, such as *Caladium* and *Colocasis*, which the Tupí Indians called taya. According to these writers, the name tayasu means "gnawer of taya." They also mentioned insects, frogs, and snakes in the diet of the collared peccary. Enders (1930) described the outside flesh of palm fruits, *Attalea gymphococa* and *Acromia sclerocarpa*, as important food of the collared peccary on Barro Colorado

Island in Panama. In Colombia, Borrero (1967) says it eats a great variety of fruits, roots, and tubers including the fruits of many species of palms. Kiltie (1979) examined the stomach contents of 17 collared peccaries from the rain forest of Manú National Park in Peru and found that the animals were largely frugivores, feeding principally on the fruits of palms and other tropical plants. Much of the material was too finely ground for identification. He found no significant difference in the plant species composition in collared and the white-lipped peccary stomachs.

Nearly all authors have mentioned mast and berries as food eaten by peccaries. Most of the nuts are highly nutritious and easily obtained when they fall from the trees. They are also available in nearly every season. For the oak woodland in Arizona, Eddy found four species of oak trees that began to shed their fruit in June and continued through December. Unlike the staple, less nutritious foods such as *Opuntia* sp., the mast-bearing plants are often sporadic in their yield of fruit, and certain years become known as "good" or "bad" mast years.

From the several detailed studies it is apparent that in most areas a few particular plants make up a substantial or staple part of the animal's diet. In addition, a wide variety of other plants are very important in the diet of the peccary when they are available.

The movement and feeding patterns of the collared peccary in Arizona have been described by Elder (1956) and Eddy (1961), Schweinsburg (1969), Day (1977b), Bigler (1974), Ellisor and Harwell (1979) and Bissonette (1976, 1978) in Texas. Both Elder and Eddy regarded the peccary as primarily an evening and morning feeder. Plotting the watering patterns of desert wildlife, Elder showed that peccaries used waterholes almost continuously throughout the night. He concluded that in hot weather feeding probably also went on through the night.

Eddy's (1961) observations, confirmed by wildlife research unit personnel, have shown definite seasonal patterns of feeding. In the hot summer months, the animals fed in early morning and evening hours. Between these feeding periods, the herds rested in sheltered areas in their home range. In autumn, as the temperature dropped, the morning feeding periods lasted longer and began earlier in the afternoon. In the coldest part of winter, feeding lasted throughout the day.

The manner in which the herds move during the feeding period has been accurately described by Eddy:

> When herds moved to feeding areas, from feeding areas to resting sites, or to water, they generally traveled in single file along game trails, fanning out when the trail was momentarily lost or when a wash or canyon was crossed. When moving, animals were often close together, although the herd column was occasionally broken into several segments....
>
> Herds fed in loosely knit units that varied greatly in compactness during feeding activity. When a particularly attractive cactus plant or tuber bed was located, the herd often assembled in a

group around the plant or bed and fed close together. Feeding herds generally moved in the same direction; if direction was altered, the herd broke up and the animals scattered unless they were in a canyon. In this case, all animals generally moved up the sides of the canyon if they were not too steep. There seemed to be no lead animal to direct movements of the herd when danger arose. Feeding generally took place while the animals were heading into the wind.

In Texas Ellisor and Harwell (1979) reported essentially the same feeding pattern but with more nighttime activity than found in Arizona; the collared peccary was found to be primarily a nocturnal feeder during spring, summer, and fall. Bissonette (1978) noted that feeding activity was closely correlated with ambient temperatures. Nocturnal feeding was common during the hot summer, while low winter temperatures delayed morning feeding in winter.

MANNER OF FEEDING

In the pens of the Arizona Cooperative Wildlife Research Unit where captive animals were kept, the manner in which the animals ate could be easily observed. Because close observation of free-roaming feeding animals is possible, observations on wild animals have also been made. From the first time that the young animals begin to nibble at vegetation, when only a few weeks of age, they show an adeptness at holding the food plants with the foot. Plants are often broken over and held with one foot while the animal picks off small pieces.

The peccary is a slow, dainty eater. It does not devour its food rapidly like carnivores or even like the domestic pig. When eating prickly pear, it usually breaks off single pads and, while holding the pad on the ground with one foot, takes out the contents and the outside layer after breaking through the skin with the feet.

Several writers have commented on the ability of peccaries to consume large quantities of spiny cacti and suffer no apparent ill effects. Knipe (1957) found numerous spines in their excrement following the consumption of small *Mammillaria* and *Echinocereus* cacti. Peccaries freely eat out the center parts of these small, spiny pincushion cacti, swallowing many spines in the process. Eddy (1959) described how peccaries also eat the soft centers of the barrel cactus or bisnaga (*Ferocactus wizlizenii*).

An important part of the collared peccary's diet is made up of roots, tubers, bulbs, and rhizomes of a variety of plants which the peccary obtains by digging (Alvarez 1952; Leopold 1959; Eddy 1961; Knipe 1957; Enders 1930). I found the collared peccary in the Chaco of Paraguay rooting out and eating the fleshy roots of *Boerhavia coccinea* Mill. This common Panotropical weed grows on disturbed soil from Arizona south to Argentina, covering practically the entire range of the collared peccary. The consumption of underground parts is greatest in

Figure 3.5. Roots and tops of *Cirsium* sp., a common food of collared peccary in Arizona. (Photograph by Thomas A. Eddy)

fall and winter, and the peccaries dig them out at the time of year when little of the above ground parts are green.

Field observations by Eddy and other workers at the Arizona Cooperative Wildlife Research Unit indicate that the peccaries are able to locate the edible underground parts by smell. It does not seem to be important whether the above ground portions of the plant are still present. The plants described by Eddy (1959) were a morning glory, *Ipomoea muricata*; a thistle, *Cirsium arvense* (Fig. 3.5); and two gourds, *Cucurbita digitata* and *C. foetidissima*. The animals usually leave small saucer-shaped excavations in places where the tubers or bulbs have been taken. Eddy described finding 704 of these diggings in seven digging sites which had been rooted by peccaries where the bulbs of covena were being sought. He reported areas as large as 10 acres that peccaries completely denuded of *Cirsium arvense*. His figures demonstrate the animals' thorough search to obtain the underground morsels. They also demonstrate the versatile nature of their feeding habits.

Writers of nontechnical articles on the peccary have often referred to it as omnivorous. Knipe (1957:34) discussed the many fallacies concerning the foods taken by the peccary and summarized by saying that he found "no evidence to support such an omnivorous and gluttonous reputation." Studies by wildlife research unit personnel, principally Eddy (1961), have indicated that classifying the peccary as an omnivorous feeder is an exaggeration. Although Eddy found grasshoppers, crickets, beetles, and some carrion in stomach contents, there is no evidence that the peccary regularly takes animal matter.

EFFECTS OF PRICKLY PEAR IN THE DIET

Nearly all investigators in the United States who have reported on the foods of the collared peccary have listed the fruits and cladophylls of the prickly pear cactus (*Opuntia* sp.) as the most common. The overwhelming emphasis on the collared peccary's consumption of prickly pear cactus has, in my opinion, given the wrong impression of its true place in the animal's diet. Knipe (1957) referred to it as a "preferred" food. The term "preferred" originated with Leopold (1933) who used it to designate the palatability sequence and the order in which the *available* foods are taken by a given species at a particular time and place. In the desert regions of the southwestern United States, where most of the studies have been done and the prickly pear is eaten in such large quantities, it is the only food available during a large part of the year. Zervanos and Hadley (1973) demonstrated that enough energy could be supplied to a peccary on a prickly pear diet if it ate 1.6 kg/day in summer and 1.9 kg/day in winter (Zervanos and Hadley 1973). Bissonette (1976) also believed that prickly pear was the most important food of the collared peccary in Texas.

These enthusiastic reports on the value of prickly pear to collared peccaries need to be tempered with a more thorough understanding of the complete nutritional value of this plant. Its value as a food for range livestock has long been known, especially as an emergency ration in times of drought. Morrison (1954) says of prickly pear that "Since they are low in protein, all the cacti should be fed with a protein-rich concentrate or roughage. Cacti alone will not maintain livestock. Though desert cattle sometimes subsist on them for three months of the year, they become very emaciated."

Because of the use of prickly pear as an emergency livestock food, numerous studies of its nutrient content have been made. Several different species of the cactus have been tested so considerable variation can be expected. A summary of the important nutritional constituents of various species of green prickly pear pads is given in Table 3.1. Data on some of the minerals available in cactus pads are given in Table 3.2.

Because of the great use of prickly pear in the peccary diet, special emphasis was placed on trying to find out the animals' reaction to prolonged diets of this low quality food. The first measurements of prickly pear consumption by captive peccaries were made in the summer of 1958. Adult peccaries were fed only prickly pear cladophylls to determine effects on general health, weight, and vigor. The animals were given water. One female was kept alone while the other two animals were in a pen together. Weighed amounts of prickly pear pads were put into the pens each day, and the uneaten remains were removed and weighed after 24 hours. The peccaries were weighed

Table 3.1. **Important Nutritional Constituents**
of Oven-dried Prickly Pear Cactus Leaves

Crude Protein %	Crude Fiber %	Crude Fats %	Carbohydrates %	Mineral Ash %	Authority
n = 4 $\overline{X}$ = 4.97 S.D. = 0.11	n = 5 $\overline{X}$ = 8.94 S.D. = 0.06	n = 5 $\overline{X}$ = 2.48 S.D. = .13	n = 6 $\overline{X}$ = 65.88 S.D. = 1.56	n = 4 $\overline{X}$ = 23.52 S.D. = 0.27	Teles (1977)
n = 4 $\overline{X}$ = 5.3 Min = 4.1 Max = 7.7	n = 3 $\overline{X}$ = 27.2 Min = 11.8 Max = 54.8			n = 4 $\overline{X}$ = 16.1 Min = 7.4 Max = 24.3	Miller (1958)
n = 7 $\overline{X}$ = 4.91 S.D. = 0.95					Sowls (unpub.) Arizona (*O. englemannii*)
7.94	11.77	2.13	53.84	2.85	Thornber and Vinson (1911) Cited by Teles (1977)
6.70					Knight et al. (1969) Cited by Teles (1977)
3.30	11.51	2.17	68.06	2.89	USDA 1920 Cited by Teles (1977)
10.00	23.26	3.64		1.60	I.N.C.A.P. 1961 Cited by Teles (1977)
3.88	7.82	6.53	64.82	0.90	McDowel et al. (1974) Cited by Teles (1977)
3.33	10.60	0.67	72.67		Church and Church (1975) Cited by Teles (1977)

seven times over the 16-week period. Because only a small number of animals could be used at one time, the trials were repeated as often as necessary to answer these questions: How long, and in what physical

Table 3.2. **Minerals Found in Various Species**
of Prickly Pear (mg/100 gm)

Magnesium	Na Sodium	Ca Calcium	P Phosphorus	K Potassium	Authority
$\overline{X}$ = 142 S.D. = 3.94	$\overline{X}$ = 9 S.D. = 0.47	$\overline{X}$ = 56 S.D. = 1.15	$\overline{X}$ = 24.3 S.D. = 0.53	$\overline{X}$ = 260 S.D. = 11.54	Teles (1977)
144	—	—	—	—	Orr (1974) Cited by Teles (1977)
—	2	20	28	166	Church and Church (1975) Cited by Teles (1977)
—	—	110	20	—	I.N.C.A.P. (1961) Cited by Teles (1977)
—	—	n = 2 $\overline{X}$ = 2.94 S.D. = 1.41	n = 2 $\overline{X}$ = .08 S.D. = .05	—	Miller (1958)

condition, can peccaries subsist on diets of prickly pear? What is most lacking in a diet of prickly pear? What levels of protein and other nutrients are necessary for a peccary to remain in good health?

The amount of prickly pear consumed and the animals' weights are shown graphically in Figure 3.6. These figures show the trend in prickly pear consumption and the decline in the weights of the animals. A slow increase in the amount of prickly pear eaten was evident at first with a sudden rise in prickly pear consumption from the fifth to eighth week of the experiment. At the tenth week, the consumption slowly went up until the fifteenth week, when consumption slowed drastically and dropped to less than one-third of what it had been at maximum consumption. Similar but shorter experiments were carried out later with six additional animals. All showed a similar response to the cactus diet.

These experiments represented situations where no other food was available. Cactus consumption in the wild reaches high levels during parts of the year when little else is available but only in extreme cases does it probably make up the complete diet. At the end of the sixteenth week, the animals appeared emaciated and weak.

NUTRITIONAL REQUIREMENTS

Protein

One of the most essential parts of an animal's diet is protein. This complex constituent of the organs and nonbony structures of the animal's body is constantly in need of new food proteins for growth and repair. With the exception of deer, little research on protein requirements and availability in the diets of wild ungulates has been done.

Preliminary trials to set the minimum levels of protein in the diet for the maintenance of general health and weight were conducted by the wildlife research unit in 1959. Three male animals were used in these trials. Two animals were put in one pen and the single animal was kept in another pen. The animals were allowed to eat as much of the feed as they wanted and were weighed once each week. Four diets were used in these trials with the protein levels as follows: 0 percent, 5 percent, 10 percent, and 15 percent. The protein supplied in these diets was soybean oil meal (42.53 percent protein). Vitamins and minerals added included: Vitamin A (in cod liver oil), Vitamin B_{12}, calcium pantothenate, folic acid, menadione, niacin, riboflavin, and thiamine. One part cod liver oil was added to four parts cooking oil to act as a binder. To this the proper ration of cornstarch and soybean oil meal (42.53 percent protein) was added to make the desired percentage of protein.

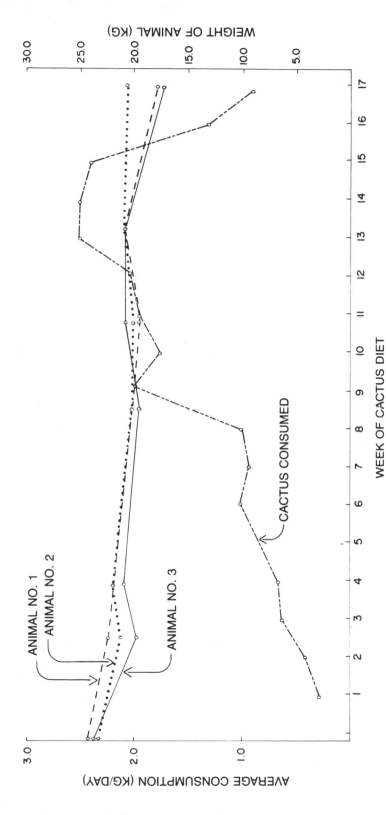

Figure 3.6. Record of cactus consumption and weight changes for three collared peccaries over a sixteen-week period

When no protein was fed, the animals lost weight, but when a 5 percent protein mixture was fed, all animals maintained their weight without further loss. Two of the animals began to gain on the 5 percent protein level and continued to gain at a progressively more rapid rate at the 10 percent and 15 percent protein levels, while the other one showed an erratic picture and did not gain weight until the protein level reached 10 percent. More research with larger sample sizes is needed to determine the protein requirements of the collared peccary.

To compare the protein level of prickly pear with that of other foods of the collared peccary, 16 other common peccary foods were analyzed. A summary of the presence of protein and phosphorus in these foods is given in Table 3.3. When compared to the protein levels of the commonly eaten prickly pear, it is readily apparent that the other foods are much higher in protein. These foods are available during periods of higher moisture and provide much higher protein levels after short emergency periods of low protein intake during dry periods when only prickly pear is available.

Vitamins

Indications that the vitamin B complex may be one of the critical deficiencies in the cactus diet for peccaries was demonstrated on

Table 3.3. Percentages of Protein and Phosphorus in Dry Weight Samples of Food Plants of the Collared Peccary in Arizona

Plant		Percentage	Composition
Common Name	Scientific Name	Protein	Phosphorus
Deervetch	*Lotus* sp.	10.81	0.328
Bee balm	*Monarda* sp.	9.42	0.726
Filaree	*Erodium cicutarium*	15.10	0.516
Lupine (dry)	*Lupinus* sp.	18.58	0.406
Lupine (green)	*Lupinus* sp.	17.82	0.344
Mesquite (pods)	*Prosopis* sp.	14.4	0.210
Beard tongue	*Penstemon* sp.	9.85	0.442
Scalloped leaf phacelia	*Phacelia crenulata*	10.53	0.500
Evening primrose	*Oenothera* sp.	8.65	0.383
Mustard	*Brassica* sp.	21.42	0.370
Arizona poppy	*Eschscholtzia arizonica*	21.90	0.576
Sow thistle (tops)	*Lactuca* sp.	21.09	0.526
Pigweed	*Amaranthus retroflexus*	16.87	0.308
Wooly tidestromia	*Tidestromia lanuginosa*	12.31	0.256
Agave	*Agave palmeri*	$\left\{ \begin{array}{l} n = 2 \\ \overline{X} = 7.52 \\ S.D. = .22 \end{array} \right.$	0.20, 0.156
Trailing four-o'clock	*Allionia incarnata*	14.66	0.188
Morning glory (tubers)	*Evolvulus arizonicus*	10.73	0.239
Mexican poppy	*Kallstroemia grandiflora*	11.42	0.262
Lambsquarters	*Chenopodium album*	7.80	0.328
Wild gourd (tubers)	*Cucurbita digitata*	10.82	0.283

three different occasions when animals became weak and emaciated after long periods on the cactus diet. Injections of vitamin B complex quickly rejuvenated them. The first animal to respond to the injections was an adult sow which had eaten cactus for 121 days and decreased in weight from 53 pounds to 38 pounds. On the 122nd day she was weak and would not eat. She was given an intramuscular injection of B vitamins (25 mg niacin, 215 mg thiamine, 2.5 mg calcium pantothenate, and 1.2 mg pyridoxine). On the 123rd day she was given a second injection. On the 124th day she was much more active and returned to normal feeding. Eleven days after the change of diet and the first injection of vitamin B complex, she weighed 41.5 pounds and on the 21st day she weighed 43 pounds and appeared to be in good health. Similar dramatic recoveries were recorded for two other weak animals.

Investigations into the vitamin content of cactus have been done by Teles (1977) and the wildlife research unit. Data from these studies relating to some of the B vitamins are given in Table 3.4 and compared to similar data on green alfalfa.

In addition to data on the B vitamins, Teles found the total carotene content of green prickly pear pads to average 31.2 micrograms per 100 international units per 100 grams. He found also a very low vitamin E content in the prickly pear pads. In milligrams tocopherol per 100 grams of material, the pads averaged 0.25 milligrams. Teles also found the vitamin D content to be low (294 I.U./100 grams where one I.U. = 0.025 micrograms per 100 grams material). Of the B vitamins Teles gives, niacin averaged between 0.441 and 0.483 mg/100 g. He found 14 mcg thiamine per 100 grams of green material and 60 mcg of riboflavin per 100 grams of green material.

Table 3.4. **Amounts of Some B Vitamins in Two Species of Cacti Compared to Green Alfalfa (except where noted, measurements are mg/100 gm)**

Forage material	Niacin	Riboflavin	Thiamine	Pyridoxine	Pantothenic Acid	Authority
O. ficus indica	0.483	60 mcg/ 100	13.79* 14.11 mcg/ 100	—	—	Teles (1977)
(green pads)	(n = 7)		(n = 4)			
O. engelmannii Sample 1	0.42	0.039	<0.02[+]	0.107	1.78	Sowls (unpub.)
Sample 2	0.35	0.033	<0.02[+]	0.106	1.57	Sowls (unpub.)
Sample 3	0.46	0.046	<0.02[+]	0.105	1.96	Sowls (unpub.)
Green alfalfa	3.7	0.90	0.55	0.64	3.4	Miller (1958)

*Two methods of analysis used.
[+] Samples exhibited "blank behavior." If present, it was extremely low.

Further work on the role of vitamins and their availability to peccaries is needed. The possibility that these animals are able to synthesize vitamins needs further investigation.

SYNTHESIS OF VOLATILE FATTY ACIDS

The peccary's unusual pouched stomach has led to considerable speculation regarding its ability to utilize coarse roughage by transforming cellulose to useable volatile fatty acids (VFA). In some cases people have labeled the parts of the peccary stomach in terms of a ruminant (Stewart 1964). Langer (1973, 1974, 1978, 1979) has described the stomach of the collared peccary in great detail and compared it to that of other artiodactyls.

Research has adequately demonstrated that microbial breakdown of cellulose is common in many nonruminants, allowing them to receive nourishment from coarse food. Several animals are capable of ruminant-like digestion, including an herbivorous marsupial (*Setonix brachyurus* Quoy and Gaimard) (Moir et al. 1956), langur monkeys (*Presbytis cristatus* and *P. entellus*) (Bauchop and Martucci 1968), feral hogs and warthogs (Longhurst pers. comm.), and rock ptarmigan (*Lagopus mutus*) and willow ptarmigan (*Lagopus lagopus*) (Gasaway 1976a, 1976b).

Hayer (1961) used an artificial rumen to determine cellulose digestion by fluids from the peccary stomach but was unable to demonstrate the digestibility of cellulose. He did, however, find volatile fatty acids in the stomach contents of captive animals on commercial diets and from wild collected animals. He found that concentrations of VFAs in captured animals showed 762 and 661 mg per 100 ml of fluid, and those on a wild diet of prickly pear had a concentration of 1,244 mg per 100 ml.

Using captive animals, Dyson (1969) did further work on digestion in the collared peccary and found values ranging from 65.9 to 6.6 micromoles per gram of wet contents with an average concentration of 33.2 micromoles of total VFAs per gram of wet contents. He found acetic, propionic, isobutyric, isovaleric, and valeric in all three areas of the tract. He fed hay and grain diets to captive animals and found the VFA concentrations higher in the stomach than in the lower portions of the alimentary tract. Dyson considered this much lower than that found in most ruminants and cited Carrol and Hungate (1954) who reported 60 to 120 micromoles of VFAs per milliliter of rumen contents in cattle.

Langer (1978), however, gave data from Prins showing volatile fatty acid concentrations in the forestomach of three captive collared peccaries. Comparing these data with those compiled by Church (1969), he showed that animals fed swine pellets had slightly higher volatile fatty acid concentrations than those for some domestic animals on roughage diets.

To determine the volatile fatty acid concentrations in the digestive contents of wild peccaries on wild diets, in 1977 we collected four animals for stomach analysis. Samples taken from various parts of the digestive tract were analyzed by gas chromatography. One animal was collected on February 7, 1977, in desert grassland at an elevation of 3,500 feet near Tucson, Arizona, where it was feeding principally on prickly pear cladophylls (*O. englemannii*). Data for the volatile fatty acid concentrations for this animal are given in Table 3.5. The other three animals were collected in February, March, and November, 1977, in the foothills of the Dragoon Mountains in southeastern Arizona at an elevation of 4,500 feet, where they were eating principally the basal leaves and pulp of *Agave palmeri*. Data on the volatile fatty acid concentrations in these three animals are given in Table 3.6.

Many variables are present in the existing data that cannot be accounted for. For example, peccaries on wild diets could take a number of species of plants that might affect the creation of volatile fatty acids in the stomach. Studies by Oh et al. (1967, 1968) showed that certain browse species taken by sheep and deer had an inhibitory effect on the microbial action in deer rumen. Langer (1978) has pointed out that the VFA concentrations in the forestomach contents examined by Prins were much higher than contents from the glandular stomach. This was also true of the material from animals on wild diets that we analyzed. Langer suggested that this may be accounted for by an absorption of VFA in the forestomach.

No studies have yet been done to reveal the presence of suitable microbes in the stomach of the collared peccary. Hayer (1961), however, found the presence of motile bacteria in the caecum. One measure of an animal's ability to harbor microbial organisms and thus be able to break down cellulose into VFA is the acidity of the stomach ingesta. This varies with the diet, time after feeding that the sample is taken, and species of animal. Hayer found the stomach contents of the

Table 3.5. Concentration of Volatile Fatty Acids in the Stomach and Intestines of a Wild Collared Peccary on a Diet of Primarily Prickly Pear (Arizona)

Digestive	Volatile Fatty Acids (μm/me)						
Compartment	Acetic	Propionic	Isobutyric	Butyric	Isovaleric	Valeric	Total
Stomach	105.90	47.92	0.52	12.11	1.67	1.35	169.41
(2 samples)	62.12	21.49	0.52	7.43	1.04	1.46	94.06
Small intestine	57.50	21.09	0.39	3.13	0.42	0.63	83.16
Caecum	88.19	42.69	0.27	11.31	1.91	1.49	145.86
Large intestine	62.92	27.80	0.26	7.43	0.63	1.46	100.08
	Volatile Fatty Acids (Molar %)						
Stomach	62.51	28.29	0.31	7.15	0.40	1.35	100
(2 samples)	66.04	22.85	0.55	7.90	1.11	1.55	100
Small intestine	69.14	25.36	0.47	3.76	0.51	0.76	100
Caecum	60.46	29.27	0.19	7.75	1.31	1.02	100
Large intestine	62.87	27.78	0.26	7.42	0.63	1.04	100

**Table 3.6. Concentrations of Volatile Fatty Acids in Stomachs
From Three Wild Collared Peccaries Feeding Primarily on Agave (Arizona)**

Digestive Compartment	N	Volatile Fatty Acids (μm/ml)										Total
		Acetic		Propionic		Butyric		Isovaleric		Valeric		
		X̄	S.D.	X̄	S.D.	X̄	S.D.	X̄	S.D.	X̄	S.D.	
Anterior blind sac	3	54.35	10.66	40.60	1.20	16.13	11.73	2.59	.70	14.28	6.90	127.95
Upper blind sac	3	37.25	22.89	28.45	20.18	7.47	4.75	1.39	.69	6.72	5.20	81.28
Glandular stomach	3	27.59	10.78	21.81	10.24	11.60	12.23	1.24	1.29	9.44	11.02	71.68
Gastric pouch	3	57.88	3.03	44.68	3.95	16.06	3.46	2.31	1.34	9.34	2.44	130.27
Small intestine	1	21.10		2.44		2.29		.70		1.55		28.08
Caecum	1	24.20		8.02		2.75		.38		.63		35.98
Large intestine	1	36.66		12.19		3.43		.68		1.00		53.96

Digestive Compartment	N	Volatile Fatty Acids (Molar %)					Total
		Acetic	Propionic	Butyric	Isovaleric	Valeric	
Anterior blind sac	3	42.47	31.73	12.61	2.03	11.16	100
Upper blind sac	3	45.96	26.74	14.20	1.53	11.57	100
Glandular stomach	3	46.02	26.70	14.20	1.52	11.56	100
Gastric pouch	3	44.42	34.30	12.33	1.78	7.17	100
Small intestine	1	75.14	8.69	8.16	2.49	5.52	100
Caecum	1	67.26	22.29	7.64	1.06	1.75	100
Large intestine	1	67.94	22.59	6.36	1.26	1.85	100

animals on a commercial diet to have a pH of 5.2, while those on a prickly pear diet to have a pH of 5.6; he considered these values too low to promote VFA production. Dyson (1969) found the following average pH values in the digestive tract of captive peccaries on experimental diets: the large fundic portion of the stomach, 6.2; extension of the fundic portion, 5.3; small intestine, 7.1; caecum, 6.8; and anterior large intestine, 6.8. We have, however, further data from wild specimens. Table 3.7 shows the pH values we found in the ingesta from six wild collared peccaries collected in 1977. These areas of the digestive tract represent those described by Langer (1978). Four of these animals are the same ones represented in Tables 3.5 and 3.6. In domestic livestock the suitable range of pH for the maintenance of active micro-

Table 3.7. pH Values of Contents From Digestive
Tract of Six Wild Collared Peccaries Collected in Arizona

Part of Tract	pH values		
	n	Mean	S.D.
Anterior blindsac	5	5.7	0.57
Upper blindsac	6	6.1	0.28
Gastric pouch	6	6.1	0.28
Glandular stomach	6	5.8	0.68
Small intestine	6	7.6	0.89
Caecum	5	7.3	0.88
Large intestine	6	7.5	0.56

bial bacteria to break down cellulose into VFA's is generally considered to vary from 5.5 to 7.5 (Hungate 1966). Thus, the pH of the digestive tract of the collared peccary should be a suitable environment for the microbial bacteria capable of breaking down and converting cellulose to VFA.

Although many unanswered questions remain regarding the collared peccary's ability to turn cellulose into volatile fatty acids, there is strong evidence that they have this ability. Table 3.8 summarizes the available data on the presence of VFA concentrations in the ingesta of the collared peccary compared to cattle and sheep. Some data on the presence of VFA concentrations in peccary included samples from unspecified parts of the stomach. These data suggest that the collared peccary, like many other nonruminants, is capable of manufacturing volatile fatty acids from cellulose and thus making a new source of energy available to them. This would be especially helpful to them in areas where they are forced to eat low quality foods such as cactus for long periods of time.

DIGESTIBILITY

Because of the large amount of prickly pear cactus and other roughage eaten, the question of how well the collared peccary can digest this material is important in determining the energy available. Shively (1979) carried out digestion trials with captive animals in metabolism cages. By giving known quantities of food and water and collecting all feces and urine over a fixed period, she obtained data on the digestibility of commercial diets (hog breeder pellets), a purified diet, and a prickly pear diet. She found that digestion coefficients for fiber were highest on the commercial pellets (26 percent) and lowest on the purified diet (4 percent). In addition, the fiber digestion on the prickly pear diet varied greatly between collections from –13 percent to 6 percent.

Table 3.8. Comparisons of Typical Quantities of Volatile Fatty Acids in Stomach Contents of Collared Peccary Compared to Other Animals

Species	Ration	Sample Size	Total VFA μ mol/ml	Volatile Fatty Acids					Source
				Acetic	Propionic	Butyric	Valeric	Other	
Cattle (*Bos tarus*)	Pasture		131–148	65–67	18–19	11–12	—	3–4	Balch and Rowland (1957) quoted by Church (1969)
Cattle (*Bos tarus*)	Ryegrass pasture		127–129	60–62	20–21	13–14	1.6–1.7	3–4	Bath and Rook (1967) quoted by Church (1969)
Cattle (*Bos indicus*)	Green berseem		94	60	18–19	14–15	—	—	Ichponani and Sidhu (1965) quoted by Church (1969)
Sheep (*Ovis gries*)	Ryegrass, Clover pasture		114	64–65	18	12–13	1	4	Jamieson (1959) quoted by Church (1969)
Collared peccary	Commercial hog feed	3	118.2	38.6	25.8	29.2	—	—	Hayer (1961)
Collared peccary	Ground milo and hay		43.7						Dyson (1969)
Collared peccary	Commercial hog feed	2	162.6	38.7	21.8	26.0	10.8	2.7	Prins (quoted by Langer 1978)
Collared peccary	Commercial hog feed and straw	1	131.7	39.9	15.4	32.3	11.2	1.2	Prins (quoted by Langer 1978)
Collared peccary	Wild cactus *O. englemannii*	1	131.73	64.3	25.6	7.5	1.46	1.2	Sowls (unpub.)
Collared peccary	Wild *Agave palmeri* plus forbs	3	102.8	44.7	29.9	13.3	10.4	1.71	Sowls (unpub.)

NOTE: Data collected after 1977 define parts according to Langer 1978.

WATER REQUIREMENTS

Elder (1956) described how collared peccaries used waterholes in the Tucson Mountains of Arizona and concluded that open water was probably necessary during the driest part of the year but was not essential when succulents were available. These waterholes were also places where artificial salt licks were available. Knipe (1957) and Elder (1956) say that the collared peccary comes to water even when succulents are available. Minnamon (1962), working in the same area, concluded that the presence or absence of permanent water did not influence the size of the home range of the collared peccary where succulents made up a large part of the diet. He concluded that some herds, whose home range did not include waterholes, did not go to water for long periods. Minnamon's observations were confirmed later when these same waterholes were eliminated. The herds remained and still used these same areas after the waterholes disappeared.

Zervanos and Day (1977) determined the water loss and water turnover of the collared peccary. They found that, under field conditions, peccaries lost 1.35 liters of water per day in summer and 1.17 liters in winter. They estimated that to do this when obtaining all their water from cactus they would have to eat 1.54 kg of green cactus per day in summer and 1.47 kg green cactus per day in winter.

During our feeding trials on green cactus, we found that the average daily consumption of green cactus reached a maximum daily intake of 3.9 kg. Specimens of cactus collected at Tucson in 1973 and 1974 averaged 82.6 percent water. Given this percentage, the total daily water intake for a peccary in summer could reach 3.0 liters, more than twice the daily water loss Zervanos and Day found. Thus, while on a diet composed largely of green cactus, peccaries would be able to obtain enough water to meet their needs.

THE OXALIC ACID PROBLEM

When the collared peccary is forced to eat large amounts of cactus, large amounts of water pass through the body. One result of the cactus diet is almost continuous diarrhea. The other problem, which could be serious when peccaries are forced to eat cactus for long periods and depend on it as a water supply, is that prickly pear cactus contains fairly high levels of oxalic acid. When analyzed, three samples collected from different sites near Tucson, Arizona, in 1977 were found to contain 518, 539, and 369 mg/100 gm (pers. comm. Francis B. Coon). Compared to common forage for livestock, these amounts are not extremely high. However, when the animal must rely on a continuous diet of cactus for both food and water, the buildup of oxalic acid may be detrimental. The effects would probably occur much faster in the absence of free drinking water such as occurs in desert situations. They could include interference with metabolism of calcium, magnesium, and other minerals (Hodgkinson 1977) and kidney failure. Twice during our cactus-feeding trials, even though free water was available, kidney failure occurred. The first time was on February 18, 1960, when an adult female, on a cactus diet with water for about four weeks, suddenly became ill and died. Microscopic examination of the kidneys revealed a chronic progressive poisoning leading to renal failure. The other occurred on May 7, 1966, when an adult male died from apparent oxalic acid poisoning after being on a diet of prickly pear for only 26 days. This same animal had previously survived for 102 days on a prickly pear diet with no noticeable adverse results.

Although ruminants may adapt to diets of high oxalates (Hodgkinson 1977), it is not known to what extent nonruminants like the peccary are able to do so. Because of the remarkable way the collared peccary survives on prickly pear in the desert areas, which seems atypical of its overall habitat, further research should be undertaken to study the role of prickly pear in its diet.

4 Reproduction

THE COLLARED PECCARY IS THE ONLY WILD UNGULATE of the Western Hemisphere which has a year-long breeding season. Until the 1960s, little was known about the reproductive pattern of this animal. Under favorable conditions the collared peccary breeds and reproduces readily in captivity. Thus it is possible to use captive animals for research in which exact details cannot be determined from wild specimens. The captive animals that the wildlife research unit studied were all kept in outdoor pens with small shelters for protection from the weather. All of the animals were taken from wild populations within 60 miles of Tucson, Arizona, where the pens were located. Some had been tamed as pets while others raised in the pens remained wild. Except for periods when captive animals were on special diets as part of an experiment, all had free access to water and a supply of commercial hog pellets which contained 16 percent crude protein, 2 percent crude fat, and 6 percent crude fiber.

In addition to the use of captive animals, information and materials were collected at established stations where hunters passed after they had killed animals. The hunting season lasted about two weeks each year in late winter. Live wild animals were handled at other times of the year during trapping and tagging operations, and their reproductive condition was noted whenever possible.

Field observations were made throughout the year to determine the season of birth. The length and frequency of the estrous cycle, gestation period, and breeding age were determined for captive animals. Studies of penned animals indicate the potential reproductive capacity. These figures are useful in comparisons with data collected from wild populations.

It was soon apparent that the external manifestations of heat, which have been successfully used as indications of estrus in some

59

domestic animals, particularly domestic swine (Struve 1911; Corner 1921; Altman 1941), are not reliable for peccary. Vaginal smears were examined to obtain information on the stage of the cycle. Sows were forced into a metal squeeze-crate, and vaginal smears were obtained by use of a rubber catheter. This was an extremely difficult procedure because the sows soon learned to avoid the crate. The method was not practical when daily information was required over a long period. Instead, five vasectomized males were used to measure the receptivity of females to determine the length and frequency of the cycle among captive animals. This technique was used by Morrison et al. (1959) to obtain similar data in the American elk (*Cervus canadensis*).

The length of the gestation period was determined by isolating the females after observed copulation with a normal boar until the young were born. Litter size and sex ratio were obtained both from animals born in captivity and from wild litters.

REPRODUCTIVE SYSTEMS

Males

The reproductive tract of the male collared peccary has been described by Low (1970). For a 3½-year-old male, he gives dimensions of the various organs: "testes are 1¾ inches long by 1¼ inches in diameter. Vas deferens is 9½ inches long, with no terminal ampulla. The seminal vesicles are well developed triangular structures 2½ inches by 1½ inches by 1 inch deep. The prostate gland forms a ¾ inch diameter sphere around the junction of the vas deferens, seminal vesicle and urethra. The well developed bulbourethral gland is an elongated tube 3¼ inches long with a diameter of 1⅛ inches. The penis is about 9½ inches from its pubic attachment and has a typical 'corkscrew' shape and reverse flexure of the domestic pig."

Low's description of the male reproductive system is accurate and very similar to that of the domestic pig described by Nalbandov (1964) and Getty (1975). Figure 4.1 shows the relative size and position of the various parts. This drawing was made of the reproductive tract from a large adult male and predates Low's description.

Females

Wislocki (1931) described the uterus of the collared peccary as bicornate with differences from that of the domestic pig, most important being the smaller uterus and its configuration; the tubes and ovaries he found materially different from that of the domestic sow. Low (1970) described the uterus of an adult pregnant sow. The anatomy of the upper part of the reproductive tract of an adult nonpregnant sow from Arizona is shown in Figure 4.2. Both Wislocki and Low give complete descriptions of the anatomy of the reproductive tract of the female collared peccary.

MATING, GESTATION, PARTURITION

Information on the breeding season is available only for very limited parts of the peccary's range. Enders (1930) believed that on Barro Colorado Island in Panama most of the young were born in the early part of the year. Miller (1930) found newborn young in the Matto Grosso of Brazil in early November. During two visits to the state of São Paulo, Brazil, where I observed large numbers of collared peccaries during July 1976 and August 1977, I saw only one pair of newborn young in August. All other young I saw indicated an October or November birth. The local game guard said that all young were born in October and November. In the Chaco of Paraguay I have observed only three-quarter grown animals in three visits in June and July. Borrero (1967) believes that in Colombia they reproduce at all times of the year.

Zuckerman (1953) gives the months of birth for thirteen litters in the London Zoological Gardens as January, May, July, August, October, November, and December. Leopold (1959) stated that they farrowed at any time of the year in Mexico, and Neal (1959) believed that breeding took place in all months of the year in Arizona. In Texas, Jennings and Harris (1953) report that breeding took place in every month except February. However, their data on breeding times were based on back-dating from times of parturition, and estimates of the ages of fetuses were based on an incorrect gestation period. Consequently, the non-breeding time which they observed probably should have been set at least 30 days earlier or during the month of January. Ellisor and Harwell (1979) gave parturition dates of the collared peccary in south-central Texas. They found births in all months except December but with peaks in April and August.

Knipe (1957) reported monthly farrowing data on 291 young peccaries in Arizona. He found that young were born in every month of the year. He concluded that the peak of parturition was from mid-summer through late fall. However, on close analysis, one sees that the unequal distribution of data throughout the year would likely influence Knipe's conclusions. Most of his observations were made in conjunction with game surveys in autumn, and comparatively few were made in July and August. Since 1956, when the Arizona Cooperative Wildlife Research Unit began to study the peccary, farrowings have been observed throughout the year. Figure 4.3 shows the frequency distribution of parturition dates in Arizona; more than half of these dates occurred in the three summer months. Breeding in Arizona, calculated to be five months earlier, occurs in winter during January, February, and March.

Information on the incidence of pregnancy during February and March was obtained from examinations of reproductive tracts saved by hunters in Arizona. In a sample of 114 reproductive tracts from adult

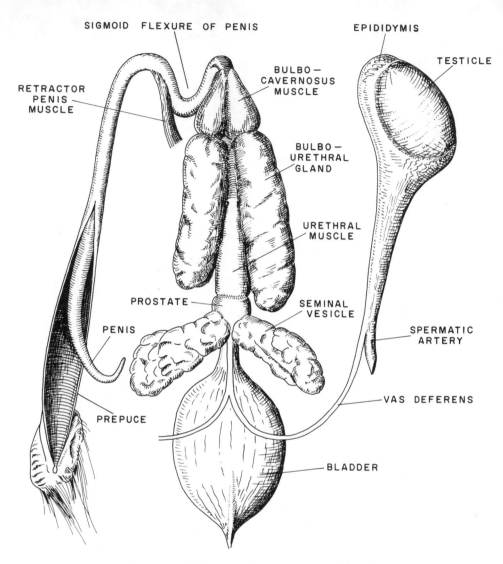

Figure 4.1. Male reproductive system of a collared peccary. (Drawing by Harold Irby)

females collected from 1956 through 1963, 21, or 18.4 percent were found to contain fetuses.

In efforts to capture animals for studies of population dynamics, young animals were often caught with their mothers. The principal trapping effort was made in the spring dry season during April, May, June, and the first half of July. During the summer rainy season, from about 1 July to early September, no trapping was done. Trapping

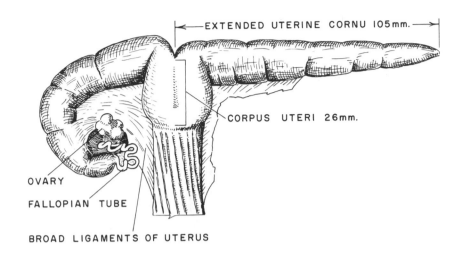

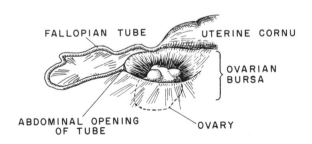

Figure 4.2. Female reproductive system of a collared peccary. (Drawing by Harold Irby)

began again each year in late September during the fall dry season. Between 1959 and 1964, 120 adult females were captured. Of 96 caught in the spring dry season, only 6.2 percent were accompanied by young less than one-quarter grown. Of the 24 caught in the fall after the summer rains, 33.3 percent were accompanied by young less than one-quarter grown.

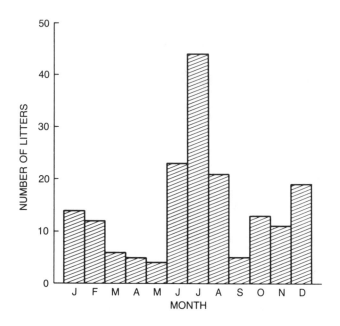

Figure 4.3. Frequency distribution of months of birth for litters of collared peccaries in Arizona

Estrous Cycle

A seasonally polyestrous type of reproductive pattern is common among wild ungulates in North America. Probably reproduction is known best in the various members of the Cervidae family, especially the white-tailed deer (Cheatum and Morton 1942) and the American Elk (Morrison et al. 1959).

Figure 4.3 shows that the collared peccary is not restricted in its breeding to any particular time of year. In captivity it was found to be a continuous breeder. If females failed to become pregnant, the estrous cycle was repeated, not just a few times, as in northern white-tailed deer and elk, but over the entire year.

The results of observations made on cycle length and duration of estrus, using the vasectomized male to detect estrus, are summarized in Table 4.1. Three of these animals were observed for more than a year, and a fourth was studied daily for 177 days. At the end of this time, she was impregnated by a normal male which broke through a fence into her pen. The average length of the cycle in the four peccaries which were observed for nine or more cycles varied between 22.6 and 24.6 days; during these cycles the average duration of estrus varied between 3.5 and 4.8 days.

**Table 4.1 Estrous Cycle in Seven Captive Female Peccaries
as Indicated by Daily Encounters With Vasectomized Males**

Animal	No. of Days Observed	No. of Cycles	Duration of Estrus (days) Range	Avg.	Range	Estrous Cycle (days) Avg.	S.D.	Remarks
1589	382	16	2–8	4.6	21–30	23.5	2.56	Age at beginning: 1 year, 9 weeks Previous litters: 1
1435	394	16	1–7	3.5	19–29	24.6	2.52	Age: 5 years, 21 weeks Litters: 3
1597	382	17	1–7	4.8	17–28	22.6	2.86	Age: 2 years Litters: 1
804	177	9	3–5	3.8	18–27	23.1	2.69	Age: 4 years, 14 weeks Litters: 4
1144	44	2	4–5	4.5	20–24	22.0	5.65	Age: 3 years, 20 weeks Litters: 1
1148	52	2	1–3	2.0	22–30	26.0	2.82	Age: 1 year, 50 weeks Litters: 1
1593	44	2	1–3	2.0	20–24	22.0	2.82	Age: 2 years, 8 weeks Litters: 1

Breeding Age and Season

Little has been published on the breeding age of the collared peccary. Information on the age of captive peccaries at first mating was collected from young females of known age which had been kept with males. In one of these instances three young females were permitted to grow to maturity in a pen with two young males of nearly the same age as the females.

Data on first known parturition for six young females are given in Table 4.2. These figures represent the first successful birth of living young, but do not necessarily represent the first estrous period or the first mating because it is possible that previous matings did not result in conceptions, or that pregnancy was terminated prematurely. Stillbirths would not necessarily have been detected because of the tendency of the mother to devour any dead young and the afterbirth. The data indicate that young females breed for the first time when they approach one year of age. In one instance (No. 1589) the weight of the breeding female was 35 pounds, and the animal was still growing. At the time of parturition she weighed 50 pounds, a weight she retained as an adult.

Little information is available on the longevity of breeding. In captivity, few females failed to bear young if left in pens where males were present. One captive female in the wildlife research unit pens gave birth to a litter of four at the age of 14 years and 6 months. Given

**Table 4.2. Ages at First-Known Breeding and Parturition
of Captive Female Juvenile Peccaries**

Animal No.	Date of Birth	Date of First Parturition	Age at First Parturition (weeks)	Calculated Age at First Breeding (weeks)
1589	11-1-59	12-19-60	59	38–39
1196	11-8-60	11-21-61	54	33–34
1557	9-17-60	10-22-61	58	36–37
823	11-9-60	11-21-61	54	33–34
1556	7-21-60	1-8-62	77	56–57
1186	6-8-60	5-20-62	80	59–60
1597	1-10-59	7-21-60	80	59–60
1228	10-22-60	6-22-62	87	66–67

the high turnover of experimental animals in our pens and the high rate of reproductive success, I believe that for most female peccaries only death or disease can end the ability to bear young.

Although not conclusive, our work indicates that young males become sexually active at about the same age as the females. The youngest male of known age that sired young was between 46 and 47 weeks of age at breeding time. An attempt was made, using an electro-ejaculator, to observe the presence of live spermatozoa in semen. This treatment seemed harsh and was used infrequently. Only two of six males yielded an ejaculate. One of these was 52 weeks and the other 65½ weeks of age at the time; both ejaculates contained live spermatozoa. The ages of the animals which did not respond to this treatment were 30, 54, 54, and 71 weeks, respectively.

Low (1970) measured and weighed the testes of 111 peccaries shot in west Texas and 41 shot in south Texas. He found spermatozoa appearing in the testicular tubules between 9 and 10 months but did not find it common until about 11 months. (Ages were determined by counting annuli in the cementum of first lower incisor.) He found a general rise in the number of spermatozoa in the testicular tubules as the animals became older. There were indications that sperm production may decline in some animals after seven years.

During our Arizona studies the testes and epididymi of 79 collared peccaries killed by hunters in late February and early March of 1965 and 1966 were examined for the presence of spermatozoa. The ages of these animals were estimated by the eruption and wear pattern of the teeth as described by Kirkpatrick and Sowls (1962), and Sowls (1961b). Results of these examinations are given in Table 4.3. These results are very similar to those found by Low in Texas — some sperm appearing at about 10 months of age and diminishing in quantity after seven years of age. The finding of more sperm in the epididymis than in the testicular tissues in our studies was similar to that found by Kerr (1965) when he measured the sexual maturity of impala (*Aepyceros melampus*).

All the data collected by Low in Texas and in our Arizona studies indicate that males could successfully fertilize sows at between 10 and

Table 4.3. Testicular Condition of 69 Male Collared Peccaries of Various Ages Collected During Late February and Early March 1965–66 in Southern Arizona

Age	N	Calculated Body Weight (lbs.)		Testes Weight (gm)		Testes Size (mm)		Epididymal Sperm	Testicular Sperm
		X̄	S.D.	X̄	S.D.	X̄	S.D.		
7–10 months	8	19.6	3.46	4.4	1.65	24.1	3.45	3 of 8 animals had 1–2 sperm per field in one side	No fields contained sperm
13–18 months	5	27.1	4.28	9.8	5.5	30.0	5.59	2 of 6 animals showed sperm. 1 showed 1–5 sperm per field. Others 10–60	Only 1 of 6 animals showed sperm. 1–2 per field
19–21½ months	2	36.7	1.76	17.7	3.8	35.7	1.76	Both animals showed 20–60 sperm per field	Both animals showed 1–5 sperm per field
2–3 years	11	35.8	7.88	16.6	7.08	34.3	6.69	10 of 11 animals showed sperm, Avg. = 18.72. S.D. = 9.36 per field	10 of 11 animals showed sperm, Avg. = 4.5. S.D. = 8.94 per field
3–5 years	14	43.2	5.95	20.0	3.77	34.9	5.31	All of 14 animals showed sperm, Avg. = 25.81. S.D. = 19.82	11 of 14 animals showed sperm. Avg. = 3.29. S.D. = 2.13
5–7 years	23	45.9	5.00	28.5	5.73	40.5	4.11	All but 1 of 23 animals had epididymal sperm. Avg. = 17.04. S.D. = 19.49	All but 1 of 23 animals showed testicular sperm. Not the same animal as showed the epididymal sperm. Avg. = 3.24 S.D. = 2.74
7+ years	6	45.6	3.00	28.4	6.91	38.6	2.35	All animals showed epididymal sperm. Avg. = 10.29. S.D. = 10.58	2 of 4 animals showed testicular sperm. Avg. = 1.90 S.D. = 2.18

*Field-dressed weight plus 27 percent.

11 months as described by Sowls (1966) for pen-reared males. Low found that there appeared to be sufficient sperm production for fertilization at all times of the year, a conclusion confirmed by evidence of parturition during all months of the year in both Arizona and Texas.

Gestation

Accurate records on the gestation period of the collared peccary appeared to be unknown before May 1959, when the first precise record was obtained in this study. Seton (1929) suggested that it was probably shorter than that of the common pig, which is 112 to 116 days. Taylor and Davis (1947) and Jennings and Harris (1953) have quoted

Seton's suggestion. Knipe (1957) reported that the gestation period was unknown but was probably between 112 and 120 days, and Leopold (1959) stated that it is variously reported as 96, 112, and 116 days.

To obtain exact data on the length of the gestation period, captive animals of known age were kept in pens where sexes were isolated. At periodic intervals males and females were brought together. If copulation followed, the female was then isolated until parturition occurred. The data on gestation periods of females which produced young in these matings are given in Table 4.4. In some of these instances only one encounter between the male and female took place. These records are given in the first part of Table 4.4. In other instances (recorded in the second part of the table) the male and female were brought together daily as long as the female was receptive.

From these data I have concluded that the gestation period of the collared peccary in Arizona is approximately 145 days. It is apparent that, except for Leopold's figure of 96 days, all of the previously published figures were probably estimates from the known gestation period of the common pig as Seton first suggested.

Table 4.4. Known Gestation Periods for Captive Collared Peccaries

Dam	Breeding Date	Parturition Date	Gestation Period (days)
Data from single encounters			
804	10-8-59	2-26-60	142
804	4-28-60	9-17-60	143
804	11-14-64	4-8-65	143
1144	4-1-62	8-22-62	144
1435	12-9-58	5-1-59	144
1435	5-13-59	10-3-59	144
1435	3-12-60	8-6-60	148
1589	6-9-62	11-4-62	149
1593	6-16-60	11-8-60	146
1597	2-29-60	7-21-60	144
101	8-1-69	12-19-69	141
958	2-24-70	7-25-70	151
969	5-28-70	1-5-70	143
*Data from multiple encounters			
804	11-18-63 (3)	4-9-64	143–145
1144	5-28-60 (3)	10-22-60	146–148
1144	7-2-61 (6)	11-28-61	145–150
1148	7-5-61 (6)	12-1-61	145–150
1589	10-31-63 (2)	3-24-64	145–146
1593	7-11-61 (3)	12-3-61	143–145
1597	5-25-62 (4)	10-18-62	143–146
1597	10-31-63 (4)	3-24-64	143–146
1600	1-19-61 (2)	6-10-61	142–143
915	5-31-66 (6)	10-24-66	142–147

*Date given in all these encounters is first day of mating. Total number of consecutive days of mating is in parentheses.

Post-partum Heat

The question of post-partum heat in a wild ungulate seldom arises because of the seasonal type of breeding pattern and the nonbreeding condition of males when most young are born. In the collared peccary, which has been shown to be a continuous breeder, the question is significant not only from the point of view of comparative biology but also from that of the population dynamics of the individual species. Post-partum heat with ovulation permits the species to produce young at a faster rate than animals unable to ovulate so quickly after parturition.

In the case of the domestic pig, Eckstein and Zuckerman (1956) say that sows come into heat shortly after weaning, and less commonly after farrowing. According to Nalbandov (1958), domestic sows come into heat three to seven days after parturition, but ovulations do not occur unless the litter dies or is removed shortly after parturition. Baker et al. (1953) found that among 17 sows which showed post-partum heat during the first seven days after parturition, none had ovulated; however, 21 of 22 that showed a post-partum heat between eight and 16 days after parturition did ovulate.

Among our captive peccaries, copulation resulting in pregnancy was known to occur within three to 17 days, five times when the young were removed. The number of days between the birth of the first litter and the second litter in these instances was 151, 154, 156, and 159. I used a gestation period of 142 to 148 days to compute the period between parturition and mating.

YOUNG

Description of Newborns

At birth, the young are a tan to yellowish gray on the limbs and underparts. The back tends to be darker but varies a great deal among individuals, often a brownish yellow mixed with black. A dark vertebral stripe, sometimes reddish, extends from the occiput to the scent gland on the rump. The collar shows at birth. With age, black gradually becomes the predominant color. Weights and measurements for animals through three days of age are given in Table 4.5.

Sex Ratio and Litter Size

Most life history accounts of the collared peccary agree that the common litter size is two. Knipe (1957) wrote that hunters reported one instance of a sow having five fetuses and another having six. Halloran (1945) reported one instance of a gravid female containing five fetuses. Among the 114 reproductive tracts from adult females shot by hunters in February and March and examined between 1956 and 1963, 20, or 17.5 percent, were pregnant. Ten of these had two live fetuses, one in

Table 4.5. Weights and Measurements of Newborn Collared Peccaries

Animal No.	Sex	Age	Wt.(g)	Total Length (mm)	Hind Foot (mm)	Ht.(mm)	Ear(mm)
1587	F	21 hours	567	254	82	138	38
811	M	21 hours	567	381	82	138	38
1556	F	4 hours	622	241	79	152	38
1591	M	4 hours	608	228	76	138	38
1592	M	2 days	681	279	89	138	38
1590	M	2 days	635	254	76	125	38
1557	F	3 days	908	254	89	137	38
807	F	3 days	681	254	76	137	38
1196	F	24 hours	706	241	82	137	44
1186	F	24 hours	678	254	82	137	38
809	F	2 days	339	215	76	102	32
1599	M	3 days	908	292	89	178	38
1600	F	3 days	908	292	89	165	38
814	F	2 days	594	228	78	165	36
907	F	12 hours	494	—	—	—	—
911	F	4 hours	379	260	71	121	36
904	M	36 hours	753	—	—	—	—
905	M	36 hours	602	—	—	—	—
941	M	12 hours	639	289	77	120	39
967	M	12 hours	662	285	70	121	36
970	M	18 hours	656	309	78	—	38
923	M	18 hours	616	312	78	—	38
927	M	36 hours	803	334	87	—	45
949	F	24 hours	760	310	80	—	38
966	F	12 hours	568	309	72	150	38
964	F	12 hours	596	320	72	155	40
955	F	24 hours	780	355	80	148	40
945	M	24 hours	795	353	79	150	45
968	M	18 hours	586	310	80	148	40
969	F	18 hours	544	314	72	140	38
928	M	36 hours	803	334	87	—	45

Table 4.6. Size and Sex Ratios of 128 Litters of Collared Peccary*

Source of Sample	Number in Litter				Sex		
	1	2	3	4	M	F	Unk.
Born in captivity	10	61	4	3	64	73	19
Born in wild	—	8	2	—	6	12	4
Record from fetuses	9	24	6	1	11	20	48
Total litters	19	93	12	4			
Total animals	19	186	36	16	81	105	71

*Records are from fetuses or from records obtained during first two days of life of the young.

each horn; four had only one fetus; two had three live fetuses; and four had two live fetuses, one in each horn, plus one dead fetus.

The sex ratio and size of 128 litters are presented in Table 4.6. Fetuses were from either pregnant females sacrificed as part of the study or from animals killed by hunters.

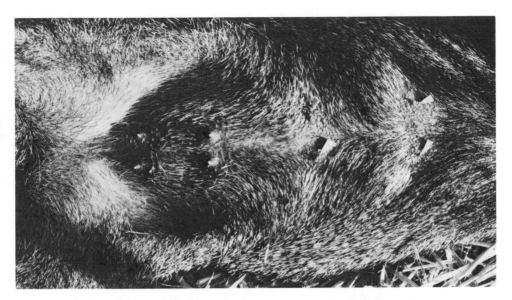

Figure 4.4. Mammary system of adult female collared peccary, a captive animal in Arizona. (Photograph by Lyle K. Sowls)

NURSING

Mammary System, Lactation

There is some confusion in the literature regarding the number of mammae present in the collared peccary. Jennings and Harris (1953) and Knipe (1957) indicate that the number is four. Wislocki (1931) says that one gravid female which he examined had only two mammae. Neal (1959) observed two pairs of functional and two pairs of nonfunctional mammae in 30 females (Fig. 4.4). Our observations agree with Neal's. At no time has careful examination failed to reveal fewer than four sets of mammae. Vearl R. Smith and Sowls (unpublished) describe the mammae position as follows: One pair inguinal, one pair postabdominal, and two pairs pectoral. Only the posterior two pairs are completely functional, although tiny droplets of milk could sometimes be obtained from the rear pair of the pectoral mammae. No galactophores were found in the forward pairs of mammae, but all other mammae contained from one to four galactophores per nipple.

The duration of lactation is difficult to determine accurately because of the very gradual decline in milk secretion in the terminal stage. In most females, the period would seem to be between six and eight weeks, but in some individuals it may vary considerably. Thus, one captive sow, which raised one of two young, was completely dry when examined 70 days later, and another, which was raising two young, was still lactating after 73 days.

The storage area for milk in the lactating sow is very small, and the conformation of the inguinal region during periods of dryness is little different from its shape during lactation.

The young peccaries nurse often. Close observations of captive litters during a three-hour period in mid-afternoon gave the following information:

Litter A (2 young, 9 days old). Nursed 48 times. The average time per nursing was 108 seconds; time spent nursing, 24 percent.

Litter B (2 young, 15 days old). Nursed 41 times. The average time per nursing was 78 seconds; time spent in nursing, 16 percent.

Litter C (1 young, 12 days old). Nursed nine times. The average time per nursing was 43 seconds; time spent in nursing, 4 percent.

These figures show considerable variation among litters of the same or different sizes. It was noted that the dam of litter C which had only one young was completely dry when examined 71 days after parturition, while the dam of litter B with two young still had considerable milk 74 days after parturition.

The chemical composition and physical properties of mature milk and colostrum milk have been described by Sowls et al. (1961), and further details on the milk fat have been presented by Brown et al. (1963). The gross composition of the milk of the collared peccary is shown in Table 4.7, and the composition is compared to that of other wild and domestic ungulates in Table 4.8.

EFFECTS OF NUTRITION

In considering the effects of nutrition upon reproduction in the collared peccary, a brief review of the peccary's year-round diet in the wild is necessary. This phase of the peccary's life history has been studied by Knipe (1958), Neal (1959), and Eddy (1961) in Arizona and by Jennings and Harris (1953), Low (1970), and Bissonette (1975) in Texas.

Table 4.7. Gross Composition of Peccary Milk

	Normal		Colostrum
	Specimen 1 Sow 1	Specimen 2 Sow 1	Specimen 3 Sow 2
Days from birth to sampling of milk	18	6	0
Fat, %	4.0	3.1	4.8
Lactose, %	6.4	6.7	5.2
Total protein, %	5.1	5.7	6.0
Casein, %	3.7	4.2	3.2
Whey protein, %	1.4	1.5	2.8
Ash, %	—	—	0.64
Total solids, %	16.7	16.2	18.2
pH	6.68	6.60	6.40
Specific gravity at 20 C/20 C	1.0441	—	1.0404
Nonprotein N (mg/100 ml)	88	75	75

Table 4.8. Comparison of the Composition of Peccary Milk With Other Ungulates

Species (Authority)	Fat	Total Protein	Lactose	Ash	Water	Total Solids
Collared peccary (Sowls et al. 1961)	4.0	5.1	6.4	—	—	16.7
Collared peccary (Sowls et al. 1961)	3.1	5.7	6.7	—	—	16.2
Collared peccary (Sowls et al. 1961)	0	6.0	5.2	0.64	—	18.2
Reindeer (Rangifer tarandus)*	22.5	10.3	2.5	1.4	63.3	36.7
Domestic pig (Sus sp.)	7.0	6.0	4.0	0.9	83.0	17.0
Pronghorn (Antilocapra americana)	13.0	6.9	4.0	1.3	75.1	24.9
Bison Sample 1 (Bison bison)	1.8	3.7	3.7?	0.9	—	13.0
Sample 2	1.7	4.2	5.7	1.0	—	13.7
Muskox Sample 1 (Ovibos canadensis)	11.0	5.3	3.6	1.8	78.5	21.5
Sample 2	5.4	5.2	4.2	1.1	83.7	16.3
White-tailed deer (Odocoileus virginianus)	8.3	—	—	1.4	79.6	20.4
Mule Deer (Odocoileus hemionus)	10.5	9.6	3.9	1.6	74.9	25.1
Mule Deer	10.5	9.0	1.3	74.6	25.4	
Cow (Bos sp.)	4.4	3.8	4.9	0.7	86.2	13.8
Water buffalo (Bubalus arnee)	12.0	6.0	4.0	0.9	77.1	22.9

*SOURCE: Data from Espe and Smith (1952) except for white-tailed deer (Hagen 1951) and mule deer (Kitts et al. 1956).

Briefly, in Arizona the food available to the peccaries varied between periods of abundance and prolonged periods of scarcity. In late July, early August, and into the autumn months, wild foods were abundant following the summer monsoon rains. The supply of winter foods largely depended on the gentler, colder, less dependable winter rains that result from frontal storms. Late spring and early summer was a period of practically no rainfall, and any annual plants soon withered. In the lower elevations the peccary depends, therefore, largely on the cladophylls of prickly pear (Opuntia engelmannii) for its food. In the higher elevations where prickly pear does not grow, it is replaced in the diet by various species of Agave. Even in periods of severe drought, the prickly pear contained about 70 percent water and remained palatable. Its nutritive value, however, was extremely low.

Evidence to date strongly suggests that nutrition plays a key role in determining frequency of estrus and incidence of pregnancy. Although the data in Figure 4.3 show that the young can be expected any time of the year in Arizona, the peccary definitely has a peak of parturition at the time of the year when food is most abundant. The timing of the birth of the largest percentage of young in Arizona follows the same pattern for the peccary that it does for the seasonally polyestrous Sonoran white-tailed deer *(Odocoileus virginianus couesii)* which drops its fawns in July and August (McCabe and Leopold 1951). The same may be said of the collared peccary in Brazil and the Chaco of Paraguay, where available information indicates a period of peak parturition following early summer rains.

That the production of young and their survival are closely linked to the rainfall pattern has been demonstrated by Sowls (1961b). An apparent direct relationship was found between the amount of rainfall and the percentage of young two to 10 months old in the sample of animals killed by hunters in February and March. This relationship was still evident a year later when animals of the same population cohort were 11 to 21½ months of age.

The exact cause of reduction in numbers of young in dry years is not known. One pregnant female in captivity was fed only prickly pear during the last 30 percent of the gestation period. The young were born on the expected date but were eaten by the female immediately, before it could be ascertained whether they were alive or dead. The same female, while on a diet of commercial food, successfully reared three normal litters in captivity. The diet of prickly pear used in this experiment approximated that encountered among wild animals under drought or near-drought conditions.

The percentage of animals that were pregnant in the February-March hunting season sample was greatest in years of high winter rainfall and good food conditions. In years when the pregnancy rate in this sample was highest, the weights of females captured in May and June were also highest.

Which nutrients are important in influencing reproduction in the peccary and which are lacking in wild diets is not yet known. Lutwak-Mann (1962) discusses the vital role of nutrition in reproduction, and lists as necessary ingredients B complex vitamins, ascorbic acid, vitamin E, vitamin A, and essential fatty acids. Ullrey et al. (1955) demonstrated the need for one of the B complex vitamins, pantothenic acid, in reproduction of domestic swine. They found that low levels of this vitamin resulted in abnormal frequency of estrus, degeneration of blastocysts, abortion, and resorption of embryos.

5 | Population Dynamics

THE COLLARED PECCARY'S YEAR-ROUND BREEDING season, coupled with the female's ability to become pregnant just a few days after parturition, gives this species a very high breeding potential. In captivity young females have been known to reach breeding condition in about eight months and easily could be ready to breed at about one year of age in wild populations. Males in breeding condition are present in herds at all times, and females continue to be reproductively active until late in life.

Thus the peccary has one great advantage over other North American ungulates, which have restricted breeding seasons and long periods of sexual quiescence. If the female peccary loses her young, she may breed again at any time of the year; deer, antelope or elk would, under similar conditions, remain barren for many months.

Compared to more common big-game animals, peccaries offer new problems to researchers attempting to gather and interpret biological data. The principal problem is their year-round breeding. The resulting year-round parturition dates mean that animals do not fit as easily into yearly age classes or population cohorts as do deer, elk, and other big-game animals.

These difficulties have shown up in all work on the population behavior of the collared peccary. For example, Low (1970), in a study of reproduction in Texas gathered age data from collected specimens. He constructed life tables from these data but encountered anomalies which he attributed to sample size, sample selection, or unequal birth or survival rates.

All information on the age structure of peccary populations has been from three sources: (1) field observations of free-roaming animals

(2) collected specimens or animals killed by hunters and (3) trapped live animals. In Arizona a great deal of useful information on age composition, herd size, and herd numbers has been gathered during game surveys conducted by the Arizona Game and Fish Department. These counts usually have been made during surveys of deer. In rugged mountainous country the counts are usually done by biologists either on foot or on horseback.

METHODS OF AGE DETERMINATION

Three basic techniques have been tried to determine the age of a peccary: (1) tooth replacement and wear patterns (2) presence of dental annulations in first lower incisors and (3) eye lens weight.

Sowls (1961b), Kirkpatrick and Sowls (1962), and Low (1970) have described the tooth replacement and wear patterns as related to age. The tooth replacement pattern is a reasonably accurate means of placing animals in the zero- to one-year and one- to two-year age class. Its application is limited, however, because of the biases in the percentage of young animals in the hunter-kill. In Arizona a combination of the classes represented in the age groups from 13 to 18 months and from 19 to 21½ months for all practical purposes represent the animals in the one- to two-year age class. The reason for this is that checking stations in Arizona were operated during the hunting season in late February and March, and very few young are born during the next three months. For our Arizona studies wear classes (Sowls 1961b) were used to give quick appraisals of the approximate age of animals at hunter checking stations. The five categories used were: (1) Slight wear on all teeth but no particular teeth show more wear (2) Wear conspicuous on first and second molars (3) All teeth show wear (4) Very heavy wear but all teeth present (5) Very heavy wear with some or all teeth missing.

Low (1970) has correctly pointed out the shortcomings in this system. The principal fault is that categories 4 and 5 overlap and cover a wide span of years. He assigned approximate ages to animals in various wear classes as described by Sowls (1961b): wear class 1, two to three years; wear class 2, three to five years; wear class 3, five to seven years; wear class 4 and 5, seven to 15 years. The system is valuable, however, because to get a large sample, data on age must be gathered from hunter-killed specimens. With more hunters not permitting the removal of teeth from their specimens, larger samples are obtained when the animal is only examined.

Richardson (1966) and Low (1970) have tried eye lens weight to determine age. Richardson did not find this technique reliable after the first year and a half of life because of the great variation in lens weights within age classes; animals below average in weight for their age had significantly lighter lens. Low also did not find it reliable.

The best method to determine the age of animals up to two years is by the tooth replacement pattern. Beyond two years the best method is by counting the annual cementum layers. Low (1970) found good correlation between cementum layers in the lower first incisor in 13 specimens from Arizona and Texas. Table 5.1 compares age determinations for the two methods.

Table 5.1. Comparisons of Age Distribution From Two Methods of Age Determination

Estimated Age	Determined by Wear Pattern (n = 2149)		Determined by Count of Annuli (n = 436)	
	No.	%	No.	%
2–3 years	453	21.0	134	30.7
3–5 years	577	26.8	145	33.3
5–7 years	590	27.5	79	18.1
7+ years	529	24.6	78	17.9

NOTE: Samples are from the same population.

AGE DATA FROM ARIZONA

Game Survey Counts

One important way to obtain population data is by annual winter counts or surveys. For the collared peccary, most surveys in Arizona are made before the late February or early March hunting season. The numbers and percentages of immature collared peccaries observed on winter game surveys from 1955–80 are given in Table 5.2. These annual counts classify the animals into two groups: adults and immatures. Unclassified animals, where the observer was unable to determine relative age, are not used in calculating the percentages. Some inconsistency exists among observers — animals that would be called adults by one could be called juveniles by another. The problem arises in animals between one and two years which, because of poor food conditions, may not appear to be adult size.

The difference in those under one year old and those between one and two years old readily becomes apparent during trapping operations. Animals less than one year old can be distinguished from those between one and two years, and both groups can be distinguished easily from animals older than two years. The weights of these animals, however, indicate that those between one year and two might be separated readily from adults in field counts.

Trapped Animals

Reliable methods of trapping and handling wild collared peccaries have been developed (Neal 1957; Day 1980; Ellisor and Harwell 1969;

**Table 5.2. Age Composition of Collared Peccaries Observed
During Annual Game Surveys in Arizona, 1955–80**

Year	Numbers			Percentage	
	Adults	Immatures	Unclass.	Adults	Immatures
1955	354	115	590	75	25
1956	335	127	101	73	27
1957	328	115	4	74	26
1958	306	106	—	74	26
1959	361	83	—	81	19
1960	391	120	166	68	32
1961	392	108	200	79	21
1962	667	267	69	71	29
1963	354	296	136	55	45
1964	598	226	1	73	27
1965	709	219	105	76	24
1966	700	362	132	62	38
1967	496	86	42	85	15
1968	601	208	11	74	26
1969	578	205	54	74	26
1970	1191	401	131	75	25
1971	1106	498	0	69	31
1972	645	251	175	72	28
1973	1137	374	178	75	25
1974	1053	308	128	77	23
1975	1303	294	0	78	22
1976	1745	609	34	74	26
1977	1119	362	173	76	24
1978	2247	667	125	77	23
1979	2348	678	75	78	22
1980	2860	760	60	79	21

Average = 74   26
S.D. = 5.87

SOURCE: Arizona Game and Fish Department reports, 1955–57, 1959–66, 1970–71, 1974–76, 1979, 1981.

Schweinsburg 1969; Low 1970). Data on age composition of populations from trapped animals have been scant because trapping usually is done for other purposes, such as herd removals or research operations. No satisfactory way has been found to remove incisors from live animals for cementum layer analysis. Consequently, ages of trapped adult animals are usually estimated on the basis of tooth replacement and wear patterns.

The wildlife unit trapped peccaries in the Tucson Mountains intermittently from May 1956 through October 1965 and obtained age information on 219 animals. Ages to the nearest year were determined by examining the tooth replacement pattern for all animals under two years of age. Of the 219 animals trapped, 120 (55 percent) were over two years of age, 34 (15 percent) were between one and two years of age, and 65 (30 percent) were under one year. Low (1970) reported similar results in Texas.

Age data obtained by trapping is the most accurate available for animals under two years of age because hunter-killed animals are strongly biased toward older animals when hunters select for size. It is much more accurate than the sight records obtained on game surveys.

Hunter-Killed and Collected Samples

Information on age composition of the hunter-kill was collected by the Arizona Cooperative Wildlife Research Unit between 1956 and 1973 and in 1977. The weekends were by far the most important times to collect data because few hunters were in the field on weekdays. A checking station was operated by the wildlife unit in Tucson from 1957 to 1973. In addition, a check station was run by Army personnel at the Ft. Huachuca Army Electronic Proving Ground during the same period. A total of 3,657 animals was examined at all stations during the period. The number of hunters in Arizona during these years varied from 13,110 in 1959 to 32,118 in 1970. The percentage of hunters bagging animals (the hunter success figure) varied from 13.4 percent in 1957 to 26.4 percent in 1974 and the total estimated peccary harvest varied from a low of 2,236 in 1957 to a high of 6,602 in 1970 (Az. Game and Fish Dept. 1977).

I have used the data collected at hunter-checking stations operated by the unit in two ways. First, crude figures on the age composition of the hunter-kill have been obtained for Arizona peccaries by classifying the age of animals according to the eruption pattern of the teeth and the relative wear on the premolars and molars. Because of the bias concerning young animals in the kill, meaningful data can be obtained from the hunter-kill only on adult animals. Table 5.3 gives the estimated age of 2,662 specimens examined at hunter-checking stations between 1957 and 1977. The data in this table are a composite of the various years and do not account for differences between years.

Table 5.3. Sex and Estimated Age of 2,662 Specimens Examined at Checking Stations, 1957–1973

| Age (months) | Age distribution by sex | | | | Estimated Age |
	Males No.	Females No.	Total (Both Sexes)	Percent	
2–6	10	15	25 ⎫		
7–10	88	85	173 ⎬	9.6	1 year
11–12	32	25	57 ⎭		
13–18	66	85	151 ⎫	8.8	1–2 years
19–21½	40	43	83 ⎭		
Wear Class					
1	242	202	444	16.7	2–3 years
2	291	293	584	21.9	3–5 years
3	324	265	589	22.1	5–7 years
4 ⎫ 5 ⎭	303	253	556	21.0	7+ years

Table 5.4. Ages as Determined by Cementum Layers
for 436 Peccaries Killed by Hunters

Age	Males No.	Males Percent	Females No.	Females Percent	Unidentified Sex No.	Unidentified Sex Percent	All Animals No.	All Animals Percent
2–3	48	35.5	41	29.5	45	27.8	134	30.7
3–4	25	18.5	23	16.5	27	16.7	75	17.2
4–5	17	12.6	25	18.0	28	17.3	70	16.1
5–6	11	8.2	15	10.8	16	9.9	42	9.6
6–7	12	8.9	11	7.9	14	8.7	37	8.5
7–8	5	3.7	7	5.0	11	6.8	23	5.3
8–9	5	3.7	3	2.2	8	4.9	16	3.7
9–10	2	1.5	3	2.2	2	1.2	7	1.6
10–11	3	2.2	5	3.6	2	1.2	10	2.2
11–12	3	2.2	4	2.9	4	2.5	11	2.5
12–13	2	1.5	0	0	1	0.6	3	0.7
13–14	2	1.5	0	0	2	1.2	4	0.9
14–15	0	—	1	0.7	1	0.6	2	0.5
15–16	0	—	1	0.7	1	0.6	2	0.5
Total	135		139		162		436	

More accurate ages of the adult animals can be obtained by a count of the cementum layers in the first lower incisor. By this method, teeth from 436 collared peccaries killed by hunters and collected at hunter-checking stations operated by the unit between 1957 and 1977 were examined. The estimated age of these adult animals based on counts of cementum layers is given in Table 5.4.

Although data from hunter-killed animals are the easiest to obtain in large quantities, they present a number of shortcomings. Caughley (1966) has pointed out that when ages at death are used as the sole source of data, the population from which the sample is drawn should have assumed a stationary age distribution. He says this is partially compensated for if the fluctuations have a wave length considerably shorter than the period over which the sample is taken. Caughley also says that data obtained from hunter-kills where meat and trophies are the goal of the hunt would probably produce too much bias for a life table. According to Deevey (1947), the use of data where only the age at death is known makes it necessary to assume that the age composition is unchanged with time. This situation is never completely true for the collared peccary because of annual population fluctuations due to changes in food supply. In Arizona the range of the collared peccary is not contiguous but is interrupted by a great many altitudinal differences. Rainfall patterns are spotty, and consequently the health and vigor of the food supplies vary greatly between areas. Samples, in order to be large enough, must come from a variety of different habitats and conditions. Thus homogenous samples are not obtainable.

Annual game surveys give rough data on the percentage of immature animals in the populations. In Arizona the surveys are conducted in January and February about six months before the main period of parturition. Consequently a high percentage of the young animals counted would be about six months of age. A smaller percentage from the group born in the fall and winter would be under six months of age. However, the survey data do not indicate whether all "red" or very young, small animals are included. Because of the difficulty of seeing all the small animals, we must assume that counts may be imcomplete. An important question concerning data from field surveys is what percentage of the young are older than 12 months at the time of the survey? The percentage of those classed as immatures — over 12 months up to 18 months of age — would consequently be very small when the annual surveys are conducted because very few young are born between January and June. The percentage of immature animals counted in the population in Arizona game surveys varied from 15 percent in 1967 to 31 percent in 1971 and averaged 25 percent for the 19-year period for which records are available.

Trapping data from both Texas and Arizona indicate that between 30 and 35 percent of the population was made up of animals under one year of age. Table 5.5 compares estimated annual recruitment in Arizona and Texas peccaries to that of other North American ungulates.

SEX RATIOS

Sowls (1966) reported larger numbers of females at birth than males (of 60 young for which the sex was known, 62 percent were females and 38 percent were males). Since these figures were first published, I have obtained additional records, bringing the total to 147 young. Of this number 50, or 0.41 percent were males. The sex of animals in individual litters has been discussed in Chapter 4.

Table 5.5. Comparison of Estimated Annual Recruitment of Collared Peccary With Other North American Ungulates

Species	Locality	Annual Recruitment Percent	Authority
Collared peccary	Arizona	15–31 (surveys) 30–35 (trapping) 35 (trapping)	Game surveys, Arizona Game and Fish Department reports, Sowls (unpub.)
Elk	Wyoming	16.3 18.8	Murie (1951)
Mule deer	Utah	38	Robinette and Olsen (1944)
White-tailed deer	Ontario	21.4	Mansell (1974)
Moose	Isle Royale	10.5–17.0	Mech (1966)
	Alberta, Canada	18–30	Hauge and Keith (1981)
Caribou	N. Canada	15.9	Kelsall (1968)
Muskox	N. Canada	0–18.0	Tener (1965)
Bighorn sheep	British Columbia	30	Cowan (1950)

Low (1970) also found the sex ratio at birth to favor females. He found that 34 sows in east Texas had 55 fetuses, of which 42 percent were males and 58 percent were females. The addition of data on 32 young born in captivity and one litter from west Texas brought his entire ratio to 47 percent males and 53 percent females. Low found that the sex ratio of his Texas sample tended to favor males as the animals became older. In Arizona this was also found to be true. The shift of the sex ratio in favor of males as demonstrated by Arizona specimens can be seen in Table 5.6.

POPULATION DENSITY

No figures are available on the population density of the collared peccary throughout most of its range. Its range is so discontinuous, with large areas of unsuitable and unoccupied habitats, that only density figures for select, carefully delineated areas are meaningful.

Schweinsburg (1969) gave density figures of 18, 22, 35, and 47 animals per square mile in selected study areas in the Tucson Mountains. These figures, however, were much too high for the entire area. The Tucson Mountains are an area of saguaro–palo verde vegetation receiving an annual rainfall of about 12 inches. Prickly pear is a common plant.

On the King ranch in southeast Texas, Low (1970) found a population density of 20.4 animals per square mile. On the nearby Welder Wildlife Refuge he found a density of 9.8 animals per square mile. These areas received 26.5 and 30.6 inches of rainfall annually. They support a brush community with interspersed bunchgrass–annual forbs. The dominant shrubs are honey mesquite and numerous species of acacias. Prickly pear is abundant.

**Table 5.6. Sex Ratio of 3,128 Animals at Various Ages
Examined at Hunter Checking Stations**

Estimated Age*	Sex		Total	Ratio
	Males	Females		
2–6 months	13	16	29	45:55
7–10 months	80	93	173	46:54
11–12 months	30	24	54	55:45
13–18 months	78	98	176	44:56
18–22½ months	63	53	116	46:54
Juveniles & immatures	264	284		
2–3 years	291	234	525	55:45
3–5 years	352	332	684	51:49
5–7 years	409	319	728	56:44
7+ years	352	291	643	55:45
Adults				
Totals	1,668	1,460		53:47

In west Texas he estimated a density of 6.4 animals per square mile in an area receiving 14.9 inches of rainfall and 3.2 animals per square mile in an area receiving 11.4 inches of rainfall annually. The first of these two areas supported scrub forest with intermittent chaparral-bunchgrass and occasional live-oak areas. The latter area was a drier site supporting desert-type vegetation of creosote bush, lechugilla, whitethorns, and ocotillo. On both west Texas areas prickly pear was common.

Mortality and
Debility

WHILE COLLARED PECCARIES HAVE BEEN KNOWN to live as long as eighteen years in captivity, such longevity does not commonly occur in wild populations. In the previous chapter, we saw that a few animals in wild populations reach 15 years of age. In the sample of Arizona data, however, 73 percent, or about three-fourths of the population, did not reach the age of six years. With a mean length of life of about four years, we cannot regard the species as long-lived. The high reproductive rate for the collared peccary and its ability to withstand severe food and water shortages for short periods enables the species to maintain good populations of vigorous young animals.

Most studies of this species, done in the northern fringe of its range in Texas and Arizona, have yielded little understanding of the effects of parasites and disease on the populations. The role of accidents, malnutrition and predation, which cause losses to populations through death or interference with reproduction, is not well known either. However, a considerable amount of information on the causes of death or lack of reproductive efficiency exists. No quantitative measurements of the various types of losses and the effects of these factors are possible. A list of them, however, is worthwhile. Some diseases and parasites cause death; others are debilitating and decrease the animal's efficiency or its ability to reproduce. Others seem to cause no effect.

PARASITES

Numerous reports on parasites in the collared peccary have been published. The most recent and most complete study was done by Samuel and Low (1970) in Texas. In all parts of its range where it has been studied, the collared peccary has been found to have a variety of parasites. Some of them, such as the sucking louse *(Pecaroecus javalii),*

Figure 6.1. Sucking louse, *Pecaroecus javalii*, a common external parasite of collared peccary. (Shown ca. 12x) (Photograph by Lyle K. Sowls)

are quite numerous and well known to hunters who bag the animals (Fig. 6.1). External parasites that have been found in the collared peccary are listed in Table 6.1 and the internal parasites in Table 6.2.

Although the collared peccary has been found to have numbers of ectoparasites and endoparasites, there is as yet little evidence that their presence causes significant losses to populations. Diseases that parasites carry and transmit to peccaries are not clearly known or prominently noticeable. Samuel and Low point out, however, that under certain conditions parasites could be important. In many desert regions of the peccary's range in the United States, where acute food shortages cause periods of stress, it is conceivable that parasites, especially endoparasites, may be significant causes of death.

DISEASES AND INFECTIONS

When animals are affected with disease in epidemic proportions, it is easy to ascribe losses to particular organisms and conditions. Thus an outbreak of hoof-and-mouth disease in domestic livestock or wild ungulates, a die-off of waterfowl due to botulism, or an epidemic of rabies in wild carnivores becomes front-page news. However, most wild animals that die from disease do it quietly, unknown, one at a time. The dead carcasses, if found, are seldom fresh enough to give accurate clues to the cause of death. The remains usually are either eaten by a scavenger or decay unnoticed. The combined effects of

Table 6.1. External Parasites Found on the Collared Peccary

Scientific Name	Locality	Authority
Class Arachnoidea		
Order Acarina		
(ticks, chiggers)		
Ambylomma cajennense	Texas	McIntosh (1932)
Fabricius	Texas	Samuel and Low (1970)
	Texas	Eads (1951)
	Panama	Fairchild et al. (1966)
Ambylomma inornatum	Texas	Samuel and Low (1970)
	Texas	Eads (1951)
Ambylomma naponense Packard	Panama	Fairchild et al. (1966)
	Colombia	" "
	Peru	" "
Ambylomma oblongoguttatum Koch	Panama	" "
Ambylomma pecarium Dunn	Belize	" "
(also on white-lipped peccary)	Mexico	" "
	Panama	" "
Ambylomma tapirellum Dunn	Panama	" "
Ambylomma varium Koch	Panama	" "
Dermacentor albipictus	Arizona	Neal (1959)
Dermacentor halli McIntosh	Texas	Fairchild et al. (1966)
	Mexico	" "
Dermacentor imitans	Panama	" "
Warburton	Guatemala	" "
Dermacentor juxtakochi	Guatemala	" "
Dermacentor variabilis	Texas	McIntosh (1932)
		Samuel and Low (1970)
Ornithodoros turicata	Arizona	Neal (1959)
Haemaphysalis leporis-palustris	Texas	Samuel and Low (1970)
Haemaphysalis juxtakochi Cooley	Panama	
Eutrombicula alfreddugesii	Panama	Brennan and Yunker
Oudemans		(1966)
Trombicula dunni Ewing	Panama	
Trombicula pecari Brennan	Panama	
and Jones		

many single instances of sickness or accident make up a significant loss. Along with accidents and predation, diseases keep the population somewhat level even when young animals are being born each year.

In the absence of records of epidemics among collared peccaries, our knowledge must come entirely from scattered evidence. Information has been gathered from the autopsy of sick animals and collection of parasites from animals killed. I will review the known or possible causes of death but not assign quantitative guesses to their importance. Most of the information on diseases comes from experience with captive animals. Table 6.3 gives details on the causes of death of nine captive animals examined soon after death and two wild animals. The known causes of loss will be discussed according to the type of disease or the parts of the body affected.

Table 6.1. **External Parasites Found on the Collared Peccary**
(continued)

Scientific Name	Locality	Authority
Class Insecta		
Order Mallophaga		
(biting lice)		
Macrogyropus dentatus	Nicaragua, Costa Rica	Ewing (1924)
Macrogyropus dicotylis	Nicaragua, Costa Rica	Ewing (1924)
	Panama	Emerson (1966)
Order Anoplura		
(sucking lice)		
Pecaroecus javalii	Texas	Samuel and Low (1970)
	Texas	McDaniel et al. (1966)
	New Mexico	Samson and Donaldson (1968)
	Arizona	Neal (1959)
	Texas	Eads (1951)
Order Siphonaptera		
(fleas)		
Rhopalopsyllus tupinus (also on the white-lipped peccary)	Panama	Tipton and Mendez (1966)
Pulex irritans	Arizona	Neal (1959)
Pulex porcinus	Texas	Jordan and Rothchild (1923)
	Texas	Jennings and Harris (1953)
	Texas	Eads (1951)
	Texas	Samuel and Low (1970)
	Texas	Babcock and Ewing (1938)
Echidnophaga gallinacea	Arizona	Neal (1959)

Respiratory

Five of the eleven animals on which complete necropsies were performed showed signs of respiratory infection and respiratory failure. All of these animals died during the colder months of the year when the effects of respiratory diseases are most serious. Respiratory diseases are probably important causes of loss along the northern fringe of the range, especially during severe winter weather.

Digestive Tracts

Five of the eleven animals whose necropsy findings are described in Table 6.3 apparently died of some type of enteritis. In three instances organisms which may at times cause severe diarrhea were isolated and identified. In two instances, *Salmonella muenchen* was identified, and

Table 6.2. Internal Parasites Found in the Collared Peccary

Phylum or Class	Scientific Name	Organ Infested	Locality	Authority
Nematoda (nematodes)	Parabronema pecariae	stomach	New Mexico Texas	Samson and Donaldson (1968) Samuel and Low (1970)
	Texicospirura turki	small intestine	Texas	Samson and Donaldson (1968) Chitwood, M.B. and M. Cordero de Campilla (1966)
	Parostertagia heterospiculum		Texas	Schwartz and Alicata (1933) Samuel and Low (1970)
	Gongylonema baylisi		Texas	Samuel and Low (1970)
	Dirofilaria acutiuscula		Texas	Samuel and Low (1970)
	Parabronema pecariae	esophagus	Texas	Schwartz and Alicata (1933)
	Physocephalus sexalatus	stomach	Texas	Schwartz and Alicata (1933)
	Trichostrongylus colubriformis	small intestine	New Mexico	Samson and Donaldson (1968)
	Capillaria hepatica	liver		Olsen (1974)
Trematoda (flukes)	Fascioloides magna		Texas	Samuel and Low (1970)
Cestoidea (tapeworms)	Moniezia benedini	small intestine	Texas	Schwartz and Alicata (1933) Samuel and Low (1970)
	Schizotaenia descrescens (in both collared and white-lipped peccaries)		South America	Schwartz and Alicata (1933)
Protozoa (protozoans)	Balantidium sp.		Arizona Texas Texas	Jacobsen (1941) Samuel and Low (1970) Alicata (1932)

in the third animal Escherchia coli was found. Although these bacteria are nonpathogenic or slightly pathogenic, they may at times cause diarrhea in very young animals which have very little resistance to severe diarrhea. Diarrhea is often present in wild animals on diets of green prickly pear cladophylls.

Kidneys

Hemorrhaging in the kidneys was noted in two captive animals that had been eating primarily prickly pear. In these two instances, oxalic acid crystals were present in the kidney. Oxalic acid poisoning may be an important cause of death under drought conditions, when

Table 6.3. Necropsy Findings and Apparent Cause of Death for Nine Captive and Two Wild Peccaries

Date	Specimen No.	Sex	Age	Necropsy Findings	Apparent Cause of Death
				CAPTIVE ANIMALS	
03-31-60	4494	F	Adult	Severe diffuse interstitial nephritis	Uremia
04-04-60	4529	M	Adult	Acute diffuse enteritis; small caseated abcesses in thorax	Acute enteritis
01-06-65	8177	F	8 yrs.	Gastric ulcers, degeneration of large arteries, chronic pneumonia, hemorrhage	Pneumonia
06-20-66*	9877	M	Adult	Subcapsular hemorrhage, prominent cortical markings and oxalate crystals in kidneys	Oxalate nephrosis
01-04-67*	644	M	Adult	Hemosiderin in spleen and liver; glomerulonephrosis; necrotic, hemorrhagic enteritis; oxalate crystals in gut lumen	Nephrosis, hemorrhage, enteritis
04-01-71	16929	F	Adult	Pulmonary congestion	Pneumonia
01-03-73	19648	F	Adult	Diffuse, severe chronic interstitial nephritis; severe pulmonary hemorrhage; chronic, diffuse gastroenteritis; edema of abdominal and thoracic tissues	Uremia
06-12-74	74-0816	M	Juv.	Acute necrotic enterocolitis	Enteritis, diarrhea
10-24-74	74-1419	F	3 mos.	Pulmonary congestion and emphysema; hepatic congestion	Circulatory and respiratory failure
				WILD ANIMALS	
11-29-71	17945	M	Adult	Hemorrhagic enteritis; pulmonary congestion; *Salmonella muenchen* isolated	Salmonellosis
02-01-72	18183			Endocardial hemorrhage, enteritis, impacted colon; *Salmonella muenchen* isolated	Salmonellosis

*Animals were on diets of prickly pear cladophylls for a prolonged period.

animals eat only agave and prickly pear cladophylls for long periods. Further investigation of this cause of loss should be conducted.

Eyes

Two types of eye conditions were noted among wild and captive peccaries in our studies. The first of these conditions was characterized by a white exudate which later turned to crusts under the eyes of isolated animals. Among captive animals, this crusting was particularly noticeable among old adults. When these adults, after living alone, were moved into pens with other animals they could get along with, constant rubbing of the jowls and face over one another's scent gland quickly rubbed off the crusty material. This was particularly noticeable when lone males were put in with females for breeding.

There was evidence that this condition, which was so common among captive animals, was also common in wild herds. Some data on the frequency of this were obtained by carefully examining the eyes of dead animals brought to the checking station. From 1971 through 1973, examinations of carcasses at the hunter checking station showed that 327 of 728, or 46 percent, of all animals showed some accumulation of exudate in the eyes. Thirty-one percent of these showed conspicuous or heavy exudate, and the remainder showed only a slight amount. Schweinsburg and Sowls (1972) attributed this exudate to chronic nonpathological eye infections but gave no real evidence that this was the cause. Byers (1978) suggests that this crusty material could be an exudate from a preorbital gland that he describes (see Social Behavior).

The other condition found among captive animals was a permanent blindness caused by an acute eye infection. This condition, easily distinguishable from that previously described, was characterized by sudden inflammation of the eye and massive drainage which, if not arrested by antibiotics, resulted in blindness.

Skin

Skin diseases were not common during our studies in southern Arizona. Of 2,662 peccary carcasses examined at hunter-checking stations, only five showed signs of some type of skin disease. Although uncommon, the ones that did appear were very conspicuous.

In 1964 two animals showing parakeratosis with heavy crusting and dry-cracking horny material on the head and body were brought through the checking station. Heavy encrusted material resembled a product of imperfect keratinization (Fig. 6.2). The epithelium was distorted by exaggerated dips with elevations, with some pedicles similar to those associated with papillomatosis.

Limbs and Body

One of the most common causes of injuries to the flesh of both wild and captive peccaries is fighting between herd members or between members from other herds. In nearly every instance some infection of the wound follows, but we have noted that the healthy peccaries have a very good natural resistance to flesh wounds and seldom succumb to infection of injured tissues.

Among the 2,662 carcasses examined at hunter-checking stations in Arizona, two examples of missing feet that had healed over were observed. One leg was severed and the wound healed at the knee joint, and the other one was severed and healed over just below the knee.

Like injury to the flesh, broken bones in javelina sometimes occur. In captivity I have seen broken leg bones occur after two herd members fought. In this instance a twisted foot completely healed. Among wild herds, I have seen three-legged animals which had lost the distal half of one leg. Six instances of broken and healed legs were observed at the checking station.

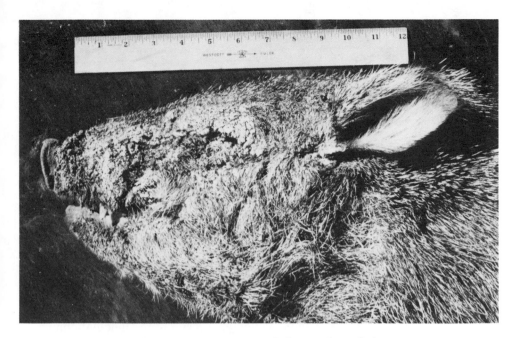

Figure 6.2. Heavy crusting and distorted epithelium on skin of adult collared peccary killed by a hunter in Arizona. (Photograph by Lyle K. Sowls)

MISCELLANEOUS DISEASES

Because peccaries have so often been associated with true pigs in various writings, they have been considered possible carriers of disease (Dardiri et al. 1969) and sources of infection among swine livestock. Diseases that have been studied include:

African Swine Fever

This acute virus disease specific to swine had been restricted to Africa, but now it occurs in Spain and Portugal. Tests at Plum Island by Dardiri et al. have found collared peccaries resistant to the virus of African swine fever.

Hog Cholera

This worldwide acute infectious virus disease has been regarded in the past as specific to the true pig family Suidae. Dardiri et al. have demonstrated, however, that the collared peccary is also susceptible to this disease.

Vesicular Exanthema of Swine

This is another serious but rare disease of swine which is caused by a virus. Dardiri et al. tested two strains of this virus on collared peccaries and found them to be susceptible to the virus.

Vesicular Stomatitis

This highly infectious viral disease affects horses, cattle, and pigs. Dardiri et al. found collared peccaries less susceptible than domestic hogs.

Rinderpest

During some years this virus disease has ravaged the herds of wild game and domestic livestock of Africa, Asia, and Europe (Scott 1964). It attacks a large number of species of ungulates, both domestic and wild. Among the animals susceptible to it are the domestic swine and wild species of the family Suidae including the bushpig, *Potamochoerus porcus*; the warthog, *Phacohoerus aethiopicus*; and the forest hog, *Hylochoerus meinertzhogeni*.

Scott describes Sainte-Hillaire's observations of the 1865 catastrophic die-off of captive animals at the Jardin d'Acclimatation in Paris. Among the animals wiped out by this epidemic were the peccaries. Dardiri et al. found peccaries susceptible to this disease, and some of the experimental animals died as a result of the inoculations. Inasmuch as rinderpest is an Old World disease and peccaries are found only in the New World, the danger of this disease to peccaries should be slight. However, it could be a serious threat to captive peccaries in European zoos or if transmitted to the Western Hemisphere a threat to both captive and wild populations. Roberts (1921) has recorded an outbreak of rinderpest in Brazil, the only cases on which I can find information in the Western Hemisphere.

Foot-and-Mouth Disease

This virus disease affects a wide variety of cloven-hoofed animals. Its absence in the United States accounts for the strict quarantine measures that are taken to avoid the admission into the United States of animals from infected areas. Dardiri et al. found collared peccaries susceptible to the disease, but they were not as severely affected as were domestic swine.

Rabies

There are no records of rabies in peccaries nor has there been any work done to determine their susceptibility to this disease. Since this disease affects a wide variety of animals, including ungulates, and the peccary is a common species in areas where rabies is common, tests should be made to determine the susceptibility of peccaries to rabies.

ACCIDENTS AND OTHER LOSSES

Under proper management the loss of animals from hunting is a planned harvest of available surplus and thus does not damage the populations. There are, however, other direct losses attributable to man which may be seriously detrimental to populations.

Until recently, the collared peccary has been considered by many as an "undesirable" animal, especially where it is living in areas occupied by livestock.

George S. Wilson (pers. comm. 1952), an early pioneer near Oracle, Arizona, told me that prior to 1940, cowboys on the range lands killed javelina whenever they found them. He vividly described a "game" or contest in which riders would make bets on the number of animals they could kill in a herd with one loading of the six-gun. Charles Beach, a pioneer rancher in the Santa Rita Mountains in Arizona, told me similar tales and described the great scarcity of peccaries in southern Arizona in the 1920s.

In many parts of Mexico and Central and South America sport hunting hardly exists. The peccary, like other wild game, is vigorously pursued for its meat and its hide (Leopold 1959). This type year-round hunting, of course, reduces populations to low levels.

Another type of loss has been described by Jennings and Harris (1953) in Texas who say, "Wardens throughout the peccary range report that numerous peccaries are killed on the smaller ranches where dogs are used to help drive cattle from thick brush. In some areas, particularly in the central parts of the range, peccary populations are decidedly on the down grade because of this slaughter which is carried on to reduce the danger to cow dogs."

Losses to automobiles, especially at night on highways through peccary country, are frequent, but probably do not significantly affect year-to-year populations except in rare cases. Animals are also occasionally killed by trains. One pair of twins that I raised in January 1959 was retrieved by a railroad crew when only a few days old. The mother was killed by a fast-moving train, and the young animals stayed near the dead carcass.

Knipe (1957) described five instances in Arizona in which he found dead peccaries in steel traps that were set for fur-bearing animals.

Aside from accidents caused by man such as losses to traffic, wild animals suffer from accidents in their natural environment. Several writers have described accidents which caused the death of wild peccaries, especially young ones. Knipe (1957) believed that such losses were high and described several types of accidents including the wedging between rocks and falling from high cliffs.

Stair (pers. comm. 1972) described finding a baby peccary only a few days old with the spiny joints of cholla cactus *(Opuntia fulgida)* clinging to it so that the animal was unable to move.

Among the animals trapped for tagging studies in the Tucson Mountains, many had scars from what appeared to be serious wounds. Others had enlarged joints and evidence that bones had been broken. This was in an unhunted area so these injuries could not be attributed to bullet wounds.

PREDATION

Little reliable information exists on the effect of predators on peccary populations because there are few techniques for objectively gathering such information. Study of stomach contents from predators does not reveal whether the stomach material represents prey killed by the predator or whether it was carrion. Also the carnivore holds material in the stomach only a short time.

Analysis of the droppings gives a clue to the animals eaten by the predator but like the analysis of stomach contents does not tell whether prey evidence found was from an animal killed by the animal that ate it or whether it was already dead.

Several authors who did extensive work in collared peccary country consider the coyote an important predator on peccaries. Jennings and Harris (1953) believe that the young are preyed upon heavily by coyotes *(Canis latrans)* but doubt whether the adults are. Knipe (1957) considered the coyote an important predator on young collared peccaries, and he describes an observation in December 1935 by A. A. Nichol who saw four coyotes kill a mature sow in a herd of 20 peccaries.

Knipe found four of 100 coyote scats had peccary remains; two of these were remains of young and two were of adults. Sumner (1951) found no evidence of peccary remains in 175 coyote droppings examined from Saguaro National Monument in southern Arizona. At that time he estimated that there were about 200 peccaries on the 46,088 acres of habitable and marginal peccary habitat.

In the Big Bend country of Texas, Krausman (1980) found that the collared peccary made up 7 percent of the diet of the coyote.

For all three species of peccary, mountain lions *(Felis concolor)* and jaguars *(Felis onca)* are probably the most important predators. Both large cats originally inhabited ranges which included nearly the entire area occupied by the three peccary species. However, little data on the predation effects of these two carnivores exist. Van Pelt (1977) describes instances in southwest Texas in which mountain lions were observed attacking adult collared peccaries. In the first instance the peccary escaped, but in the second the peccary was killed and partially eaten by the mountain lion.

Krausman (1980) reported two known lion kills in the Carmen Mountains in southwest Texas. He also reported an injury to an adult peccary in poor physical condition, which he attributed to a mountain lion. Dominguez et al. (1972) gave the collared peccary as a food of the mountain lion in Chihuahua, Mexico. Young (1946) gives records of mountain lions killing peccaries in Arizona and quotes earlier authors who refer to the collared peccary as a favorite food of the mountain lion. Leopold (1959) lists the peccary as a regular item in the diet of the mountain lion where it occurs.

Leopold (1959) says that the jaguar is fond of wild peccaries. A large part of the natural range of the peccaries was once inhabited by the jaguar. They are often found in the same habitat, consequently peccaries and jaguars are in constant contact wherever the two still exist. This predator-prey relationship has been often described in the popular literature. In 1979 I interviewed rural people in the Chaco of Paraguay to obtain information on the status of the jaguar. I found that people familiar with the peccaries and the jaguar regarded peccaries as a principal item in the jaguar diet. I collected 11 scats of either mountain lion or jaguar in the Chaco in Paraguay in 1981. All but three contained peccary hair (species unidentified). Two of the eight also contained hooves of young peccaries.

TOOTH WEAR

In some species of animals, the wearing down of the teeth and their eventual loss or infection is a major cause of death. The importance of the loss of teeth as a mortality factor among ungulates is suggested by the fact that some species exhibit a survivorship index approaching a convex curve. This is true of the Dall sheep *(Ovis dalli dalli)* studied by Murie (1944) and interpreted by Deevey (1947) and Hickey (1952).

Barrett (1978) found that the main cause of old-age deaths in feral hogs in California appears to be related to the slow process of tooth deterioration which eventually leads to septicemia. In such species an accelerated death rate is sudden and correlates with a marked decline in the animal's ability to chew its food.

Such a situation does not seem to exist with the collared peccary. The survivorship curve for Arizona peccaries, instead of approaching a convex pattern with a sudden increase in the death rate in old age, compares more closely to a concave curve where there is a more even rate of loss in the various age classes.

Although tooth wear is severe and dental caries are common, they do not seem to have the kind of damaging effect in Arizona peccaries that Barrett found in California feral hogs. Over several years old animals in good health with very worn teeth showed no noticeable change in the tooth pattern. The main reason that the tooth wear pattern is a poor criterion of age is that the wear pattern in the old animals changes so slightly each year in the last half of the lifespan of the longest-lived animals.

Malocclusions are another pattern of tooth wear sometimes seen in peccaries. Canine teeth grow continuously until the peccary is about four or five years old. The sharp edges on the teeth are maintained by the wear of the rear surface of the lower canines against the front surface of the top canines. A good fit is necessary; when the teeth do not meet, the lower canine grows through the skin of the upper jaw and protrudes above it. This condition, observed in one captive male in the summer of 1973, made it necessary to saw off the end of the canine. Among wild peccaries such a condition could cause death. Neal and Kirkpatrick (1957) described an anomalous canine development in which a lower left canine tooth divided and curled back through the lower jaw, resulting in an infected lower jaw.

General
Behavior

CERTAIN ASPECTS OF PECCARY BEHAVIOR ARE GENERAL or nonsocial. These can be defined as behavioral actions that the animal does by itself without obvious influence from other members of the herd, for example, how it moves, eats, drinks, and many other important actions in the daily and seasonal life of the individual.

ACTIVITY PATTERNS

Daily

The daily activity pattern of the collared peccary has been described by several writers who have all made the same general conclusions. Jennings and Harris (1953) observed that:

> The daily activity schedule of the collared peccary appears to follow the same pattern each day. The herd moves out of the bedding area about daylight and feeds until mid or late morning. On hot days, the herd may quit feeding as early as 9:00 a.m., and on cool or cold days feeding may continue until noon. During the heat of the day the herd moves back into dense brush for a mid-day rest period. Feeding is resumed by late afternoon and continues until after dark.

Eddy (1961) elaborated on the seasonal variations in feeding patterns as the temperature changed:

> Peccaries in the Tucson Mountain Park and the Santa Rita study areas showed seasonal patterns of feeding activities. In summer, feeding took place only in morning and evening hours. During the interim the herds returned to caves or bedded down in well-shaded canyons, under rock outcrops, or in dense shrubs. When temperatures dropped and the days became shorter in autumn, morning and evening feeding periods increased in length. The animals

usually bedded down in canyons or in washes in dense palo verde, hackberry or mesquite.

During the winter months, feeding activity generally lasted throughout the day, but rest periods were of shorter duration. On extremely cold days in the Tucson Mountains study area, herds sought the shelter of caves or tunnels, presumably to avoid cold and wind. When the weather again became warm in spring, feeding periods became shorter. Movements were similar to those of summer.

There seems to be considerable variation in the amount of movement of peccaries at night. Ellisor and Harwell (1969) have made the strongest statement for nocturnal movements when they say that "Peccaries on both study sites were mostly nocturnal except during the winter months when no feeding pattern was followed. Feeding activity began about sunset and continued throughout the night with occasional resting periods." Not all observers have found night feeding to the same extent. Jennings and Harris (1953) and Eddy (1961) both thought that nighttime feeding was not the general rule. In the hot dry months of May and June in Arizona, Elder (1969) found herds of peccaries moving to the waterholes most commonly from early evening until shortly before sunrise.

Seasonal

Most writers agree that the activity patterns for the collared peccary vary little at different seasons of the year except concerning time of feeding and moving about. Eddy (1961) concluded that in southern Arizona from late April until mid-October the morning feeding activity terminated when the air temperature rose to above about 90°F and resumed in the evening when the temperature dropped below this. In the winter when temperature was not a limiting factor, however, they did not regulate their hours of activity so rigidly. In Texas Bissonette (1976) showed the quantitative relationship between movement, feeding activities, and temperatures.

Eddy (1959) observed that peccaries did not feed during high winds or storms. Schweinsburg (1969), however, reported feeding and other activity during the winter rains in Arizona. In the Texas brush country, Ellisor and Harwell (1969) found that peccaries fed and moved at night during the summer months but during the winter months followed no particular feeding pattern. Day (1977b) and Bissonette (1976) reported feeding activity throughout the night in summer.

DRINKING AND EATING

Eddy (1956), Knipe (1957), Neal (1959), Schweinsburg (1969), Bigler (1974), Ellisor and Harwell (1969), and Bissonette (1976) have discussed the feeding behavior of the collared peccary. All agree that, when feeding, the herd spreads out in loosely knit units. When the food species being sought is a large single plant such as the agave, or sparsely scattered barrel cactus or prickly pear cactus plants, a number of animals converge on one plant. In such instances some "squabbling" is common as the animals compete for food. When food plants are more abundant, the herd members are scattered over a considerable area.

Eddy (1959) tallied the types of terrain in which peccaries fed and concluded that in the low desert country of Arizona, on 99 observations, peccaries were found feeding on wash bottoms 43 times, flat ground 28 times, hillsides 20 times, and in canyons 8 times, but they avoided extremely rocky areas such as talus slopes.

The manner in which peccaries eat depends largely on the plant species taken. When tubers or other underground plant parts are taken, the animals root the ground with the nasal disk in the same manner as hogs. However, unlike domestic hogs and contrary to common belief, they do not devour their food rapidly. Both in the wild and in captivity, the observer is readily impressed with the careful and "dainty" approach peccaries take toward their food.

Plants such as prickly pear cactus have many large, sharp spines and many small glochids. With great care and with the help of the front feet to hold the prickly pear pads against the ground, the peccaries skillfully eat large amounts of this material. Although the manner of eating is not always the same, the peccary usually peels the skin off one side of the cladophyll and eats the soft juicy pulp, thus avoiding the spines and leaving one side uneaten (Fig. 7.1). Sometimes the bite is through the entire cladophyll but this method of feeding, as illustrated by Bissonette (1976), was not generally used by our captive animals.

Over much of the peccaries' range, open water is scarce and these hardy animals subsist for long periods on the water obtained from succulent plants. When fresh water is available, however, the peccary regularly comes to drink.

In much of the arid southwestern United States and northern Mexico these water sources are *charcos*, tanks constructed for the use of domestic livestock, or natural *tinajas*. One of the most common types of watering places is a simple basin made by building an earthen dam across a ravine or arroyo in a runoff area. If well constructed, many of these will collect enough water to last the livestock and wildlife for the entire year during all but the driest years.

Elder (1956) gave considerable detail on the watering patterns of peccary in the deserts of Arizona. He found that peccaries came to watering areas during all months except August, September, and December, with the highest use of waterholes being in June, July, and October. In Arizona there are normally two rainy seasons during the year. Summer thunderstorms come in late July and August, and rainy periods resulting from frontal storms occur in the winter from December until March. Winter storms are undependable, and during many

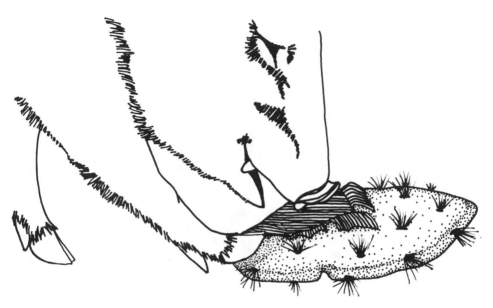

Figure 7.1. Collared peccary eating cactus and avoiding spines. (Illustration by Deboragh McDonnell)

years there is very little rain. Following both rainy periods, there is an abundance of new vegetation growth and standing pools of water. When such moist conditions exist, peccaries do not frequent the tanks and other watering areas.

In the higher areas of the peccaries' range, near the bases of mountains and in the foothills, many seeps and springs are available as watering places of peccaries.

Because many water areas used by peccaries were built for domestic stock, some ranchers have claimed that peccaries pollute waterholes. Knipe (1957), however, observed a total of 140 peccaries drinking at open waterholes and said that none entered the water, but drank and immediately left. The waterholes observed by Elder were made of concrete, and there was no possibility of animals wallowing in the mud or going into the water.

Being a herd animal, the peccary approaches waterholes in a group. Peccaries often stood silently scattered in the brush near the waterhole and only seldom did the whole herd water together at one time. Figure 7.2 shows a herd drinking at a waterhole. Elder (1956) observed that when watering herd members seldom squabbled. At the waterhole the peccaries normally pay little attention to other species that come to drink. Edler noted an exception, however. On two occasions peccary herds quickly left waterholes when a bobcat approached. In both instances, suckling young peccaries, which could be considered prey of the bobcat, were in the herds.

Figure 7.2. Herd of collared peccaries at a manmade waterhole in the Tucson Mountains in Arizona. Night photograph
taken with flash attachment. (Photograph by James B. Elder)

RESTING

Collared peccaries most commonly rest in small groups of three or four
with their bodies often touching. The close contact between animals is
more common in cold weather and especially at night. Resting animals
recline in several positions. Like all ungulates, they lack the supple
spine characteristic of many carnivores and therefore cannot curl into
a round posture while resting. The most common resting postures are a
belly-down, feet out front, head alert posture and a horizontal
stretched-out posture in which the animal lays on its side. In this
position the animal may or may not be sleeping.

WALLOWING

Wallowing in either mud or dust is a common activity among mammals.
This form of grooming is particularly noticeable among pigs and piglike
animals. Some species have permanent, specific wallowing places
within their territory (Hediger 1950).

The peccary uses both dust and mud wallows when available in
its home range. It does not normally enter the water to bathe but
wallows in the mud near the water areas. Among our captive animals,
whenever a water tap leaked, the resulting puddle was used quickly
as a wallow.

Dust wallows are present in all areas inhabited by the peccary. They usually consist of a simple depression in the ground burrowed out by the animals. They are common in bedding areas under low trees and bushes and sometimes under overhanging rocks.

GROOMING

With the exception of mutual rubbing, which is a social action, the collared peccary spends little time or effort grooming. Rubbing the scent gland against rocks, trees, and other objects is also a social act. One action that may or may not have social significance is rubbing the jowls or cheeks against inanimate objects. If the area was previously a scent post, the action may be social. If it is not a scent post, the rubbing is simple grooming.

Both adults and young animals occasionally scratch their cheeks and jowls by a rapid up and down motion of a hind leg against the cheek. Shaking of the hair and skin is a common type of grooming seen among peccaries emerging from a mud wallow or a dusty area.

LOCOMOTION

The peccary, like most four-footed mammals, has what is often referred to as a diagonal type of locomotion (Hildebrand 1960, 1962). For example, the front left foot moves forward at the same time as the rear right foot while the other two feet support the weight of the animal. As the first two feet to move land on the ground, the other two feet move foward. Figure 7.3 shows a typical walking stance of a young collared peccary.

We charted the foot-fall pattern of peccaries moving in long runways and saw three basic types of movement: walking, trotting, and running. To determine the distance between steps, we covered the runway with a thin layer of soft, moist soil. Measurements were taken between the footprints, and results are shown in Table 7.1.

In 1965 we obtained information on the speed of the peccary plotted at various gaits. Captive animals, either brought into the pens from the wild or born and raised in the pens and untamed, were used in these trials. The animals born and raised in the pens showed a

**Table 7.1. Nearest Distance Between
Tracks or Groups of Tracks for the Collared Peccary**

Gait	No. of Samples	Distance Between Tracks (inches)		
		Range	Average	S.D.
Trot	8	16–23.5	18.4	14.6
Run	12	46–79	61.0	10.2

Figure 7.3. Six-week-old collared peccary in typical walking stance. (Photograph by Lyle K. Sowls)

tendency to escape and to run in the alley way in the same manner as wild animals.

The tendency to return quickly to the pen with which they were acquainted and to show fear of man when excited made it possible to use the runway as a speed measuring area. A ninety-foot-long runway was used for the running trials. To obtain speeds a Doppler radar Model FTB X (1) was placed at one end of the runway. The animals were released from the opposite end of the runway. As they ran down the alley, the radar recorded the speed of movement. The various speeds recorded are given in Table 7.2.

INTERACTIONS WITH OTHER SPECIES

Several writers have commented on the reactions of other animals to the presence of peccaries. Knipe (1957) observed that deer and peccaries come into close contact at waterholes but pay little attention to each other. He further states that peccaries pay no attention to quail, cottontails, or jackrabbits. Elder (1956) made similar observations on the interactions of peccaries with mule deer, cottontails, jackrabbits,

Table 7.2. **Speeds Recorded for Five Adult Collared Peccaries**

Animal Number	Radar Speed (mph)	Kind of Gait
1	14	gallop
	18	gallop
	18	gallop
	6–10	trot (10 = rapid trot)
	4–5	walk
2	6–10	trot
	18	gallop
	16	gallop
	18	gallop
3	20	gallop
	18	gallop
	16	gallop
4	10	trot
	18	gallop
	22	gallop
	18	gallop
	16	gallop
5	14	gallop
	14	gallop
	20	gallop
	20	gallop

quail, and white-winged doves around desert watering areas. Ellisor and Harwell (1979) describe four encounters between peccaries and feral hogs in Texas. On each occasion the hogs fled from the pursuing peccaries and never tried to defend their position.

Neal (1959) has described an experiment to test the popular myth (Hornaday 1908; Seton 1929; Cutright 1940) that peccaries kill and devour rattlesnakes whenever they find them. He says

A captured rattlesnake (*Crotalus* sp.), approximately one and one-half feet in length, was tethered to an iron stake by a cement waterhole in the Tucson Mountains on October 22, 1956. The waterhole measured 4 x 5 feet in length and width. Three peccaries approached the waterhole at 7 p.m. (after dark) and proceeded to drink about a foot away from the tethered rattlesnake. The snake "buzzed" and the three peccaries withdrew rapidly from the area. Two of the peccaries came back to the waterhole ten minutes later, but this time they approached the waterhole on the side opposite the snake. The rattlesnake "buzzed" the entire time that the peccaries were drinking at the waterhole.

Some interesting observations on the interactions between peccaries and various other species have been noted in the field and among our captive animals. For example, in May 1969, a female domestic cat gave birth to kittens in the hay pile about 30 feet from the pens where captive peccaries were kept. The mother cat moved all of her kittens to a new location before weaning time except one which remained behind and grew to adult size. The cat lived in and around the peccary pens, and from the age of about two months freely moved about in the pens without being molested by the peccaries.

Ferocity

Stories relating the ferocity of the peccary in the popular literature are numerous. Finley (1947) says, "Having plenty of time on their hands, they liked to tree a man and keep him there for hours at a stretch." Ligon (1927) says, "A bunch of peccaries when at bay present such a scene of vicious fighting energy that few dare press them." Nichol (1936) believed that "if the young are threatened or other members of the herd endangered the animals often attack fearlessly."

However, many observers do not agree with those who claim that the peccary is ferocious. Carr (1946) says that "like other wild animals it will usually keep to itself and is only anxious to escape." Speaking from long-time experience in Arizona, O'Connor (1939) says, "I have seen thousands of javelina and without a single exception all of them were convinced that homosapiens was a bad hombre and to be avoided."

From his many years of contact with this animal, Knipe (1957) describes two instances that may, by less experienced observers, be considered ferocity on the part of a peccary. He concludes, however, that the words "ferocious" and "vicious" are not applicable. From our contact with peccaries in wild herds and in trapping and handling wild animals, I have concluded, like many other writers, that the main aim of the peccary in its relationship with man is to escape from him. It may seem strange that this has been found true even of adult sows in herds when accompanied by their young. Several authors (Anon. 1849; Seton 1929; Knipe 1957; Neal 1959) have described taking very young animals away from their mothers, only to see the mothers forsake the young and flee. I have seen this type of behavior on several occasions.

SHELTER SEEKING

References to the collared peccary seeking shelter in burrows, caves, or under logs are common, especially in tropical areas (Buffon 1787; Azara in Hunter 1838; Gaumer 1917; Seton 1929; and Cabrera and Yepes 1940). Roosevelt (1914) describes the collared peccary in Brazil seeking refuge in holes and hollow logs when it is pursued or is seeking shelter from the weather. Miller (1930) found the collared peccary in Brazil living in burrows made by other animals. He described one instance in which peccaries used the burrow of a giant armadillo. Hanson (pers. comm.) found collared peccaries using similar burrows and hollow logs for shelter and hiding places in Honduras. In Arizona the collared peccary appears to be adept at finding adequate shelter from cold winter nights or hot summer days. To escape the heat the herds spend the hot part of the day in the cool shade of desert trees and shrubs, under rock overhangs or similar natural features. During the winter many cold nights are spent in caves or mine tunnels. The animals paw and root excavations in the soil and lie in them. Often several animals lie in these areas together during cold weather in close contact with each other.

TAMING AND IMPRINTING

The collared peccary tames quickly if removed from the mother and handled at an early age. This readiness to taming has been described by many writers (Azara in Hunter 1838; Orton 1876; Mearns 1907; Cook 1909; Grant 1916; Gaumer 1917; Nelson 1918; Goldman 1920; Seton 1929; Cabrera and Yepes 1940; Lowie 1946; Handley 1950; Bennett 1962; Noguiera-Neto 1973; and Smole 1976). In a book entitled *Sketches in Natural History of Mammalia* (Anon. 1849) the author said, "it is domesticated with more facility than the wild hog, and becomes troublesome from its familiarity." This author, like others, is talking about pet-keeping rather than true domestication, which implies the taming of many successive generations of subjugated animals. The peccary, if properly treated, could perhaps become a domesticated animal. Two essential characteristics of a potential domesticated animal (Zeuner 1963) are that the animal first be a social or herd animal and that it tame easily. However, there is no evidence that man has ever truly domesticated the peccary, although evidence of taming individuals as pets is common.

There appears to be a period in early life when following reactions are important. If taken when very young, peccaries will follow a person just as they follow their mother. The age after which taming became difficult was found to be about three days, although the length of this period must be regarded as variable. Those born in captivity that stay with their mother and are not handled remain wild.

In the summer of 1959 I received a pair of two-to-three-day-old litter mates (both females) from Arnold Kester. These young were fed the usual diet of canned milk but were not handled frequently. They remained fairly wild. At about five weeks, one died. At this point it was decided to tame the other animal. Daily and repeated handling had no effect upon this animal; it remained very wild. Sometimes it seemed to be terribly frightened and would run against the wire fence and injure its nose. What appeared to happen in this case was that when the two were together, they were content, but by the time one died the period of easy imprinting in the other had passed.

Generally it appears that a young peccary which has been hand-raised and tamed remains so and will be tame to almost all people. There are certain exceptions to this rule, however, as the penned captives that are tame will often threaten strangers or stay away from the wire.

In November 1958 one notable exception to this general tameness was noted. A young animal was hand-reared by Mrs. Hal Gras of Tucson and was extremely tame. At the age of 26 weeks, it was given to the wildlife unit collection and put with a mature male with which it was compatible. For over a month, however, it appeared wild in its new surroundings. It avoided its new handlers and would not come up to the wire like most hand-reared animals. Of more than 20 tamed pets taken from various handlers and put in the unit's collection, all were tractable and showed little or no discrimination toward specific handlers.

STANDING WATCH

Probably no interpretation of an animal's action is more subject to error than that of leadership and "guard duty." At least one writer has referred to "guard animals" watching the other herd members eat or drink (Seton 1929). Elder (1956) cites instances in which individual animals seemed to take up a guard station while others drank at desert waterholes.

SENSES

Numerous writers (Olin 1959; Knipe 1957; Neal 1959) have said that the peccary has a rather poor sense of sight but a good sense of hearing and smell. Neal waved arms, handkerchiefs, and other objects in the air to attract the attention of peccaries and concluded that peccaries do not readily see moving objects over 100 yards away. I observed an example of light-orientation among young peccaries on March 5, 1968, when I moved twin baby peccaries (eight days old) from an indoor pen to a pen that included both an outside and an inside run with a small hole in a wall dividing the two parts. I found that at night they could not find their way back into the inside nest without a light to guide them. When a light was furnished, they quickly followed it.

Social
Behavior

PECCARIES ARE SOCIAL ANIMALS THAT LIVE in herds or groups. Although "solitarios" (Leopold 1959) are sometimes found, generally they are old, sick, or disabled and no longer able to keep up with the herd. Unlike most ungulates, whose group size and composition change during the year, the collared peccary is a herd animal throughout its life (Seton 1929; Jennings and Harris 1953; Knipe 1957; Neal 1959; Sowls 1966; Schweinsburg and Sowls 1972; Sowls 1974). No temporary male bands or female harems interrupt the yearly cycle of social relationships in this species except when herds are temporarily fragmented. The sex and age ratios of individual herds represent a sample of the population as a whole and are not a result of particular behavioral divisions.

Frädrich (1967) and Schweinsburg (1969) were the first to describe the various behavioral postures of the collared peccary. Schweinsburg and Sowls (1972), Dobroruka and Horbowyjova (1972), Sowls (1974), and Diaz (1978) described the social behavior of captive penned and wild animals. Bissonette (1976, 1982) described the social behavior and organization of the collared peccary in wild herds and quantified some of his field observations. Byers (1980) and Byers and Bekoff (1981) described the social behavior of the collared peccary in a wild situation, and they give the most detailed and quantitative analysis of social interactions for this species and the development of these interactions.

HERDS

Size and Composition

Since the herd is the most common social unit in the life of the collared peccary, its size, variation and makeup are, therefore, important. Numerous writers have reported on the herd size of the collared peccary. Knipe (1957), reporting on 127 herds in Arizona, found that herds ranged from one to 21 animals and averaged 8.5 between 1948 and 1954. He also gave estimates of three additional herds which numbered from 40 to 53. His figures represent the largest amount of published information based on accurate counts of undisturbed herds. Seventy percent of the herds Knipe observed were of 10 or fewer animals. He reported only nine percent with more than 15 animals. Knipe observed only four instances of lone peccaries. In the Tucson Mountains in Arizona, Minnamon (1962) found an average herd size of seven. Bigler (1964) found that 12 herds in the Tortolita Mountains in Arizona averaged 7.2 animals each. From 1959 to 1971 in Arizona, hunters were interviewed at checking stations operated by the Arizona Cooperative Wildlife Research Unit. The 851 herds from which hunters took animals averaged 7.9 animals per herd. Of 48 herds which I observed in southern Arizona where the animals were undisturbed, numbers varied from one to 18 and averaged 8.0

In south Texas, Jennings and Harris (1953) reported herds of 10 to 30. In Big Bend National Park in west Texas, Bissonette (1976, 1982) reported on 10 herds which ranged from five to 27 and averaged 14.4. In Saguaro National Monument in Arizona, where hunting is prohibited, Day (1967) reported average herd sizes of 8.9, 11.1, 13.3, 10.5, 13.5, 11.3, and 14.4 between 1961 and 1967. Day (1972) found that, on the hunted part of the Three-Bar Wildlife Research Area in Arizona between 1967 and 1972, herds averaged 16.5, 9.6, 7.2, 16.6, 5.6, and 7.6. On the unhunted part of this area during the same years, he found an average herd size of 15.0. 9.8, 16.8, 18.6, 20.0, and 11.8. Supplee (1981), working the same general area, reported herd sizes of 22, 18, 16, and 11 before the handgun hunting season; sizes of the same herds after the hunting season were 12, 16, 14, and 10. Byers (1980) reported that the average size of nine herds in the Three-Bar area was 11.2

Few records on herd size for the collared peccary are available from Mexico, Central America, and South America. Both collared and white-lipped peccaries are frequently mentioned in early explorers' reports and, although there are few references to the herd size of the collared peccary, frequent mention was made of the large size of white-lipped peccary herds. Numerous writers have reported small herd size for the collared peccary in South America. Azara (in Hunter 1838), Anon. (1849), Alston (1879), Cook (1909), Roosevelt (1914), Gaumer (1917), Miller (1930), Enders (1930), Murie (1935), Siskind (1973), Carneiro (1974) and Kiltie (1980) all reported that the collared peccary in the rain forests of South America was found in small groups. One wild group of collared peccaries which I observed in the state of São Paulo in southern Brazil in June 1975 and August 1976 had more that 40 animals. This herd was drawn into a baited, protective area, however, making actual size of individual herds difficult to determine.

Several reasons may account for the smaller herd size of the collared peccary in the tropical rain forests than in the more open, northern part of its range. The forest growth of the tropical and subtropical areas makes visibility difficult, possibly causing many animals to go unnoticed. Also, most observers who have reported on herd size of the collared peccary have seen animals near settlements where they are heavily hunted. Some authors have attributed the smaller herd size of the collared peccary in the tropical rain forest to the heavy hunting pressure near these villages (Gaumer 1917; Leopold 1959; Borrero 1967) which causes the herds to break up into smaller units.

The number of animals in the herds varies greatly in different areas and at different times. It is influenced by the amount and effectiveness of rainfall, which influences reproduction and survival, and by the severity of the winter weather, especially at the higher elevations at the northern fringe of the animals' range. Concentrated hunting pressure also causes the number of animals in herds to vary. There is some evidence that herds today are not as large as they were in earlier years. In 1893 Roosevelt reported herds in Texas numbering 20 to 30 animals. Many hunters in Arizona have told me that herds in that state are not as large as in former years. Unfortunately these accounts are hard to evaluate, and data on early herd size are lacking. From the standpoint of studies of social behavior, I have concluded that herds could vary from 2 animals to over 50. Most herds encountered, however, range from about 5 to 15.

Stability

The most common changes in herd size occur because of deaths or births, but occasionally animals move out of a herd or new animals join. Schweinsburg (1971) concluded that two types of changes occur. The first are temporary fluctuations resulting from animals leaving the herd after fighting or scattering after a disturbance. When temporary fluctuations occurred, members stayed within the home range of the herd and later regrouped. The second type he termed "herd alterations," which included permanent changes — members either left the herd's home range or wandering animals joined a herd and remained with it. Schweinsburg studied movements between two herds during two years and reported that five animals left the home range of one herd and stayed within the home range of the herd they joined. He found no instances in which animals shuttled between herds. Ellisor and Harwell (1969) marked and observed 66 individuals in five herds in southeast Texas and observed eight instances in which males left their respective herds and moved to another herd or eventually returned to their original herd.

Bissonette (1976) reported that the territorial groups he studied were stable, but smaller subgroups did change, possibly because of intraspecific competition and vegetative cover.

Home Range

The home range of the collared peccary has been described by several writers. By retrapping and field identification of 143 marked animals, Minnamon (1962) concluded that the home range of the collared peccary in the Tucson Mountains of Arizona was less than 388 hectares. Bigler (1964), who carried out a similar study in the Tortolita Mountains of Arizona, found home ranges that varied from 260 to 800 hectares. A study based on individually marked animals in the Texas brush country (Ellisor and Harwell 1969) revealed average home ranges of 111, 187, 92, 73, 167, 188, and 255 hectares in two other study areas. These authors obtained a total of 1,333 sightings of 66 marked animals by attaching bells to collars to help find the animals in heavy brush. They found that peccary herds established definite territories which overlapped from 90 to 180 meters, and that no more than one herd was observed in this overlapping edge at one time. Schweinsburg (1969, 1971) placed plastic harnesses on individual animals to identify them in the Tucson Mountains and used radio transmitters attached to these collars to rapidly locate herds. He concluded that the home ranges of four herds were 150, 64, 83, and 171 hectares in size. Day (1977) placed radio transmitters on animals in 20 different herds on the Three-Bar Wildlife Area and six on animals in the Tortolita Mountains and found that the home ranges averaged 285 hectares and 313 hectares respectively. Schweinsburg (1969, 1971) spoke of "core areas," parts of the home range most commonly used, a concept first put forth by Kaufman (1962) and enlarged upon by Jewell (1966).

Castellanos (1982) put radio transmitters on collared peccaries in the central llanos of Venezuela to study their home ranges. He emphasized the use of core areas. During the dry period one animal covered a daily average of 9.83 hectares and another covered 10.93 hectares, or 28 and 29 percent of the total area estimated for each individual during the entire dry period. He estimated that these same measurements for the transition period were 8.65 and 9.53 hectares, or 21 percent of the total area covered during the period. During the rainy season he found that the average daily area of utilization was 10.02 and 9.28 hectares which represented 10 and 16 percent of the total.

In the Tucson Mountains, where several herds drank from the same waterholes during the dry seasons, home ranges overlapped. Schweinsburg (1971) found boundary overlaps of up to 184 meters where home ranges of individual herds met at waterholes and desirable bedding areas, but more than one herd did not use a bedding area at one time. A herd's definite and strong affinity for specific areas seems to hold true despite the presence of other herds in the area. Scent marking within the home range informs other animals that the area is already occupied. Ellisor and Harwell (1969) used the words "home range" and "territory" interchangeably and discussed the overlapping of the home ranges of different herds. In describing their

Texas study they say (p. 427): "Territorial behavior made it possible to accurately define home range boundaries by plotting points at which herds repeatedly refused to venture farther from the center of activity." Bissonette (1976, 1982) studied five territorial groups in Texas and found that territories of all groups to be about the same size, 245 hectares.

Supplee (1981) found that herds of collared peccaries maintained home ranges with territorial markings and defense. Although she found areas of overlap around waterholes, most herds maintained corridors to these places of joint use. She found that herds of seven or more had home ranges averaging 374 hectares while herds of two to four had home ranges averaging 147 hectares.

AUDITORY COMMUNICATIONS

Numerous writers have given subjective interpretations of the vocalizations of the collared peccary (Enders 1930; Neal 1959; Schweinsburg 1969; Schweinsburg and Sowls 1972; Sowls 1974; and Bissonette 1976, 1982). Tembrock (1968) has been the only one to describe a sonogram of a peccary sound, but he does not say which of the many vocalizations is shown. Byers (1980) spoke of only three vocalizations of the collared peccary—the bark, distress call, and low grunt. He ranked the vocalizations along with 19 other categories of motor patterns and assigned to this category an incredibly low 0.3 percent of all actions. This figure may be accurate for those particular vocalizations that Byers heard, but it indicates that he arrived at the low figure because he did not recognize all of the calls. In my opinion, vocalizations should not be considered as a component comparable to movement patterns but should be regarded as accompanying these other actions.

The necessity of recording calls and expressing them as sonograms has been recognized by most students of animal communication. The tape recorder is the best solution because sounds can be played back repeatedly for study. Significant portions of the tape can be selected for analysis on the sonograph, which gives a general visual picture of the sound, with frequency graphed against time. Loudness is to some extent rendered by variation in the darkness of the graph, but it can be measured only relatively, since the loudness of the recording depends on the closeness of the microphone to the subject and the setting of the recorder.

To hear many of the vocalizations adequately, I found that captive animals had to be accustomed to their handlers and to the environment. Some common vocalizations are too low for the sound to travel far, and they are impossible to hear among wild herds. Between 1965 and 1974 I tried to obtain tape recordings of as many vocalizations as possible from captive animals. I found that the best time to record sounds at the captive pens was around 3 a.m. when extraneous noises were minimal. Because extraneous noises, even at this hour, were still excessive we built a sound chamber into which we placed some of the animals. Because of the animal's sharp teeth and tendency to bite, they had to be placed behind a wire fence within the chamber. This eliminated most of the outside noises, but other noises caused by the animals appeared. The animals rubbed their noses on the wire fence which, in the enclosed chamber, made loud noises. They attempted to lift the wire with their nose disc, made "smacking" sounds with the lips against the wire, and rubbed their sides on the wire barrier. Young animals had a tendency to rub on the handler.

Because many aggressive sounds are heard only when a number of animals are involved, sounds of single animals were hard to separate. A number of distinct calls, however, could be separated and described. I will attempt to describe these and illustrate, by sonograms, their frequency, length, and appearance. Besides a descriptive term which we found useful, I will also give my interpretation of how these vocalizations sounded to me and my colleagues. Lastly, I will summarize the possible uses and responses to these vocalizations in the manner used by Carpenter (1964), Struhsaker (1978), and others (Table 8.1).

Togetherness Vocalizations

Herd animals which commonly become dispersed when alarmed must depend on rallying calls to know where the other herd members are while trying to reassemble. This is especially true of the collared peccary which has poor long-range vision and often lives in densely vegetated areas. One of the most common types of vocalization evident in all species of peccaries is nonaggressive, heard in situations where young and mother attempt to stay together or where herd members "keep in touch" with each other. These calls play an important part in group cohesion, a very important consideration for a herd animal in a forest environment. Smith (1977) called these vocalizations "seeking to associate" calls. Two separate vocalizations fit this category — purring and complaining.

"Purring." One of the most common vocalizations is what Schweinsburg (1969), Schweinsburg and Sowls (1972), and Sowls (1974) have called "purring" or the contentment vocalizations. It is a constant, repetitive series of sounds heard from young animals in captivity and some adults all through life. Young captive animals responded by increased purring when they were scratched or their bellies were rubbed. I have never heard tooth-clicking or aggressive vocalizations accompanying these purring sounds. Illustrated in Figure 8.1, the purring sounds which I have described fall in the range of about 500 to 1,000 Hz.

Table 8.1. Vocalizations in the Collared Peccary and Probable Functions

Type	Subjects	Vocal Patterns	Responses	Probable Functions	Situation and Remarks
TOGETHERNESS CALLS					
Purring	All young with mother—some adults	Short repetitive sounds to ca. 660 Hz	Closes distances mother to young	To hold animals together—especially mother and young	Heard only at close range. Up to about 10–15 m
Complaining	Young animals with mother	Caused by inhaling and exhaling air; To 2,000 Hz	None visible	Continuation from purring to keep animals together	Heard if mother tried to get away from young
"Low grunt"	Any herd member	A low grunt, repetitive	May be answered	To reassemble herd members	When herd members have become separated
"Bark"	Any herd member	Loud, sharp, "dog-like"	Alerts other herd members which may answer	To locate other herd members after dispersal	When herd members are trying to regroup
AGGRESSIVE AND ALARM CALLS					
Continuous grumble or "growl"	Any herd member	Repetitive grunts	Retreat or return threat	Both intraspecific and interspecific; important in establishing dominance order	Heard in crowded situations such as feeding, ceases with increase in distance
Tooth clicking	Any herd member	In series of 2–8 clicks	Retreat or return threat	Both intraspecific and interspecific; Important in establishing dominance order	In close situations; in aggressive only
Squeal	Any herd member but usually young or subordinate	Loud, sharp call	Signal of submission	Both intraspecific and interspecific; important in establishing dominance order; also reaction to danger	Distress and alarm call during intensive play and close feeding
"Whoof"	Any herd member	An explosive, short call, usually in a series	Alerts herd for retreat	To warn other herd members	When herd is surprised and takes flight

"Complaining." The other common sounds which often accompany the purring are what I call a "complaining" sound. The reason for this name is because the sound is an evident change from the purring; it occurs when a mother pulls away from the young or when the food dish is removed from the young when they are eating. Figure 8.1d illustrates purring sounds interrupted by complaining calls. Kathy Groschupf, who made these sonograms from my tapes, has pointed out that these calls, with harmonics reaching slightly over 2,000 Hz, are made by an inhalation and exhalation. Figure 8.1d is labeled to show this exchange of air.

The "low grunt." Numerous references have appeared in the literature describing the "grunts" of the collared peccary (Enders 1930; Knipe 1957; Neal 1959; Schweinsburg 1969; Schweinsburg and Sowls 1972; Sowls 1974; Bissonette 1976, 1982; Byers 1980; and Byers and Bekoff 1981). Many references to the grunt of the peccary have also appeared in popular writings, no doubt because some authors automatically associated peccaries with hogs. Although the word "grunt" has been generally used in reference to the collared peccary, it has undoubtedly been applied to many different vocalizations. Despite the confusion, one call seems distinct enough that it can logically be separated as a specific sound with a very specific place in the repertoire of the species.

Neal (1959) has described a low grunt and its answer as a way for herd members to contact each other. He spoke of the increasing loudness of such a call until a response was heard. Byers (1980) described the low grunt as a nonaggressive, low pitched, repetitive flat sound with a sharp onset and duration of about one-fourth to one-half a second. Both Jerry Day and Vashti Supplee (pers. comm.) agree with Byers. These three, who spent a great deal of time in the field, were able to imitate the call well enough to bring lone peccaries to them. Apparently they are describing the same nonaggressive call that Neal had earlier described. I have no sonogram to illustrate this vocalization. I have placed it with other "togetherness" calls and classified it as a herd reassembly call.

The "bark." Like the "low grunt," a number of people have described a "bark." Sowls (1974) described a bark as being like that of a dog. Bissonette (1976) said that the bark was more resonant than a dog's and was associated with a growl. He classified it as an agonistic vocalization. Byers (1980) described the bark as sounding quite similar to that of a dog but gave no description of the situations under which he heard it.

I disagree with Bissonette that this is an agonistic vocalization. Rather I consider it a "togetherness" call used by lost animals to find other herd members during reassembly. Day (pers. comm.) calls it a

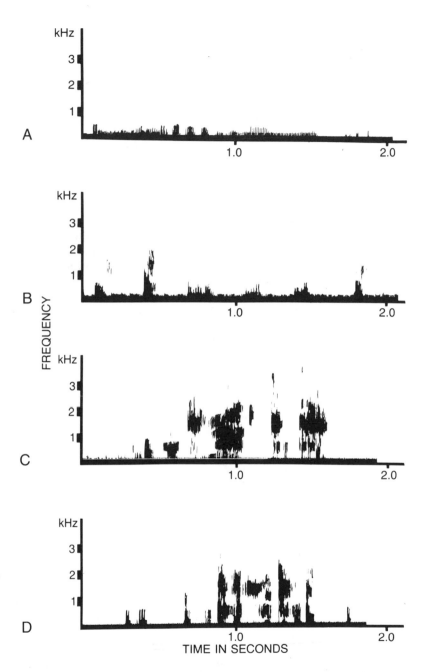

Figure 8.1. Sonogram of nonaggressive vocalizations of the collared peccary. A, adult "purring"; B, young "purring"; C, young "complaining"; D, young "complaining" intermittent with "purring"

bark because it is the only one he believes sounds like the bark of a dog. He too considers it as a call made by a lost herd member trying to find other herd members.

Alarm and Aggressive Vocalizations

This category includes three aggressive vocalizations and one alarm call. Two of these aggressive calls accompany each other and will be discussed together (the continuous grumble and tooth-clicking).

The continuous grumble or "growl" and tooth-clicking. One of the most aggressive sounds of the collared peccary is a continuous grumbling or series of rapid grunts heard from animals feeding together. Sharp clicking sounds from the teeth accompany the grumbling. When a number of herd members gather around a restricted food source, such as an agave, an aggressive situation results; and the animals can be heard long before they are seen. This is especially true in heavy vegetation, such as in Arizona's live oak-juniper vegetation type. Experienced hunters use this knowledge in finding herds in early morning when they are feeding. The continuous grumble and tooth-clicking have been described by a number of writers including Neal (1959), Schweinsburg (1969), Schweinsburg and Sowls (1972), Sowls (1974), and Bissonette (1976). A sonogram of these sounds is shown in Figure 8.2. I have never heard clicking sounds except in aggressive situations. These clicking sounds come in short groups. Of a series of chatterings made by a female with young, the average number of tooth impacts was 3.4 and varied from two to eight in a series.

The "whoof." Several writers, including Knipe (1957), Neal (1959), Schweinsburg (1969), Schweinsburg and Sowls (1972), and Bissonette (1976), have applied this term to an alarm call of the collared peccary. All these authors describe this as an alarm call emitted as the herd runs away. Bissonette (1976), who most completely describes this sound, says it is a series of rapid short breath exhalations made while the animal is usually in motion. He also describes it as a challenging sound made while an isolated animal is trying to ascertain the location of the intruder. Bissonette says that the exploring animal stamps its feet while sniffing the air and emitting this sound and exhibits pilo erection of the hairs on the back.

INTRASPECIFIC BEHAVIOR

Frädrich (1967) has described some aspects of the behavior of the collared peccary and compared its behavior to that of some species of Suidae. Schweinsburg (1969), Schweinsburg and Sowls (1972), and Sowls (1974) have described other aspects. Bissonette (1976) has given detailed descriptions of his interpretations of these same behaviorisms and, in some instances, has expanded and divided these into more

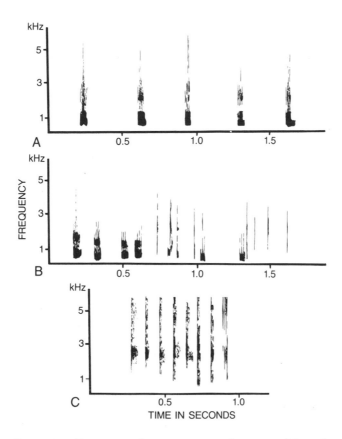

Figure 8.2. Sonogram of aggressive vocalizations of the collared peccary. A, repetitive grunts; B, repetitive grunts and clicks; C, tooth-clicking without repetitive grunts

detailed actions. Byers (1980) has described a repertoire of 146 motor patterns which he placed in 20 larger categories. Many of these are the same as those described by earlier writers, some are new and have not been described before, and others are variations of previously described actions. Some in his groupings have been placed in the category of general behavior by other writers, even though a social situation may have existed.

Many of the behavioral postures, actions and vocalizations grade almost imperceptibly from one to another depending upon the intensity of a situation. For that reason many interpretations are arbitrary and subjective and not all people give the same interpretation. Many times several behavioral actions are taking place at the same time leading to complex interactions. For example, an animal could be vocalizing, exhibiting hair display, marking behavior, or some other action simultaneously. The behavioral actions I have described here are my interpretations of some of the most common ones. For fine detail and other interpretations the reader should refer to the above cited sources, especially those of Bissonette (1976, 1982), Byers (1980), and Byers and Bekoff (1981).

Friendly Meetings

Approach. Frädrich (1967) described some forms of greeting for the collared peccary, specifically what has often been called mutual or reciprocal rubbing between friendly animals. He also described the meeting of animals and their touching of nasal discs as a form of greeting. I have shown a nose-to-nose meeting of friendly animals in Figure 8.3. Various parts of the body can be touched during these behavioral actions. Figure 8.4 shows an adult animal touching the side of a reclining animal which it had just approached. Included in the areas that are commonly touched by the nose is the scent gland of another animal (Fig. 8.5)

Schweinsburg (1969) and Schweinsburg and Sowls (1972) described the resting of the entire snout on the head or neck of another animal as "nuzzling" and considered it an important contactual experience between two friendly animals (Fig. 8.6). Byers (1980) gave a detailed account of the use of the nose in probing both other animals and the environment. He classified these under olfactory investigation and contact and included licking, nibbling, nose contacts, and what he has called "nuzzling" — the movement of the nose up and down against the body of another animal.

Bissonette (1976) described a "walk toward" movement of the collared peccary. Byers (1980) also described a similar movement and divided the larger category of approach into five subdivisions: (1) approach, front, side (2) approach rear (3) approach trot (4) approach run and (5) follow.

Aggressive Meetings

Dominance. Considerable confusion remains in the literature regarding the role of dominance and establishment of a social hierarchy among collared peccary groups. This is probably because no one has yet studied a sufficient number of marked animals and watched them long enough in wild herds. Bissonette (1976) stressed the importance of the alpha male; he noted that peccary groups have a linear dominance hierarchy including both sexes and that males always ranked highest in the social hierarchy. He observed animals in wild herds, but he marked only a small percentage of the animals. Diaz (1978), working with a herd of captives in a large pen, recognized certain animals as being dominant.

Byers (1980), who has spent more time than anyone else observing animals in wild herds, questioned Bissonette's belief that a social hierarchy exists. Byers, like Bissonette, did not have a significant number of animals marked and thus was unable to differentiate quickly either the individual or its sex. By observing the actions of marked known animals, I found that among 14 small herds of penned animals

Figure 8.3. Nose-to-nose greeting between
two adult collared peccaries

that had lived together for several months or more, certain animals
retained definite dominance over others (Sowls 1974). Following a technique previously described by Beilharz and Cox (1967) for domestic
swine, I withheld food or water for a time before testing. I either withheld water to create a competitive situation or furnished particularly
desirable fresh weeds and green vegetables, chopped into fine pieces
that could not be carried away. I considered an animal in a herd to be
dominant if it displaced another animal when eating or drinking. Interactions between herd members were classed into the two categories
used by McHugh (1958) for the American buffalo: (1) passive dominance, when one animal responded to another without show of force;
and (2) aggression, when force or threat was used to displace another
animal or when a subordinate animal was blocked from access to
the food.

   Following the methods previously described, data on social ranking in small penned herds was gathered. Results are given in Table
8.2. Ten adult males and 21 females were involved in these trials.
Usually females dominated males. Only in two herds did I observe
instances of females definitely being subordinate to males. These two
females had been raised as pets as had the males that dominated
them. In one instance, a small young male was consistently dominant
over a larger and older female.

   At least two factors may contribute to a difference noted between
the captive and wild animals: (1) the tameness or wildness of captive
individuals; the influence of this factor on behavior may contribute to
observations of captive animals. Hand-reared animals were not afraid

Figure 8.4. Adult collared peccary grooming another adult with its nose. Brazil. (Photograph by Lyle K. Sowls)

Figure 8.5. Adult female collared peccary sniffing scent gland of adult male

Figure 8.6. Two adult collared peccaries "nuzzling"

Table 8.2. Results of Tests to Determine Dominance in Small Herds of Penned Animals

Herd No.	Composition	No. of Trials	Interactions Aggressions	Passive Dominance	Remarks
1	5 immature F	2	5	0	Situation vague. One female definitely dominant over two others.
2	3 adult F 1 adult M	2	5	0	One female dominant over one other female. All others ate peacefully at 12' apart without apparent aggression.
3	2 adult F	6	7	2	Same female always dominant.
4	2 adult F 1 adult M 1 juvenile F	7	21	3	One female clearly dominant over all others in pen. Male dominant over subordinate adult female.
5	1 adult F 1 adult M 1 juvenile F	1	2	1	Adult female dominant. Situation between male and juvenile female vague.
6	3 adult F 1 adult M	2	1	4	One adult female dominant over all others. Position of others not clear.
7	2 adult F 1 adult M	3	6	3	Definite order with same female always dominant; male subordinate to both females.
8	2 adult M 2 adult F One has 2 young	5	25	1	Female with young aggressive and dominant. Other female dominant over both males. No aggression between the two males.

of man, while those not hand-reared remained farthest from the observers and from the food piles. This resulted in a lack of decisive encounters between individuals in some pens. For this reason many vague dominance positions existed in our picture of the dominance in these herds; (2) the sex ratios and numbers in the captive herds did not necessarily represent the same situations found in wild herds.

The "squabble." Schweinsburg and Sowls (1972) described some of the aggressive actions of the collared peccary, the most common of which is what they have termed "the squabble." In this action (Fig. 8.7) two animals face each other in a "sparring" position. Canine teeth are usually brought together in a sharp clatter. Both animals flatten their ears against the back of the head. Occasionally animals receive cuts on the face and head during squabbles. The squabbles are commonly seen and heard both in wild and penned herds.

Byers (1980) found the squabble to be the most frequently observed type of agonistic action, making up 22.2 percent of the agonistic behavior he observed and 1.07 percent of all social behavior encounters. He described a separate motor pattern which he called the growl or snarl. This sound I have described under vocalizations.

Figure 8.7. Head-to-head "squabble" between two adult collared peccaries

Threatening actions. Even before their canine teeth are well-developed, young peccaries bring their jaws together making the threatening staccato sound. Tooth-chattering is an intraspecific and an interspecific threat. A "close range" threat, which is also either intraspecific or interspecific, is the opening of the mouth and showing of the teeth. This is usually a defensive or threatening action made by a subordinate animal.

Byers (1980) listed and described in detail a number of social actions which I regard as threatening. These included the "butt" where one animal strikes another with its snout or forehead; the "fast head turn with mouth open" where an animal quickly turns to another in such a position; the "fast head turn with mouth closed"; the "gape" (opening mouth and showing teeth); and the "lunge," where an animal leaps toward another in a close encounter.

Fighting. The fighting actions of several species of Suidae, which are closely related to the collared peccary, have been described by Frädrich (1965, 1967). He found two basic fighting positions: (1) a frontal attack which is used by the warthog, *Phacochoerus aethiopicus* P.; the bushpig, *Potamochoerus porcus* L.; and the giant forest hog, *Hylochoerus* sp. and (2) a lateral attack used by the European wild boar, *Sus scrofa.* In the first type of fighting the opponents come directly at each other with hair bristled and push each other backward. In the lateral attack the opponents circle each other and press their shoulders together and bite each other about the shoulders, throat, forelegs, and ears and try to overturn each other. Frädrich observed that warthogs seldom bite each other in these encounters but that the European wild boars and bushpigs do.

In order to determine the type of fighting pattern of the collared peccary Schweinsburg and Sowls (1972) studied penned peccaries which were placed together in neutral enclosures. They described the "whirl-around" motion in which the two became locked together at the jaws and circled around each other. This action was often followed by a "throw-down" because both animals became exhausted, fell to the ground, and finally released their hold. The retreat of one of the animals usually followed.

These observations have indicated that the fighting of the collared peccary is primarily frontal, but in some respects it resembles lateral fighting. The peccaries we observed bit their opponents with their long sharp teeth. When they attacked, they "charged" head-on but did not push. Most of the biting was directed toward the head, neck, and shoulders. As they became tired they tended to bite their opponent's flanks and hindquarters. The advanced stages of fighting, which included the whirl-around and the throw-down, were seldom seen unless antagonistic animals, which did not normally live together, were placed in the same enclosure.

Neither I nor any of my coworkers have seen fights of this type among wild collared peccaries. In commenting on our description of these fights, Byers (1980) correctly concluded that they must indeed be rare occurrences among wild animals. He and workers in the Arizona Game and Fish Department spent hours in the field and none saw such fights.

Submission. In the encounters just described, subordinate animals showed their position by retreat when threatened. In most cases, this meant backing away from the threatening dominant animal. Schweinsburg and Sowls (1972) and Sowls (1974) have described the elevated position of the head among dominant animals during face-to-face encounters. Earlier I discussed "nuzzling" between friendly animals (Fig. 8.6). The same position can be seen between hostile animals, and it may lead to the submission of the subordinate animal. In such an instance the subordinate animal relaxes and sits on its hindquarters (Fig. 8.6). Schweinsburg (1967) and Schweinsburg and Sowls (1972) also showed a kneeling animal in a subordinate position. Figures 8.6 and 8.8 were copied from successive photographs. A small adult male was being encountered by a larger, older male which was clearly dominant. In this particular encounter fighting was avoided. Figure 8.6 also resembles closely the "nuzzling" during courtship described by Schweinsburg and Sowls (1972). Diaz (1978) has described a similar action as adult play. Thus the "nuzzling" action we have described, the snuggling together while standing, seems to be either part of a friendly encounter, an aggressive encounter, or part of courtship and, as Diaz has described it, a part of play.

DISPLAY

A great deal has been written about display in animals, especially birds (Hochbaum 1944; Armstrong 1947; Tinbergen 1952, 1961; Lorenz 1970, 1971). Display in mammals, too, has been described for a number of species, including the ungulates. Schaller (1967) has described

Figure 8.8. Subordinate animal taking submissive posture

display for a number of Asian deer and antelope, including the barasingha (*Cervus duvauceli*), the chital (*Axis axis*), the hog deer (*Axis porcinus*), the sambar (*Cervus unicolor*), the blackbuck (*Antilope cervicapra*), and the nilgai (*Boselaphus tragocamelus*). Geist (1971) has described rump display and hair display for the bighorn sheep (*Ovis canadensis*). Walther (1974) has described various displays for a number of species of African antelope.

Displays among the ungulates may consist of either showing a particular marking or the horns, or erecting bristlelike hairs or mane.

Hair Display

The collar, which gives the collared peccary its name, runs from the top of the shoulder down both sides to the lower edge of the body. It is made up of lighter hairs than those surrounding it. The dorsal stripe, which has been described by Schweinsburg (1969) and shown here in Figure 8.9, is conspicuous when the dorsal hairs of the back are erected. The stripe results from the alignment of lighter portions of the hairs when the very stiff hairs are raised into erect position. Schweinsburg also described a dorsal band at the base of each ear which can be seen from the front. The dorsal band can also be seen from the front when the hairs on the back are in erect positions. Thus, the natural characteristics of the collared peccary lend themselves to display. Interspecific display is common in the collared peccary as a defense against another species or it can be intraspecific during courtship or aggressive encounters.

Hair display in the collared peccary apparently serves to make the animal appear larger than it actually is. Either in an intraspecific or an interspecific situation, this is generally regarded as definitely valuable to the species (Schweinsburg 1969; Schweinsburg and Sowls 1972; Wallace 1979).

OLFACTORY COMMUNICATION

The role of scent in marking the territories of mammals has been described for numerous species. Probably the best known is that

Figure 8.9. Adult collared peccary rubbing scent gland on a rock. Note display of dorsal stripe. Saguaro National Monument, Arizona. (Photograph by Lyle K. Sowls)

employed by certain Canidae, including the male domestic dog which deposits urine on conspicuous objects (Schenkel 1947; Lorenz 1945; Kleiman 1966). Other mammals that commonly use urine as a scent marker are the hippopotamus (*Hippopotamus amphibius*) (Frädrich 1967) and the bush-baby (*Galago senegalensis*) (Eibl-Eibesfeldt 1967). The methods by which mammals mark their territories vary with the species (Hediger 1949, 1950; Ewer 1968). Some mammals not only mark locations but also other members of their own species, for example, male tree porcupines (*Erethizontidae*) drench the female with urine (Eibl-Eibesfeldt 1967; Ewer 1968). Some mammals also use feces to describe their territory. Schaller (1967) has discussed the use of feces and urine as territorial markers by the Indian tiger (*Panthera tigris tigris*). A wide variety of mammals possess a scent used in this manner.

Among ungulates, scent marking of pathways and territorial locations is well developed. Some species mark areas by urination and defecation, either separately or in combination. Among other species there is an elaborate system of scent marking from glands. The use of the preorbital gland has been described by Walther (1968) for several species of African antelope; by Ralls (1974) for Maxwell's diuker (*Cephalophus maxwelli*); Müller-Schwarze (1974) for mule deer (*Odocoileus hemionus*). Similar scent marking of territories has been described by Schaller (1967) for the sambar deer (*Cervus unicolor*), chital deer (*Axis axis*), barasingha (*Cervus duvauceli*), and blackbuck (*Antilope cervicapra*).

The Scent Gland

Among the members of the superfamily Suoidea, only the three members of the family *Tayassuidae* possess a scent gland. The gland appears as a raised area of skin measuring approximately 2 x 3 inches along the dorsal midline about 6 inches from the base of the tail. The nipple-like protuberance, from which the scent is emitted, is located in the center.

The anatomy and histology of the collared peccary's scent gland has been described by Werner et al. (1952) and Epling (1956), who describes it as a compound storage gland complex composed of numerous sebaceous and sudoriferous glands that empty their secretions into a common storage area. Epling says "The fact that the entire gland complex is surrounded by a capsule that attaches to the voluntary cutaneous trunci muscle gives credence to reports that the secretions may be ejected at will."

Some early writers called the scent gland of the collared peccary an extra navel because of its superficial appearance (Restrepo 1960; Anon. 1763; Orton 1876). In 1795 Father Ignaz Pfefferkorn (Treutlein 1949) described the scent gland this way: "In the middle of its back is a navel-shaped hole from which is exuded a heavy odor of musk, which spreads throughout the flesh and makes it distasteful. For this reason, almost all the Spaniards have an aversion to it." One early writer, however, commented on this misinterpretation. Even earlier, however, Tyson (1683) described it as a scent gland: "... whereas our musk hog has its scent gland seated on the back, and it has been, by most, hitherto mistaken for a navel." Seton (1929) considered the scent gland part of a signal system and noted that animals rub their scent on low limbs to mark their range.

Werner et al. (1952) believed that the scent gland served to keep members of the herd together. A similar conclusion was reached by Neal (1959). Frädrich (1965), Hediger (in Grzimek 1968), Ewer (1968), Schweinsburg and Sowls (1972), Sowls (1974), Bissonette (1976), Diaz (1979), and Byers (1980) have described its use for marking areas within the home range. The peccary's rubbing the scent gland on objects within its range and depositing scent there appears to be the same type of behavior common in many species.

On several occasions I have seen captive peccaries squirt a stream of liquid scent several inches. Similar instances of scent release have been described by Neal (1959), Mohr (1961), and Schweinsburg (1969). This was commonly seen among penned animals when strange animals came near or when animals were moved to new quarters. When animals were moved to other pens, they usually explored the area and marked the fences, posts, and other objects. Where posts were marked, a conspicuous brown coloration usually remained. When an animal rubbed against a fence, short streams of musk were often emitted. Often we saw the animals back into objects and leave scent on them. Penned and wild animals were seen doing this. Rocks, tree trunks, and stumps having dark areas of oily material on them were common within the home areas of wild herds. Very often the skin around the scent gland was wet with the dripping liquid. When first emitted from the scent gland, the liquid has an amber color but quickly turns to jet black when exposed to the air.

Reactions to Scent of Strange Animals

Müller-Schwarze (1974) and Brownlee et al. (1969) have found that scent from the tarsal gland of the mule deer was important in individual recognition and that males and females reacted differently to scent. Tembrock (1968) suggested that in the collared peccary the composition of the secretion changes, thus different information is transferred.

To determine reactions to the scent of another animal, and to see if any differential reaction could be detected because of sex, I brought penned animals into contact with scent from other animals. A neutral area with removable posts set in line were treated with scent from animals in pens 250 feet away. Individual peccaries were then released into the enclosure to observe their reactions to scent from strange animals.

Reactions of four males and three females were observed. Three of the four males showed more bristling when they approached the posts having male scent than they did when approaching the post with female scent on it; however, all rubbed one post as freely as another. One female showed much more excitement over the post with the scent from a female than a post with male scent. No definite conclusions can be drawn on how the reactions of an individual peccary are influenced by the sex or some other characteristic of another peccary's scent. Clearly, however, all peccaries responded in some way to marked areas.

I used additional animals to study investigative behavior and to obtain the photographs from which Figures 8.10 and 8.11 were sketched. They sniffed areas where other animals had left scent (Fig. 8.10), and often rubbed their cheeks and jowls over these scented areas (Fig. 8.11). They not only reacted to the scent of others, but also reacted similarly to their own scent which had been left on a post previously. An observation of this was made on August 3, 1971, when I placed a fresh new post in an open pen; the post had been rubbed on the scent gland of an adult female. When she was put into this pen, she immediately sniffed the marked part of the post and rubbed vigorously with her scent gland.

Effects of Scent Gland Removal

The scent gland of the collared peccary is a skin gland and can be easily removed. To determine how removal would affect the behavior and health of animals, the gland was surgically removed from two animals in 1968. When they were 33 days old, two, hand-raised, female orphan twins had their scent glands surgically removed. After the age of six weeks, these animals regularly rubbed objects when put into enclosures, appeared to have normal coats, mutually rubbed each other, and rubbed other animals (see Mutual Grooming). Both mated several times, one bore young three times and the other twice in two years. There was no behavioral evidence that these animals acted or responded differently from animals possessing a scent gland, or that other animals responded differently to them.

Mutual Grooming

Mutual grooming in peccaries has been described by several writers (Knipe 1957; Neal 1959; Frädrich 1967; Schweinsburg and Sowls 1972; Sowls 1974; Bissonette 1976, 1982; and Byers 1980). Frädrich refers to the mutual grooming in peccaries as a form of greeting and as pleasure-oriented. In this action two peccaries stand in opposite directions with sides touching while each vigorously rubs the side of its head against the others hindquarters and scent gland (Fig. 8.12).

Mutual grooming is not restricted to animals of either sex or a particular combination of sexes. Sometimes males and females rub each other, sometimes both are males, and sometimes both are females. The grooming was most often seen among penned animals when compatible animals were brought together. In the case of males and females that were isolated but brought together daily, mutual rubbing nearly always occurred as soon as the animals met. When single males were brought into the same enclosure with several females, the male usually went from one female to another and mutual rubbing occurred. For example, when a lone male was placed in a pen with five adult females, he immediately rubbed reciprocally with one female and successively with three more. The fifth female stayed in the shelter and did not encounter the male.

The most detailed analysis of the frequency with which certain sex and age groups rubbed with the other sex and age groups has been given by Diaz (1978). He studied a group of 14 captive animals, where the identity of each was known, and found that all age groups engaged in rubbing with all other sex and age groups. He found that adult males ʾand females rubbed each other more than adult females did. In addition, there was a significant tendency for juvenile animals (six months old) to rub more with sub-adults (eight to 12 months old). His results indicate that smaller animals tend to initiate rubbing with larger animals, but larger animals do not tend to initiate or to return the rubbing with smaller animals.

Figure 8.10. Adult collared peccary sniffing scent mark on post

Figure 8.11. Adult collared peccary rubbing cheeks and jowls over scent on post

Sometimes the rubbing is done by only one animal (Fig. 8.13). This may happen between friendly animals, but Schweinsburg (1969) points out indications that dominant animals may rub submissive animals without reciprocation. I observed this behavior on July 19, 1971, when two adult males, which previously had lived together compatibly, were again put together after being separated for 78 days. One animal rubbed the other animal, but the second animal did not reciprocate. In this instance the animal which did the rubbing was dominant when interactions were observed later. Diaz (1978) has called unreciprocated rubbing "ignored rubbing."

Reciprocal rubbing begins at an early age. Frädrich (1967) says that the mutual grooming behavior in peccaries appears during the second month of life. Among our penned animals, one pair of twins began rubbing each other when 27 days old.

PLAY

Although a great deal has been written about play in other animals, very little has been written about play in peccaries. Loizos (1966) has pointed out that play in animals has generally been thought to be without function. She says that this attitude has arisen from a false analogy with the word as it applies to human behavior, where play is opposed to work. She reviewed the most commonly accepted theories of the function of play: that practice is necessary to develop skills needed as an adult, and that it provides the young animal with necessary information about its environment. She pointed out the merits and shortcomings of both these concepts.

Symons (1978) has discussed conflicting opinions on what play is and whether it constitutes a valid component of behavior. He suggests that the category of "play" could include behavior patterns that "(1)

Figure 8.12. Two adult collared peccaries in reciprocal rubbing action

Figure 8.13. Unreciprocated rubbing by one adult collared peccary against another

are similar to agonistic patterns of fighting, chasing, and fleeing; (2) are inhibited compared with these agonistic behaviors; and (3) are not associated with stereotyped agonistic signals of threat and submission."

Knipe (1959) describes play among young, wild peccaries. Neal (1959) says he has never seen adult peccaries playing, though playing among young peccaries is common. Schweinsburg (1969) likewise describes playing among young animals but does not mention it concerning adults. Frädrich (1967), from observations of captives, says that young peccaries like to play but adults rarely do. Bissonette (1976), who extensively studied the social behavior of peccaries in a wild situation, does not mention play. Dobroruka and Horbowyjova (1972) observed play only in young peccaries. On the other hand, Byers (1980), who made a detailed study of the social behavior of the collared peccary in wild herds, found play to be extremely common. He found the play category made up 13.6 percent of all motor patterns observed. Under the category of play he grouped different actions: play chase, play chase in circle, dash, dash in circle, fast turn, flip down, flop, head toss, leap, open mouth, paw other animals, play dashing, play, general, play snap, tumble, play squabbles, roll onto back, and roll onto side.

Byers found that play tended to occur at specific sites as a coordinated herd activity. He found that sequences of actions occurred too fast and too close together for a complete recording of them. He did, however, show that the rates with which acts of play occurred dropped off drastically after animals reached the age of 12 to 16 weeks. He showed graphically that the number of play acts divided by the number of hours of observations fell from a high of 4.0 at eight to 12 weeks to a low of about 0.1 at about 12 to 16 weeks of age and never again rose above 0.5. He gives an adult rate of only 0.3. The data given by Byers (1980) could explain the remarks of Knipe (1959), Neal (1956), Frädrich (1967), Schweinsburg (1969), and Dobroruka and Horbowyjova (1972) who observed play commonly among juveniles but not adults. It could also explain the lack of any mention of play among the animals observed by Bissonette (1976).

More significant, I believe, is the fact that Byers (1980) and Byers and Bekoff (1981) have demonstrated the importance of amiable interactions during the early years of life as a necessary preparation for life in a social animal. It seems likely that some of the actions which Byers and Bekoff recognized as play have been regarded by others as aggressive.

DEFECATION STATIONS

The use of certain sites for defecation is a well-known phenomenon among certain animals. Hediger (1950) differentiates between diffuse excretion and localized excretion. Localized excretion is common among ungulates. For example, Koford (1957) says that the New World camels, the alpaca *(Lama pacos)*, the llama *(Lama peruana)*, and the vicuña *(Vicugna vicugna)* use the same dung piles and normally visit the closest piles available. Franklin (1974) describes this behavior in the vicuña. Owen-Smith (1974) described the use of defecation stations by the white rhinoceros *(Cerathotherium simum)*, saying that defecation is nearly always at one of the numerous dung heaps within the territory. I have found nothing in the literature to describe such behavior in the tapir, but from the evidence I have observed in the Gran Chaco of Paraguay where it is a common species, it follows closely the defecation behavior in the white rhinoceros.

In captivity, the collared peccary leaves its droppings in one part of the pen. All members of a group in one pen do so. The collared peccary does not always use the same stations in the wild, however, and scattered droppings will be found along trails and in feeding areas. There are, though, very frequent sites that can certainly be referred to as defecation stations.

In Arizona these are often located near bedding grounds. Eddy (unpublished manuscript), while studying the food habits of the collared peccary in the Tucson Mountains of southern Arizona, kept careful notes on the scat stations in a 300-acre (121.4 ha) study area where two herds (one of 12 and one of 17 animals) were observed. In this study area Eddy found 42 scat stations, all of which were considered permanent because of an accumulation of considerable fecal material. Of the 42 stations, 22 were located on "saddles" or ridges, 15 were on hillsides, and five were along washes. Generally the stations were under tangles of hackberry and palo verde trees, and in wash bottoms and cave entrances.

CONTACT BEHAVIOR

Frädrich (1967) has described the peccary as an animal in which voluntary physical contact is common, as in the Suidae and Hippopotomidae. I have noticed this to be true both among captive animals and in wild herds. Usually the herd sleeps in small groups in close contact with one another. I have previously shown a drawing made from a night photograph of a captive group sleeping (Sowls 1974). Night observations, even among penned animals, are hard to make because the least amount of disturbance startles the animals and causes them to leave their resting positions. To overcome this, I photographed a group, using remote control, in January 1971. The nighttime low temperature was about 15°F (–9.4°C), and the animals huddled together in the shelter hut (Fig. 8.14). Another type of contact behavior is the constant grooming of all parts of the body as animals rub each other with their noses (see Fig. 8.4).

The most common situation in wild herds is for two or three animals to be sleeping or resting together. This occurs both in summer and winter but would be more valuable to the animals during cold weather. Eddy (1959) described the shallow depressions in the ground in which a few animals lay side by side. This same behavior was often noted among penned animals. Byers (1980), observing wild animals, placed olfactory investigation and contact in one category, which made up 4.9 percent of all the motor patterns he observed. In this category he placed 30 acts, including licking, nosing, and nuzzling parts of the body.

LEADING AND FOLLOWING

There is no evidence that members become leaders within herds of the collared peccary. Knipe (1957) says, "There is no apparent leadership." A strong tendency is seen in young peccaries to closely follow their mother from the moment they are born. If a person takes a newborn peccary (under three days) away from the mother, it will follow the person closely. All of the more than 20 young peccaries that I

Figure 8.14. Sleeping herd of five adult collared peccaries

have hand-reared as pets exhibited a following action. The young tried to stay close to whatever they were following, whether it was their mother, a person, or a dog. One young peccary could run up to 7 miles per hour, following me over a measured course.

Schweinsburg (1969) pointed out that young animals in the wild followed their mothers until they were more than one year old; captive animals did the same. Schweinsburg also described how adult animals followed each other while scattered or in a loose group, and how they filed into line when alarmed or when following a narrow trail. We recorded several instances in which young animals seemed to be following their mother, but on closer examination we found that they were following an animal other than their mother. For example, young animals often followed old males. One instance of this was seen on June 26, 1958, when an adult and a one-quarter grown peccary were observed at a waterhole in the Tucson Mountains. At first this pair appeared to be mother and young. On two later sightings, however, it was found that the adult was an old male. The sex of the juvenile was not determined. Similar instances of young traveling with adult males were encountered while we were trapping and tagging peccaries. In June 1965, during our trapping operations in the Tucson Mountains, an adult male was captured four times; each time a one-third grown female animal accompanied him. Companionship seemed often to be determined by an "acquaintanceship" between individuals. Penned orphan twins showed a strong tendency to stay together, as did litter mates in the absence of their mother.

From the information, it seems likely that leadership as it is known in some animal species, such as the red deer (Darling 1937) and domestic sheep, which have a strong matriarchal organization, does not exist in the collared peccary. Although no particular animal may be the leader, herd members do follow each other on a single trail or if some stimulus, such as noise, affects all herd members at the same time. As Etkin (1963) has pointed out, leadership within a herd is not necessarily associated with social hierarchy.

REPRODUCTIVE BEHAVIOR

Collared peccaries breed year-round. The chief period of parturition is during the summer rainy seasons, and the main breeding is about five months earlier in late winter (Seton 1929; Jennings and Harris 1953; Knipe 1957; Neal 1959; Sowls 1966; and Schweinsburg and Sowls 1972). They have no harems, long-term pair bonds are not formed, and conflict among males in wild herds is not noticeably greater when receptive females are present than at other times (McCullough 1955; Neal 1959; Sowls 1966; Frädrich 1969; and Sowls 1974). The behavioral patterns of courtship have been described by Frädrich (1967), Schweinsburg (1969), Sowls and Schweinsburg (1972), Sowls (1974), Bissonette (1976), and Byers (1980).

One of the principal aspects of the Arizona Cooperative Wildlife Research Unit's work with the peccary has been a study of reproduction. In 1956, when the research unit began work on this animal, even the gestation period was unknown. To determine this, males and females were brought together daily for brief encounters and then kept apart after copulation occurred (Sowls 1961a). Later vasectomized males were used to determine the length and frequency of the estrous cycle (Sowls 1966). Bringing together males and females on this systematic schedule allowed an opportunity to observe sexual behavior of the peccary in considerable detail and at various stages of the cycle.

Many female domestic animals, especially cows and hogs (Hafez and Signoret 1969), exhibit great restlessness when in heat. They commonly pace ceaselessly in their paddock or cage during this period. In hundreds of observations of female peccaries in heat, hardly any restlessness was observed. A few instances have been exceptional. For example, on December 9, 1958, I noticed a female pacing in her pen, appearing very restless. A male was already in the pen with her. On May 1, 1959, 143 days later, this female gave birth to two young. At that time we did not realize that the gestation period for the peccary is 142 to 145 days.

When penned males and females were brought together, certain basic behaviors typical of most meeting situations were mixed with behavioral patterns exclusively associated with reproduction. The basic behavioral actions common to most meeting situations include a nose-to-nose greeting previously described by Frädrich (1967), (Fig. 8.3), sniffing the scent gland, (Fig. 8.5), and "nuzzling," in which each animal leans its head and nose heavily into the shoulder and neck of the other (Fig. 8.6). Mutual grooming between the male and female accompanies all these actions when friendly animals meet. Actions almost entirely associated with reproduction were a sniffing of the vulva by the male (Fig. 8.15), "inhibited" biting about the neck and shoulder by both male and female (Fig. 8.16), and sniffing the male's penis as the female puts her head under the male's body (Fig. 8.17).

Females in heat rode males and occasionally rode other females (Fig. 8.18). Sometimes copulation (Fig. 8.19) was almost immediate with no mutual grooming or nuzzling behavior. The time between initial encounter of the two sexes and coitus was recorded in 277 instances. On 185, or 67 percent of the encounters, coitus occurred less than five minutes after meeting. On 26 of these encounters, copulation occurred as soon as the animals met. In 89, or 32 percent of the encounters, coitus occurred five to 10 minutes after meeting. In only 3, or 1 percent of the encounters, was the male with the female more than 10 minutes before copulation took place.

Both Bissonette (1976) and Byers (1980) described the "thrust" and considered this as evidence of copulation. From my numerous observations of copulation among captive animals, I believe that this term may be misleading to those familiar with the breeding habits of other ungulates. Unlike many ungulates, where there is a violent thrust of the male during a very short copulation (Morrison 1960 [elk]; Geist 1964 [mountain goat, *Oreamnos americanus*]; Schaller 1967 [barasingha, chital, blackbuck]; McHugh 1972; Lott 1974 [American bison, *Bison bison*]; and Bromley and Kitchen 1974 [pronghorn, *Antilocapra americana*]), the male peccary often almost imperceptibly comes into the copulatory position and remains still for a relatively long period of time. The duration of copulation in 66 timed instances varied from 52 seconds to four minutes. It lasted less than one minute only once (1.5 percent), between one and two minutes 16 times (24.2 percent), between two and three minutes 39 times (59.0 percent), and between three and four minutes 10 times (15.0 percent).

McHugh (1972) has suggested that the grass-eating ungulates, which are in constant danger of predators, have developed an efficient, extremely brief period of copulation as contrasted to many prey species which remain attached for several hours. Although peccaries have a relatively long copulation period, they are partially protected from predation because they are in a herd situation where herd alarms could make the pair's flight possible.

Penned females were found to copulate with several different males in succession. For example, one female copulated with three males in succession as one at a time was put in the pen with her. No information on polyandry in wild herds has been obtained nor has it been observed among penned animals where several males were in the same pen with a female in estrus. Unreceptive females prevent copulation by holding the very short but strong tail over the vulva. Receptive females raise the tail during courtship and copulation.

BEHAVIOR OF MOTHER AND YOUNG

The usual litter size in the collared peccary is two (Knipe 1957; Neal 1959; Sowls 1966). The female has four active mammae, and the young are precocial (Sowls 1966).

When very young, the babies stay close to or underneath their mother. The mothers and young communicate constantly, and the vocalizations play a vital role in keeping them together. When other animals approach too closely, aggressive vocalizations and tooth chattering follow. While nursing her young, the female peccary is usually

Figure 8.15. Male collared peccary sniffing vulva of female

Figure 8.16. Inhibited biting of female about neck and shoulders by male collared peccary

in a relaxed, standing position. The young stand or kneel under her and usually feed at the same time (Fig. 8.20). I have never observed sows lying down while nursing as members of the Suidae commonly do. Day (pers. comm.) says, however, that on several occasions he has observed young nursing while the mother was lying in a resting position during the daytime. This is probably much more common than has been reported. Bedded animals in resting positions are seldom closely observed because of the dense vegetation that hides them.

The young nurse often. Sowls (1966) describes nursing among penned peccaries. He found that a litter of two (nine days old) nursed 48 times in three hours and spent 24 percent of their time nursing. Another litter of two (15 days old) nursed 41 times in three hours and spent 16 percent of their time nursing; however, a single young (12 days old) nursed only nine times in three hours and spent only four percent of its time nursing.

Weaning occurs at about six weeks. It can, however, vary considerably. One captive female had no milk 71 days after parturition, while another female still had a good supply of milk 74 days after parturition. Knipe (1957) and Neal (1959) described the collared peccary as a poor mother. Schweinsburg (1969) disagrees, giving several instances in which mothers defended their young against other adults which came too close.

Among penned animals mothers were found to guard the young closely against other peccaries and other species, including man. Whenever young were born in the pens, we examined them to determine sex and tried to obtain weights and measurements as soon as possible. It was a difficult task because the female invariably charged anyone who came near. A long-handled net was used to scoop up the

Figure 8.17. Female collared peccary sniffing penis of adult male

Figure 8.18. Female collared peccary in heat riding a male

Figure 8.19. Collared
peccaries copulating

young while the operator was behind a woven wire fence. The young
usually stayed under their mother (Fig. 8.21) and could not be netted
until they could be separated from her. After the young were in the net,
the mother often bit at the net and the handle.

The mother's close guarding of young penned animals has not
been observed closely in wild herds. Usually, when disturbed, a
female peccary runs away with the herd and leaves the young behind
(Knipe 1957; Neal 1959). The young then normally lay quietly hidden
among the rocks and vegetation. I first noted this behavior on July 8,
1955, when a group of students and I tried to capture a young javelina
from a herd. We surrounded a herd in which one female had two young

Figure 8.20. Twin collared peccaries nursing

Figure 8.21. Young collared peccaries under mother in defense position

just a few days old. The two young then lay motionless and quiet on the ground while the herd and the mother fled. A second young peccary, a few days old, was captured by us on August 3, 1955, by the same method; the reaction of the mother was the same. A number of similar incidents have since been described by my students and cooperators.

This usual reaction of very young animals to "freeze" and hide on the ground has great survival value, but it is not always followed. When herds are disturbed and the mother leaves, the young, on at least some occasions, call loudly in an apparent attempt to attract their mother. On October 27, 1961, I was sitting on a high hill in the Pinal Mountains of Arizona. There was a strong, shifting wind and I could hear the distant sound of what seemed to be a baby javelina. After tracking down the sound, I found two baby peccaries between one and two days old. The sound, which traveled clearly about 600 yards, could attract coyotes, bobcats, and mountain lions that inhabit the same country.

Unlike many ungulates, the mother peccary does not appear ever to lick the newborn. I have seen three females, two in pens and one in the wild, give birth to young. In all instances the young were born while the mother was standing. On numerous occasions I have noted a mother with newborn young. One common behavior of all sows observed at this time was a rolling or tumbling of the young just after birth. This practice serves to disconnect the afterbirth from the head of the young animal and to dry and possibly to stimulate the young. On some occasions among penned females, this exercise does not cease and the young animal becomes exhausted. Possibly this can be attributed to the captive status of the female and a sense of nervousness on her part.

Figure 8.22 shows a wild female that had just given birth to young on a cold morning in February 1979 in Saguaro National Monument

Figure 8.22. Adult female collared peccary nosing and tumbling young, about an hour after they are born. Arizona. (Photograph by Lyle K. Sowls)

near Tucson, Arizona. This female rolled the young vigorously, but only for a short time.

VALUE OF BEHAVIORAL STUDIES

To many people, the detailed descriptions of the behavior of animals may seem unnecessary and excessive. Some may think that animal behavior is studied only because a few investigators become obsessed with the details of an animal's actions but is of no real value. Such is not the case.

Knowledge of an animal's behavior gives clues to its evolutionary relationship to other species; this knowledge is necessary in order for conservationists to conduct accurate censuses or to obtain population trend figures needed for the successful management of a species. Behavioral information is also valuable in setting the boundaries of home ranges and assuring the wildlife manager that all the species' requirements are available in the areas available for a particular population. As Geist and Walther (1974) have pointed out, shortcuts to the conservation of endangered species can possibly be found if we better understand the species behavior.

No group of animals better demonstrates the value of behavioral information for management than do peccaries. Being a herd animal, it is vulnerable to overhunting if hunters concentrate in areas where herds have limited movements. Thus it is necessary to disperse hunters into management units to prevent local elimination of a peccary population.

In this chapter I have tried to review all of the existing literature on the behavior of the collared peccary. The reader will notice that different workers have given different interpretations to the various actions. This is to be expected because many of the behavioral postures, actions, and vocalizations grade almost imperceptibly from one to another depending upon the intensity of a situation. For that reason interpretations are subjective. Many times several behavioral actions are taking place at the same time leading to complex interactions. For example, an animal could be vocalizing or exhibiting hair display, marking behavior, or some other action simultaneously. I have found, also, that some of the vocalizations which I have recorded from captive animals could not have been recorded from free-roaming animals without great difficulty. The behavioral actions I have described here are my own interpretations of some of the most common ones.

White-Lipped and
Chacoan Peccaries

The White-Lipped Peccary

ALTHOUGH LITTLE RESEARCH HAS BEEN DONE on the white-lipped peccary, I will attempt to review the existing literature here and add my own observations from Brazil and Paraguay. In 1975, and again in 1976, I watched a herd of about 60 white-lipped peccaries at a bait station at the edge of the forest in the state of São Paulo, Brazil. These animals fed in the forest but used the open clearing as a place to rest in the sun in the middle of the day. Each day they were fed small amounts of maize and squash to acquaint them with the bait station and to train them to come in without fear.

A herd of collared peccaries fed there too, as well as a troop of capuchin monkeys (Cebus sp.). Each morning that I came to the forest the collared peccaries were already at the station. The arrival of the white-lipped peccaries was announced by the single sharp clicks of their teeth as they approached the open area. It was clear from the small amount of food they ate at the bait station that they had already eaten in the forest. At the bait station their behaviorisms could be observed. Also in 1976, I watched a herd of white-lipped peccaries feeding in the scrub forest in the western part of the Chaco of Paraguay.

DESCRIPTION

The white-lipped peccary is considerably larger than the collared peccary. Only meager information on its size has been published. Gaumer (1917) reported that the total length of males from Yucatán ranged from 1,110 to 1,190 mm; tail, 50 mm; and height at shoulder, 400 to 500 mm. From Honduras, Murie (1935) gave the live weight of a male as 60 pounds and an adult female as 62 pounds. Goodwin (1946) gives the total length of a female from Costa Rica as 1,040 mm; hind foot, 190 mm; and the ear, 80 mm. Measurements of average adults from Guatemala were given by Handley (1950): total length, 1,180 mm; hind foot, 230 mm; and weight, 75 pounds. Leopold (1959) gives head and body length as 1,100 to 1,200 mm and tail, 50 mm. The measurements of one large old female that I collected on July 14, 1976, in the western Chaco were: total length 1,020 mm; hind foot, 220 mm; tail, 65 mm; ear, 80 mm; height at shoulder, 530 mm; and weight, 83.6 pounds. Husson (1978) reported the measurements of 11 white-lipped peccaries from Surinam (Table 9.1).

The white-lipped peccary varies in color from a reddish to dark tan for immature animals to jet black as they become older. Adults have a white along the mouth and under the jaw which, in most adults, gives the impression of white cheeks. The nasal disc, typically hoglike, is flesh colored. Above the nasal disc in most older adults are some short white hairs. As in the collared peccary, the white-lipped peccary has slender legs and relatively small feet in proportion to its body. The front feet have two dew claws and the hind feet only one. The scent gland in the white-lipped peccary is located in relatively the same position as in the collared peccary — in the center of the back about 120 mm from the base of the tail. The gland is larger than in the collared peccary. The gland of the adult female that I collected in the western Chaco measured 54 mm by 99 mm.

The dental formula of the white-lipped peccary is the same as that for the other two living species of peccaries:

$$I = \frac{2}{3} \, C \, \frac{1}{1}, \, P \, \frac{3}{3}, \, M \, \frac{3}{3} \times 2 = 38$$

(pers. observation). As in the collared peccary, canine teeth point up and down and are extremely sharp and pointed. They appear to serve the same purpose for both species: for defense, for display in interspecific situations, and as an acoustic instrument to generate loud clacking or chattering as sounds of threat.

Wetzel (1981b) points out differences between the skull of the collared and white-lipped peccaries. He says that the rostrum of the white-lipped peccary's skull is flattened rather than rounded. The supraorbital canals are not as deep in the white-lipped peccary and are well separated by the flattened rostrum.

For chromosome numbers of the white-lipped peccary, Wetzel (1981b, from Hsu and Benirschke 1974 and Giannoni and Ferrari 1976) gives the karotype as 2n = 26, 20 metacentric or submetacentrics, 4 acrocentrics; X and Y chromosomes are both acrocentric.

HABITAT AND DISTRIBUTION

The range of the white-lipped peccary is more restricted than that of the collared peccary. Leopold (1959) gives its range in Mexico as the dense tropical forest country from southern Vera Cruz eastward through the Yucatán peninsula. This includes the states of Yucatán, Quintana Roo, Campeche, Chiapas, Tabasco, Oaxaca, and Vera Cruz. It is found in the lowland areas of Guatemala, principally in the state of Petén (Handley 1950), in all the Central American countries, and in the rain forests of South America as far south as Paraguay. The range of this species is shown in the introduction along with the ranges of the other two species.

According to most writers, the white-lipped peccary is restricted to the humid tropical forests of Central and South America. In Costa Rica, Goodwin (1946) describes the habitat of the white-lipped peccary as the thick forests of the tropical lowlands. Handley (1950) gives its habitat in Guatemala as the coastal lowlands. Leopold says it occupies dense tropical forest country. Its habitat in Colombia has been described by Borrero (1967), who says that it inhabits the humid forests and marshy areas surrounded by woods. Klein and Fujino (1977) describe the habitat of the white-lipped peccary in Honduras as the tropical virgin rain forest. They further state that it is not found in the cut-over forest as is the collared peccary.

Figure 9.1 is a climatograph made from data from various parts of the range of the white-lipped peccary. I have selected areas in widely separate parts of its range, where the white-lipped peccary is known to exist. No weather data are available for the drier part of the range in the western part of the Chaco in Paraguay and eastern Bolivia. These figures do not show nearly as much variation as those for the collared peccary's range. Annual rainfall varies within the white-lipped peccary's range from as low as 32.7 inches per year at Mariscal Estigarribia, Paraguay, to as high as 127.3 inches at Colon, Panama. Winter temperatures did not drop below a monthly average of 67.1°F at any of the locations.

Contrary to the commonly accepted belief that the white-lipped peccary occupies only heavily wooded, humid forests, I found it common in the dry scrub forest of the western Chaco of Paraguay. It occurs there in large herds near desert waterholes where the forest floor is covered with numerous species of cactus and desert shrubs such as mesquite.

FOODS

Like the collared peccary, the foods eaten by the white-lipped peccary vary from one area to another depending on what is available. Inasmuch as its habitat is not as diverse as that of the collared peccary, however, the diet probably varies less. Several writers have given brief descriptions of the foods of the white-lipped peccary. Gaumer (1917) lists roots and fruits as the most common foods taken and says that both species are able to break the hard seeds of the cocoyol or palm. Roosevelt (1914) reports opening the stomachs of three white-lipped

Table 9.1. Measurements of White-Lipped Peccaries From Surinam

	Head and Body			Hind Foot			Ear			Tail		
	mm	$\bar{X}$(mm)	S.D.	mm	$\bar{X}$(mm)	S.D.	mm	$\bar{X}$(mm)	S.D.	mm	$\bar{X}$(mm)	S.D.
	995–1,080 (7 males)	1,040	28.3	215–225 (7 males)	218.8	3.9	78–90 (7 males)	81.8	4.0	30–50 (5 males)	36.2	8.9
	950–1,100 (4 females)	1,043	67.5	207–225 (4 females)	216.7	7.7	80 (4 females)			35–60 (4 females)	38.0	12.0

Source: Husson 1978.

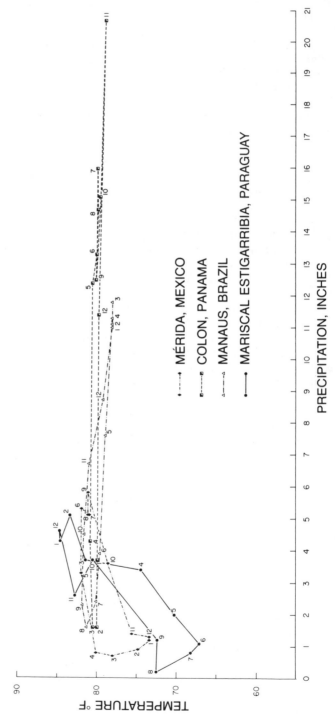

Figure 9.1. Climatograph for various locations within the range of the white-lipped peccary

peccaries from the Matto Grosso of Brazil and finding wild figs, palm nuts, and bundles of fibers. Leopold (1959) says that in southern Mexico it eats a wide variety of foods including fruits, greens, and roots of plants. Ihering (1968) lists fruits, roots, and small animals as food for the white-lipped peccaries. Mendez (1970), in Panama, lists but does not quantify fruits, roots, leaves, seeds, dead animals, eggs of birds and turtles, lizards, and frogs as the food of the white-lipped peccary. Klein and Fujino (1977) say that the white-lipped peccary in Honduras eats roots, seeds, greens and, at times, eggs and meat, but they do not give quantitative data. Kiltie (1980) analyzed the contents of 17 stomachs of the white-lipped peccary from the area of the confluence of the Mann and Madre de Dios rivers in Peru. He found coats of fruits of *Mauritia flexuosa, Astrocaryum* sp., and *Jessinea* sp., all palm fruits. Whole seeds of *Socratea durissima* were also found. Animal parts found by Kiltie included snail operculi, tissues from unidentified vertebrates, parts of adult invertebrates, and larvae. The major portion of the stomach materials found by Kiltie was unidentified vegetative material. He found no significant difference in the contents of the stomachs of the white-lipped peccary and the collared peccary and concluded that both species are omnivores.

One large female white-lipped peccary which I collected in July 1976 in the dry thorn forest near the Trans-Chaco highway in Paraguay, was filled with mesquite (*Prosopis* sp.) seeds and pods (Fig. 9.2).

REPRODUCTION

There is little published information on reproduction in the white-lipped peccary. Leopold (1959) reports that newborn young have been observed at all seasons of the year. He reports on specimens killed by O. P. Pearson in Panama and Peru. Of four killed in March 1938 in Panama, three were pregnant, containing two fetuses each, while another collected by Pearson in Peru in February 1971 had two and another had three fetuses. Miller (1930) reported seeing young only two or three days old on September 24, 1925, in the Descalvados area of the Matto Grosso in Brazil. At the bait station in the state of São Paulo, Brazil, where I observed peccaries in July 1975 and August 1976, I saw only young animals estimated to be about eight to 10 months old. Salvador Selva, the forest guard who had worked in the forest for many years and knew the peccaries well, said that the young are always born in the spring months of October and November.

The gestation period of the white-lipped peccary has been determined by Roots (1966) from the observations of three captive females in the Dudley Zoo in England. He observed births at 156, 157, and 162 days from the time of observed breeding. Zuckerman (1953) gives the litter size for two births in the London Zoo as two each. Litter sizes which established the gestation period at the Dudley Zoo (Roots 1966)

Figure 9.2. Stomach contents, entirely seeds of *Prosopis* sp., from a white-lipped peccary collected in the Chaco of Paraguay. (Photograph by Lyle K. Sowls)

were also two. A large adult which I collected on the Trans-Chaco highway in Paraguay on July 14, 1976, contained two well-advanced fetuses. Existing information indicates that the white-lipped peccary has very nearly the same gestation period as the collared peccary and also the same litter size (see Chap. 4). The young are reddish brown at birth, the coat slowly turns to a tannish brown which, from my observations in Brazil, is retained until the animals are about one-third grown.

Breeding in Captivity

While the litter size and gestation period of the white-lipped peccary and the collared peccary seem similar, female white-lipped peccaries do not reproduce readily in captivity as do collared peccaries (Sowls 1966, also see Chap. 4). Records of white-lipped peccaries which have reproduced in captivity are few. The International Zoo Yearbooks from 1959 through 1980 reported that collared peccaries were born in captivity in 104 zoos located in 27 countries on six continents. During the same period only six zoos had births of white-lipped peccaries: São Paulo, Brazil; São Leopoldo, Brazil; Georgetown, Guyana; Dudley, Great Britain; Paignton, Great Britain; and Lima, Peru. One reason for this difference in number of zoo births between the two species is that white-lipped peccaries have been unavailable to many zoos because of the low numbers raised in captivity and because laws in certain countries prohibit their import (Hill 1970). In spite of this, the evidence for low reproduction in captivity is convincing.

Roots (1966) regarded the white-lipped peccary as a difficult species to establish and breed in captivity, partly because they do not go through regular estrous cycles as frequently as do collared peccaries. McDonald and Lasley (1978) tried to determine why one male and two female captive white-lipped peccaries in the San Diego Zoo did not reproduce. They found that spermatogenesis in the male was deficient with only a few sperm cells, mainly spermatogonia, being produced. They did not say whether the females exhibited regular estrous cycles.

Hybridization

Although there are no records of hybridization between collared and white-lipped peccaries in the wild, there are positive instances of hybridization in captivity. Zuckerman (1953) described three instances of such crosses in the London Zoo. Dr. Edino Camoleze, Zoologico CIGS at Manaus, Brazil, has had the two species hybridize in captivity on three separate occasions (Russell A. Mittermeier, pers. comm. 1981). Figure 9.3 shows one of these hybrids. Except for the absence of the collar in the hybrid, all three superficially look alike.

BEHAVIOR

Movements

Several writers have commented on the long distances that white-lipped peccaries travel (Roosevelt 1914; Gaumer 1917; Leopold 1959; Borrero 1967; and Mendez 1970). It wanders so far that some observers have called it nomadic or migratory (Borrero 1967; Mendez 1970; Lathrop 1970). If one spends much time in "white-lipped country," this conclusion is understandable. The diggings and tracks of the large herds are very conspicuous, and it is easy to note the frequency of their visits. Near lagunas in the thorn forests of the Chaco of Paraguay I found that herds moved through only periodically.

The best information on the movements of the white-lipped peccary has been furnished by Kiltie (1980) and Terborgh and Kiltie (in press). He and his colleagues at the Cocha Cashu Biological Station in Peru's Manu National Park in the upper Amazon basin kept a record of locations and times that all groups of peccaries in a specific study area were encountered. He determined that during the dry season (June through September), white-lipped peccaries appeared at the observed site an average of once every $4\frac{1}{4}$ days, while in the wet period (October through May) they appeared an average of every $14\frac{1}{2}$ days. Kiltie considered the white-lipped peccary to have a fleeting behavior and an almost continuous movement, even after nightfall. In his observations he did not find them to turn sharply but to keep on a straight line. From Kiltie's observations and those of others it is apparent that the white-lipped peccary moves long distances and has a rather large but definite home range.

Figure 9.3. Animal on right is hybrid between collared and white-lipped peccary. Manaus, Brazil. (Photograph by Russell Mittermeier)

On their extensive movements the herds did not follow definite trails but instead were spread out. I found this to be true in the Chaco of Paraguay where local people knew about certain crossings or particular sites where white-lipped peccaries occasionally could be seen. Kiltie (1979), from his observations in Peru, took the repeated usage of certain spots as evidence that the white-lipped peccary followed the same routes on successive visits through an area. My observations in the Chaco of Paraguay and the forests of southern Brazil suggest the same. In the dry Chaco their travel routes were always near lagunas.

Ferocity

Early explorers almost always described peccaries as vicious beasts, ever ready to attack man and dogs. The white-lipped peccary is reported as being more vicious than the collared. An example of a typical report appeared in an anonymous publication in 1849: "When attacked they surround the man, dog, or jaguar, and if there is no means of escape, their enemy is soon torn to pieces." M. Schomburgh, in a narrow escape from an infuriated herd, shot the herd leader as it rushed at him. Similar reports were given by Soares de Sousa (1587: in Nogueira-Neto 1973), Alston (1879), Orton (1876), Grubb (1911), Whiffen (1915), Cutright (1940), and Santos (1945). Miller (1930) reported one instance when his party was charged by a band of white-lipped peccaries in the Matto Grosso of Brazil. He reported that dogs which were accustomed to hunting the collared peccary refused to approach within several hundred yards of the bands of white-lipped peccary. Roosevelt (1914) reported similar experiences, saying that his dogs would not even follow a wounded white-lipped peccary. He also described the experience of a friend who "came on the body of a jaguar which had evidently been killed by a herd of peccaries some 24 hours previously. The ground was trampled by their hooves, and the carcass was slit into pieces." Handley (1950) says "This species travels in larger packs than does the collared peccary, and is reported to be more vicious and dangerous when molested." Chapman (1936), from experience in Panama, considers the white-lipped peccary more pugnacious than the collared peccary; he also found that it is primarily nocturnal and that it moves in larger bands than the collared peccary.

Some writers, even a few early ones, describe the stories of the reputed ferocity of the peccaries as exaggerations (Azara, in Hunter 1838; Furneaux 1969). Others have attributed this reputed ferocity to the animal's desire to flee from an intruder (Cabrera and Yepes 1940).

Kiltie (1979), who has done the greatest amount of scientific research on white-lipped peccaries, says: "The aggressive behavior for which white-lipped are famed was never observed in the herds at Cocha Cashu."

At a bait station in southern Brazil, located at the edge of the forest, I was able to observe the animals' reactions to the forest guard and to me. The guard wandered among them with no apparent aggressive reactions on their part. This could probably be expected since he usually had food for them and they were accustomed to him. When I approached them, however, I often had animals threaten me by jumping a short distance in my direction. I always found that if I then quickly moved toward them they slowly turned aside and walked away.

The slow movement away from an intruder seems to be similar to what Kiltie (1979) found. When wild collared peccary herds were approached in the forest at Cocha Cashu in Peru they invariably fled, but when he and his coworkers encountered white-lipped peccary herds, the animals moved off slowly, allowing Kiltie to maintain contact by following the herd for several hours. This same reluctance on the part of herds to be pushed to flight has been described by Nietschmann (1972), who says that when the peccaries attacked they assume a "covered wagon defense."

Despite numerous references to peccaries and their hunting by South American Indians, anthropologists with firsthand knowledge do not say much about the ferocity of the white-lipped peccary. Some refer to it as a dangerous animal (Smole 1976; Harner 1973).

One report of an attack on man by a herd of white-lipped peccaries that I know is accurate is from Dr. Stephen M. Russell, an ornithologist who was collecting birds in Belize. Dr. Russell was on the west slope of the Cockscomb Mountains (highest in the country at about 2,000 feet elevation) in a tall uncut "rain" forest with a rather open under-story. His account (pers. comm.) follows:

> Paul Scott, my local assistant, and I were returning from an ascent of the Cockscomb Mountains on May 30, 1959. It was mid-afternoon when Paul smelled a group of "wari" (white-lipped peccary) and asked if I would like to catch one. The animals were over a slight rise and out of view. We approached the rise quietly and were within 25 yards of the animals when Paul urged "drop the packs." Then we rushed at them, Paul barking loudly like a dog. In theory, the wari were to flee and we would pick up one of the slower moving ones. But in an instant the herd charged us. We sought refuge on the buttresses of a very large tree. Most of the group veered away but about 20 animals milled below us, some rearing on their hind legs to get closer! After a few minutes, the animals dispersed. Our packs were not molested during the fracus and we were soon on our way but without a young peccary.

Foraging

Leopold (1959), Mendez (1970), and Kiltie (1980) have commented on the large volume of food needed by a herd of foraging peccaries. Fejos (1943) and Kiltie (1979) have described the very noisy nature of their feeding. Kiltie (1979, 1981a, 1981b) found that they moved long distances over large areas in the quest for food. Through detailed studies of their foraging pattern, he determined that they concentrated their search behavior near tree trunks, fallen logs, and other objects. He described their search as a bulldozing of the top few centimeters of the soil surface. From a series of tests he determined that the inter-locking jaws helped prevent dislocation of the jaws when the animals ate hard seeds. He also found that the white-lipped peccary is capable of breaking harder seeds than is the collared peccary.

Swimming

For an animal that must travel long distances for its food in a wet tropical environment, it would be highly advantageous for it to be able to swim. The excellent swimming ability of the white-lipped peccary has been described by numerous writers (de Buffon 1787; Anon. 1849; Gaumer 1917; Cabrera and Yepes 1940; and Vanzolini pers. comm. 1974). All of these people describe seeing herds swim across rivers. Vanzolini saw a herd of 300 to 400 swim across the River Purus in Brazil in September 1973. A few references simply say "both species of peccaries" (Anon. 1849) swim, but most specify the white-lipped peccaries. Hershkovitz (1972) says the two species: "Both are excellent swimmers and cross the largest of South American rivers routinely."

Wallowing

Like the collared peccary, the white-lipped peccary commonly wallows in mud. This behavior has been described by several writers (Enders 1935; Chapman 1936; Alvarez del Toro 1952; Kiltie 1980). Kiltie described both permanent and ephemeral wallows, depending on the availability of moisture. He noted also that certain wallows were only occasionally visited, similar to the infrequent visits to these areas I have seen in the Chaco of northern Paraguay, where wallows along the lagunas formed by old oxbow river courses are common.

SOCIAL BEHAVIOR

Like the collared peccary, the white-lipped peccary is a highly social animal. Unlike most ungulates of the dense tropical forests, it lives in large herds (Kiltie 1979). Kiltie referred to the herds as "raucous." Others have described the animals' strong smelling musk that serves to reinforce a strong social instinct. The importance of both a complex system of vocalizations and the use of scent can be easily seen in a herd while it is feeding and resting in a forest opening. My discussion of the social behavior of the white-lipped peccary is based on the sketchy literature and from my observations of a herd of about 60 white-lipped peccaries at a bait station in southern Brazil in July 1975 and August 1976.

Herd Size

According to all available accounts, the white-lipped peccary forms much larger herds than does the collared peccary. Roosevelt (1914) describes a herd of several hundred in Costa Rica. Leopold (1959) says that in southern Mexico they travel in herds of hundreds. Miller (1930) describes seeing a herd of at least two hundred in the Matto Grosso of Brazil, Mendez (1970), Meggers (1971), Klein and Fujino (1977), and Kiltie (1980) reported herds of more than 100 individuals. In addition to the herd of 60 animals that I studied at Fazenda Paraiso, I observed another herd in the drier Chaco at kilometer 674 of western Paraguay on July 14, 1976, that contained between 40 and 50 animals.

These large herd sizes in the white-lipped peccary show it to be an exception to the rule for distribution of ungulates in the tropics — that forest-dwelling species live in small groups and plains-dwelling species live in large groups (Meggars 1971; Eisenberg and Lockhart 1972; Bourliére 1973; Eisenberg and McKay 1974; Estes 1974; Geist 1974; and Leuthold 1977).

Contact

Because of the dominant role of this type of behavior and because it overshadows aggressiveness, it is, in my opinion, worthy of great attention. Unlike the collared peccary which exhibits contact behavior while resting and rejoining the herd, members of white-lipped peccary herds almost continuously draw together. One aspect of this is displayed in the constant nosing of other members of the herd. This probing may be directed at any part of the animal's body. While watching the herd at the bait station I observed 54 such contacts in about three hours. Of these contacts, 10 were on the back, nine on the neck, seven on the side, seven on the scent gland, five on the groin, four on the shoulder, three on the face, three on the front leg, two on the belly, two on top of the head, one on the ear, and one on the hip. Some typical examples of nosing other herd members are shown in Figures 9.4 and 9.5.

Grooming

A number of writers have described mutual grooming in peccaries (Knipe 1957; Neal 1959; Frädrich 1967; Schweinsburg and Sowls 1972; Sowls 1974; Bissonette 1976, 1982; Diaz 1978; and Byers 1980). Frädrich, however, who refers to it as a form of greeting and as pleasure oriented, described it as an action of both the collared and white-lipped peccaries. I have seen it many times among the white-lipped peccaries I observed at the bait station at Fazenda Paraiso. In all respects it was the same as I have observed in the collared peccary. Two peccaries stand facing

Figure 9.4. Adult white-lipped peccary nosing juvenile. Brazil. (Photograph by Lyle K. Sowls)

Figure 9.5. Resting white-lipped peccaries tend to pile into groups with bodies touching. (Photograph by Lyle K. Sowls)

opposite directions, with their sides touching, while each vigorously rubs the side of its head against the hindquarters and scent gland of the other (Fig. 9.6). As in the collared peccary, I found that the rubbing action was not restricted to animals of any particular sex or age. Non-reciprocal rubbing, where one animal rubs another but the animal rubbed does not reciprocate, is also common in white-lipped peccaries.

Aggression

While feeding, the most common aggressive action which I saw in the herd at the bait station was a face-to-face "argument" between two animals. During these encounters, aggressive sounds are common. These encounters end either in a quick chase or in the subordinate animal slowly turning away to increase the distance between the animals.

The Chase

One common aggressive action which I have seldom seen among herds of collared peccaries but which is common among white-lipped peccaries is the chase. These sudden actions involve one animal chasing another entirely from the herd. They usually begin with a frontal encounter. The distance of the chase was always sufficient to take the animals well outside the feeding herd. At the Brazilian bait station this was usually about 50 to 100 meters. At this point, beyond the mass of animals, the pursuer broke off the chase and returned to the feeding herd. I did not determine the sex of animals involved in this behavior pattern.

Figure 9.6. Mutual rubbing between two adult white-lipped peccaries and non-reciprocal rubbing by a juvenile. (Photograph by Lyle K. Sowls)

AUDITORY COMMUNICATION

Being primarily an animal of the dense tropical forest, the white-lipped peccary depends to a great extent on vocalization to maintain contact with other herd members. When I carefully watched and listened to a feeding herd for many hours in Brazil, it was clear that the white-lipped peccary had a far more elaborate repertoire of vocalizations and a closer tie to other herd members than the collared peccary. I found that its vocalizations were not only more elaborate but also much louder than those of the collared peccary. Its aggressive vocalizations were quite similar to those of the collared peccary, but the "togetherness" vocalizations of the white-lipped peccary were much more varied.

In the crowded herds, especially at feeding places, aggressive sounds became so mixed that they were difficult to separate. Inasmuch as these sounds are only made when two or more animals are together, the sound of a single individual cannot be determined.

As with the vocalizations of the collared peccary, I have classified the various sounds of the white-lipped peccary into "togetherness" vocalizations, illustrated by sonograms and by my subjective interpretation of the sound.

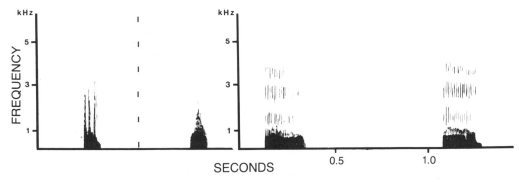

Figure 9.7. Sonogram of the low "rumble," a togetherness vocalization

"Togetherness" Vocalizations

In the heavy, dense forest where visual contact is very limited, auditory contact becomes extremely important. This, along with their powerful scent, keeps the animals in touch with each other. One characteristic of the togetherness call is that it always obtains an answer.

One of the most noticeable sounds I heard from the feeding herd in the Brazilian forest was a low rumble. Figure 9.7 is a sonogram of this sound. It is repeated by other members of the herd at random and appears to be contagious. I found that animals commonly used this call when they traveled in loose groups (more than a few meters apart) through the forest. When herd members were closer and feeding, aggressive grumblings and tooth clickings were more common. An illustration of how spatial changes determined the calls is shown in Figure 9.8.

Another togetherness vocalization that always received an answer is a loud bark that occurred either singly or in a series. This call varies a great deal and is shown in Figure 9.9.

The whine or complaining call is shown in Figure 9.10. This call is drawn out in time and does not receive a response. I first heard this call in August 1975; young animals emitted this long complaining call when the mother walked away or laid down when they were trying to nurse.

Aggressive Vocalizations

Grumbling and tooth-clicking are the most common vocalizations one hears when animals are feeding close together. This grumbling in a feeding herd is a blending of many sounds that are difficult to separate. Figure 9.11 shows some of these aggressive grumbling sounds. Tooth clicking sometimes accompanies these sounds or is heard alone as in Figure 9.12. Unlike the collared peccary which clicks three to eight

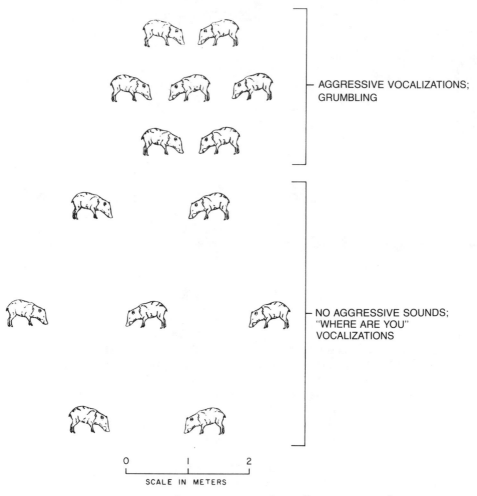

Figure 9.8. Spatial arrangement and its influence on vocalizations in the white-lipped peccary

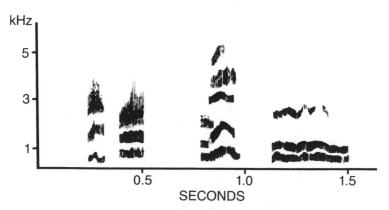

Figure 9.9. Sonogram of the "bark," a togetherness call of the white-lipped peccary

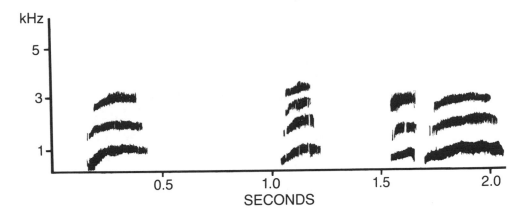

Figure 9.10. Sonogram of the "whine," or complaining call, of the white-lipped peccary

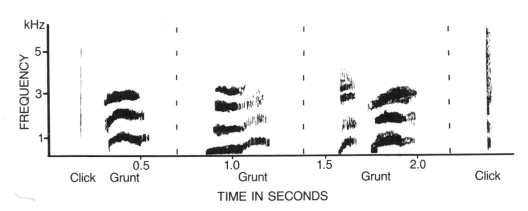

Figure 9.11. Sonogram of aggressive grumbling and tooth-clicking of white-lipped peccary

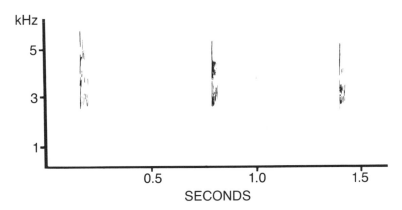

Figure 9.12. Sonogram of tooth-clicking of white-lipped peccary

times in series (see Chapter 8), white-lipped peccary usually made single clicks.

In a crowded feeding situation the white-lipped peccary emits many snorts, wheezes, and other noises as it inhales and exhales. These are impossible to separate on a sound recording because of the many different sounds being made at one time. I have never heard these noises except in an aggressive or alarm situation.

STATUS OF THE WHITE-LIPPED PECCARY

Unlike the collared peccary, the white-lipped peccary is a wilderness animal, seldom thriving in second growth or cut over forest. Also it is not as adaptable to as wide a variety of climates. Inasmuch as it moves much farther, it requires a much larger area of undisturbed forest. Consequently the fate of the white-lipped peccary over much of its range is not assured. The rapid, wholesale destruction of the tropical forest for lumber and livestock grazing lands are threatening the habitat of this interesting animal over a large area. This subject will be discussed in more detail in Chapter 11.

10 | The Chacoan Peccary

DISCOVERY

The indigenous people of the Gran Chaco in Paraguay, settlers, and hide buyers knew the Chacoan peccary, or taguá, well. (Wetzel, pers. comm.) They clearly differentiated between the three species of peccary and had names for each of them. Scientists, on the other hand, were late in knowing about the largest of the three peccaries. Not until 1972 did mammalogists first discover that this species existed. In that year Ralph M. Wetzel and his colleagues found it in the Chaco Boreal of Paraguay. Wetzel, et al. (1975) reported that this species, for which they had collected 29 skulls, was the same species Rusconi (1930) had previously described as a fossil form. Wetzel (1977) gave a detailed description of its cranial characteristics and its relationship to the other members of the family *Tayassuidae*. Mayer and Brandt (1982), Wetzel's co-workers in the Chaco, have written about the identity, distribution, and natural history of the peccaries. They described the morphological characteristics of all three extant peccaries, as well as their distribution and habitat, density, reproduction, winter food habits, predation, and behavior.

Discovery of the Chacoan peccary by science was the first time since 1900 that a new large mammal was added to the list of known mammals. The answer to why the Chacoan peccary was undescribed for so long seems to lie in the fact that the Chaco remained an almost untouched wilderness. The northwestern half of the Chaco, a vast area of thorn forest was, until about 1970, relatively undisturbed. Native vegetation and wildlife had not been greatly changed by man's intrusion. Since 1970, however, a greatly accelerated program of forest clearing has been underway, designed to turn large sections of the Chaco into grazing land for livestock. The attendant human encroachment and changes have threatened the existence of the Chacoan

Figure 10.1. Adult Chacoan peccaries. (Photograph by Lyle K. Sowls)

Figure 10.2. Adult Chacoan peccary in natural habitat with two half-grown young. (Photograph by Lyle K. Sowls)

Figure 10.3. Young pet Chacoan peccary about eight months old. (Photograph by Lyle K. Sowls)

peccary. As a result, in 1980 the Survival Service Commission of the International Union for the Conservation of Nature first listed the Chacoan peccary as vulnerable.

DESCRIPTION

The Chacoan peccary, *Catagonus wagneri* (Rusconi), has been thoroughly described by Wetzel (1977): it is "a large brownish-gray peccary with faint collar of lighter hairs across the shoulders. Hair on ears and legs is longer and paler in color than in *Tayassu*. Head is larger, and ears, legs, and tail are longer" (see Figs. 10.1, 10.2, 10.3). Wetzel points out further that, like the other two species of living peccaries, there are vestigial hooves or dew claws present on the front feet; unlike the other two related species, there are no dew claws on the hind feet. Wetzel gives the external measurements of five freshly killed adult specimens and one young adult from the western Chaco of Paraguay as: length of head and body, average 1,026 mm; length of tail (three specimens), 86.7 mm; hindfoot (five specimens), 227.6 mm; length of ear (five specimens), 119.4 mm. He gave the weight of only one animal, a female, which weighed 37 kilograms (81.4 pounds).

Four more adult specimens which were collected at kilometer 580 of the Trans-Chaco highway in western Paraguay were measured. An adult female — total length, 1,155 mm; hindfoot, 223 mm; tail, 50 mm; ear, 120 mm; and weight, 42 kg (92.4 lbs.) Three adult males — total length, 972, 1,120, and 1,040 mm; hindfoot, 250, 225, 240 mm; tail, 72, 85, 68 mm; ear, 110, 120, 120 mm, and weight, 40 kg (88 lbs.); 42 kg (92.4 lbs.); 34 kg (75 lbs.). The first two of these measured: neck, 630, 620 mm; girth 830, 780 mm; and height at shoulder, 690, 580 mm. Further details on measurements of specimens collected by Wetzel's group have been published by Mayer and Brandt (1982).

RANGE AND STATUS

Although the exact range of the Chacoan peccary and its numbers are not known precisely, a composite estimate from all available sources indicates that the entire range of taguá probably covers about 139,600 square kilometers (53,904 sq. mi.), an area about the size of North Carolina. Wetzel (1977, 1981a) and Mayer and Brandt (1982) have described its range as extreme northwestern Argentina, southeastern Bolivia, and northwestern Paraguay. Some of this range has already lost its population of taguá and parts of it may never have had high populations. Areas of former high populations which no longer have the Chacoan peccary are now well known. In the vicinity of Copogro, a small village at kilometer post 580 of the Trans-Chaco highway, there was a high population of taguá in 1976. In 1981, however, there were hardly any taguá or sign of taguá because of land clearing and heavy hunting. Table 10.1, a summary of taguá seen by me and my assistants from 1976 through 1981, shows this decline.

Few wild animals are as vulnerable to local extinction as the Chacoan peccary. Its habit of fearlessly walking into the road to investigate a passing vehicle or standing and watching intruders has led to its disappearance in newly cleared areas.

CLIMATIC TOLERANCES

The Chacoan peccary inhabits the dense, arid thorn forest and is strictly a wilderness animal. When a climatograph (Fig. 10.4) is constructed for taguá's range and compared to climatographs for areas within the ranges of the collared and white-lipped peccaries, it is clear that the taguá does not thrive in as wide a variety of climates as do the other two. Unfortunately, there are few long-term records from weather stations within the range of taguá. Both rainfall and temperature can vary widely and location will still be suitable for the collared peccary. The white-lipped peccary can tolerate a wide range of moisture conditions but cannot tolerate low temperatures. Taguá, on the other hand, requires areas of both low rainfall and high temperatures. With its narrow climate needs, its range is by far the smallest of the three species.

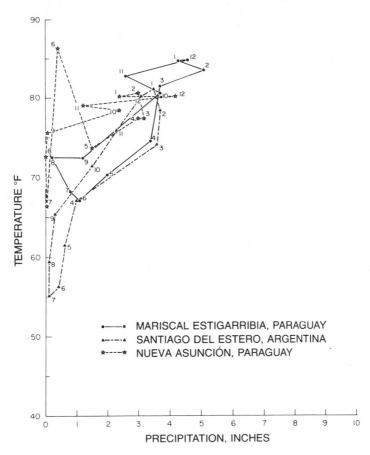

Figure 10.4. Climatograph for the range of the Chacoan peccary

Table 10.1 Taguá Seen Near Kilometer 580 of Trans-Chaco Highway (Copogro)

Year	Observation Time (Days)	Number of Herds Seen	Number of Individuals
1976	19	18	72
1977	21	4	22
1979	13	2	10
1981	19	2	6

HABITAT

Short (1975) has described the Chaco as a vast low plain with a xeric-adapted woodland. From its eastern border at the Paraguay River westward there is a moisture gradient and a resulting change in the vegetation. At the eastern border of the Chaco there are broad open grasslands with scattered palms (*Copernicia* sp.). Depending on the amount of rainfall of the previous rainy season, the land may be entirely dry or have areas of standing water. At the eastern border the

Figure 10.5. Gallery forest. Large trees, mostly quebracho, are found along old streambeds and depressions. (Photograph by Lyle K. Sowls)

average annual rainfall can range up to 1,450 mm (57 in.) (Gorham 1973). In areas of such heavy rainfall there are, apparently, no taguá. Somewhere between this eastern part of the Chaco and Villazon, about 275 kilometers north of the river, the habitat becomes suitable and taguá have been found (Wetzel 1977). To the north palm trees and grassland give way to thorn forest. A point at about kilometer 580 on the present Trans-Chaco highway appears to be the center of the taguá range. Here the average annual rainfall is about 800 mm (31 in.). The forest is dense and scrubby except for scattered large trees. These are principally the quebrachos (*Aspidosperma quebracho blanco* and

Figure 10.6. A laguna in the Chaco of Paraguay formed in an old streambed. Peccaries often use them as watering holes. (Photograph by Lyle K. Sowls)

Schinopsis quebracho colorado). These species reach their greatest size and abundance along oxbows and old river channels which collect water during the rainy season (Figs. 10.5, 10.6). In these places they form small patches of gallery forest. Scattered lone bottle trees (*Chorisia insignis*) are common on the level dry land. As one proceeds northward the average annual precipitation drops to about 387 mm (15 in.), and few large trees grow there. In this drier area, the dominant trees and shrubs are various species of *Prosopis*, *Cercidium*, *Condalia*, *Ephedra*, and *Mimosa*. Cacti become more abundant and large forms of *Cereus* and *Opuntia* are conspicuous (Fig. 10.7).

The habitat where we found taguá is an impenetrable thorn forest with few openings. To measure the density of what we believed was optimum taguá habitat, we selected a study area on the Parque Nacional Teniente Encisco near kilometer 684 of the Trans-Chaco highway. For these analyses, a 10-meter line was stretched out at 100-meter intervals at right angles to the Old Chaco War Road which runs through the park. Readings of the percentage of either ground cover or overhead coverage by vegetative type were estimated for each segment of the transect line. The results of these observations are shown in Table 10.2. The high figures for bushes and shrubs best indicate the density of the vegetation and the difficulty of seeing or

Table 10.2. Percentage of Ground Covered With Various Plant Groups in 31 Sample Transects Parque Nacional Teniente Encisco, Paraguay. June 1981

	Bare Ground	Leaf Litter	Moss, Lichens	Cactus			
				Creeping, Course	Creeping, Fine	Low, Heavy	Tree Types
Range	0.1–9.5	60.6–96.6	0.0–16.3	0.6–17.8	0.0–19.5	0.0–5.8	0.0–21.5
Mean	2.69	87.6	1.5	5.48	3.68	1.45	1.95
Standard deviation	2.58	7.72	3.59	3.82	6.02	1.56	5.98

	Herbs, Forbs	Grasses	Brome-liads	Bushes, Shrubs	Trees
Range	0.0–10.0	0.0–10.4	0.5–45.2	66.0–100.0	0.0–100
Mean	0.63	2.84	16.78	93.2	59.1
Standard deviation	1.85	2.8	14.28	8.5	31.21

Table 10.3. Chemical Composition and Physical Properties of Soil Samples In and Near Salt Licks Used By Chacoan Peccary

FROM SOIL IN LICKS (ppm)						
Cl	Na	Ca	Mg	K	pH	EC x 10^3
1560	624	132	32	42	7.5	6.55
3240	816	1270	320	336	7.8	8.56
120	344	1540	464	48	7.7	6.65
632	124	610	164	400	7.6	4.95
700	688	1000	240	50	7.5	11.90
FROM SOIL OUTSIDE LICKS						
52	16	110	38	80	6.4	1.05
125	24	1380	288	50	7.7	1.41
352	27	325	92	164	6.9	2.62

Figure 10.7. Many species of cactus are present in the thorn forest, range of the Chacoan peccary. (Photograph by Lyle K. Sowls)

studying taguá in this habitat. The two groups of creeping cactus, which are important food for taguá and the collared peccary, are compatible with nearly all other groups except the plants in the family Bromeliaceae. These plants form dense stands which appear to keep out these two species of cacti (Fig. 10.8).

FOODS

Mayer and Brandt (1982) studied the winter diet of the taguá in the Chaco of Paraguay. From 70 stomach samples they found that various species of cactus made up the winter diet. These included *Cleistocactus baumannii*, *Eriocereus* sp., *Opuntia discolor*, and *O. canina*. The species of cactus taken by taguá are low species that are easily available near the ground (Fig. 10.9).

Taguá regularly come to salt licks. The herds' predictable appearance at these places is one reason they are so vulnerable to hunting. In 1976 and 1977 soil samples from these licks were obtained for analysis to determine which elements the animals were seeking. Although more samples are needed for a definite indication of these elements, it seems likely that common salt (NaCl) was probably the compound they were seeking since both sodium and chloride were definitely more abundant in the lick area than in the surrounding country (Table 10.3).

Figure 10.8. One of many species of *Bromelia* that grow in the range of the Chacoan peccary. These plants often form impenetrable thickets and exclude other plants. (Photograph by Lyle K. Sowls)

These salt licks occur in two ways. First, there are natural salt licks maintained by the taguá over a long period of time. Second, new licks are available when road building, land clearing, or other disturbances tear down large mounds created by leaf-cutting ants (*Atta sexdens*). In the natural upward movement of soil, the ants apparently bring salts to the surface in their mound. These mounds, when disturbed by bulldozers and road machinery, quickly expose areas where salts are available to the taguá (Fig. 10.10).

HERDS

Size

Taguá herds contain fewer individuals than the other two species. Wetzel (1981a) gave the average herd size as five. Mayer and Brandt (1982) give an average of only 3.8 animals per herd. The 26 herds on which my associates and I have obtained counts in the Chaco ranged from one through nine and averaged 4.3 animals per herd with a standard deviation of 2.18. These herds which my colleagues and I observed, however, as well as the herds previously reported by Wetzel and Mayer and Brandt, were in disturbed country that was also heavily hunted by local people. Information on the herd size of the Chacoan peccary is sketchy. It tends to be biased to the low side because few

Figure 10.9. Several low species of cactus common on forest floor. This species of *Opuntia* is important food for the Chacoan peccary. (Photograph by Lyle K. Sowls)

observations of taguá have been made in their undisturbed habitat. In the disturbed habitat, hunting quickly reduces the herds. Local residents, who knew the Chaco before the present accelerated land-clearing and settlement, have told me that herds of up to nine individuals were common. My informants included Venancio Sanchez, a camp guard at an advanced road construction operation; Eurides Fidalski, hotel operator and hunting guide at Copogro and Nueva Asuncion; Roglio Cateveque and Raul Macchi, ranch foremen at Copogro: Heinrich Epp, who ran a land clearing business, and several other hunters, surveyors, and travelers in the most remote parts of the Chaco. Although the herd sizes so far reported are low, the combined information available indicates that taguá generally travel in smaller herds than either the collared or the white-lipped peccary.

Population Structure

The health of an animal population can be partially determined by its age structure. A population with too high a percentage of old animals indicates a static situation, which is typical for many threatened or endangered species. On the other hand, vigorous populations with a balance of different age classes indicate a dynamic, healthy situation. One way to determine the age structure of an animal population is to gather age information at random on as many animals as

Figure 10.10. Salt lick for Chacoan peccary in a disturbed ant mound made by bulldozing a new road through the thorn forest. (Photograph by Lyle K. Sowls)

possible to determine the percentage of the different age groups in the population.

Techniques for gathering age information include counting the cementum layers of the incisors, developed by Low (1970) and Low and Sowls (unpub.) for the collared peccary. These techniques are based on the earlier work of Scheffer (1950) and Laws (1952, 1953) on northern fur seals and elephant seals; Low and Cowan (1963) on mule deer; Lowe (1967) for red deer, and many other researchers who have used these techniques on various species of ungulates. Low described the technique based largely on the use of teeth of wild collared peccaries and captive-reared animals of known age (Low and Sowls, unpub.). The same technique was used to determine the age of 454 collared peccaries in Arizona.

To try this technique with taguá, I collected all of the first lower incisors that I could from taguá skulls found in the Chaco. (Unfortunately, no teeth from known-age animals have been available for this species.) I found a total of 44 skulls of adult taguá and four skulls of immature taguá under two years of age. All of these skulls were thrown out by hunters who had killed the animals for meat. Incisors from the adult skulls were sectioned and cementum layers examined. Without known-age reference material, it is not clear in what season the dark band formation occurs and the age at which the first band is formed in the permanent incisor (Gary Matson pers. comm.). There are, however, good distinct cementum rings in the incisors which require only further research for a determination of accurate aging. Estimates of the age structure from all 48 specimens were as follows: Under two years = 13; two and three years = 15; three and four years = 2; four and five years = 6; five and six years = 3; six and seven years = 3; seven and eight years = 2; eight and nine years = 2; nine + years = 2. These figures indicate that 58 percent of the sample was under three years of age; 23 percent was between three and six years old, and 19 percent was over six years of age. The population from which these animals came was being exposed to exploitation by overhunting resulting from land clearing operations. These figures on the age composition show that the local population is a healthy, young, reproducing population in the Paraguayan Chaco in places where there is still enough habitat for them.

Social Behavior

During my trips to the Chaco I found that heavy hunting pressure made studies of taguá social behavior very difficult, especially during 1979 and 1981. Observations in 1976 and 1977, when animals were more numerous, have shown that taguá has behavioral patterns similar to the other two species. It is a highly social animal which depends upon its scent gland for marking territories and marking other herd members. It also has a repertoire of vocalizations to stay in contact with other herd members. The mutual rubbing among collared peccaries, which has been described by many writers (Knipe 1957; Neal 1959; Frädrich 1967, Schweinsburg and Sowls 1972; Sowls 1974; Bissonette 1976, 1982; Diaz 1978; and Byers 1980), and which I observed in the white-lipped peccary, is also found among taguá. I have seen this mutual rubbing in three different herds of taguá and also among captive pets. The scent gland in taguá is located in the same relative position as in the other two species. It is in the center of the back, about 6 inches above the base of the tail. The rubbing action, as among the other two species, is performed as two animals, with sides touching, simultaneously rub their cheeks over each other's scent gland. In the same manner as the other two species of peccaries, the Chacoan peccary rubs its scent gland against trees and other objects to leave scent. The particular places are continually used by the same animals to mark objects within their home range.

Mayer and Brandt (1982) recorded 820 minutes of observations on taguá herds. In most interactions, their findings on social behavior were similar to those related for the collared peccary. They classified aggressive interactions as squabble, tooth-chattering, charging, biting, and whirl-around. Tooth-chattering, however, was uncommon among taguá.

There is a need for more quantitative data on social interactions of taguá, and it is hoped that further work may be successful. Also, a description of vocalizations should be made, including obtaining sonograms of the various calls as has been done with the other two species.

RESEARCH AND MANAGEMENT NEEDS OF TAGUÁ

Like the white-lipped peccary, taguá is a wilderness animal which quickly disappears when its habitat is disturbed for agricultural development. Of the three peccaries it is by far the least adapted to a variety of climates. Its habitat needs are thus very specific, making it the most vulnerable to exploitation of all the peccaries.

The creation of nature reserves within the range of taguá, such as Parque Nacional Teniente Encisco in Paraguay, are badly needed. The required size of these preserves is not known to date because an adequate study of the range and movements of these animals has not been done. Detailed studies of taguá by use of radio telemetry also are needed to determine the home range and area requirements of this species. The techniques used by Day (1977b), Byers (1980), and Supplee (1981) on collared peccary would likely provide the needed information on this species.

There is only meager information on the reproductive pattern of taguá. From the time of appearance of the young they seem to have a limited breeding season. A captive breeding program in a favorable climate following the study methods used by Sowls (1966) and Low (1970) would not only furnish valuable information on reproduction but also animals for zoos and for eventual restocking programs.

Peccaries
and People

11 | Peccaries and Indigenous Man

MAN'S FIRST ENCOUNTER WITH MEMBERS of the family Tayassuidae probably occurred thousands of years ago, following the migration of the first Paleo-Americans into what is now middle North America. It is likely that the peccaries that man first knew were not any of the three living species. It is far more probable that it was one of the many species now extinct. Two genera which lived until the late Pleistocene were *Mylohyus* and *Platygonus*, shown in the introduction.

Indigenous people over a large area took peccaries for food and for pets, and included them in their culture and mythology. Although their numbers eventually were decimated by disease, slavery, and murder, a few tribes, primarily in Central and South America, largely retained their original culture. Anthropological studies of these indigenous groups provide the best case studies of the importance to these people of hunting peccaries.

To some extent the economically poor mestizos of Mexico and Central and South America may be included with Indians, since subsistence is also the most important aspect of their relationship to wildlife.

CENTRAL AND SOUTH AMERICA

Game Meat in the Subsistence Diet

The importance of meat as a source of protein for the Indians of Central and South America can hardly be exaggerated. The literature on these tribes is crowded with references to hunting, leaving no doubt concerning its place in these societies. Carneiro (1970), speaking of the tribes of Amazonia in general, stresses the importance of hunting when he says, "...it is hunting, not fishing, which must be relied upon for the bulk of the protein in the diet."

177

Few writers have placed the need for wild meat among the Indians as high as Wilbert (1972): "...for a Yanoama to be forced to go without meat is tantamount to suffering hunger, and if the choice is between remaining close to a producing garden and migrating to a promising new hunting territory, the later most of the time wins." This same conclusion is expressed by Nietschmann (1972) when he says, "Hunting and fishing activities form the core of village life. Meat is the single most sought after food and is the center of interest in the village. Deprived of meat, many women refuse to cook; or they are indifferent about it at best."

The importance of meat in the diet of the Jívaro of the upper Amazon basin has been described by Harner (1973) who says, "Hunting is the chief source of protein, and is more important to the food supply than fishing or gathering, contributing an estimated 20 percent of the diet."

Many writers divide the tribes into groups of hunters and gatherers as contrasted to agricultural types. The dependence upon wild meat in the diet thus varies greatly. Even to those who practice extensive agriculture, wild meat is still an essential of the diet. For example, speaking of the Campa Indians of eastern Peru, Denevan (1974) says, "No meal is considered complete without meat." Métraux (1948a) says of the primitive contemporaries of the Guaraní of Paraguay, "Because the Cainguá prefer meat to any other food, their main concern when they move their village is to choose an area with abundant game."

Heavy stress on the value of wild meat in the diet of the Indians of the headwaters of the Rio Orinoco was expressed by Smole (1976): "All Yanoama are very fond of eating fresh meat, the flesh of animals being a 'real' food, like plantain. Their language even has a special term for meat hunger as opposed to the word for 'hunger' in general."

Peccaries As a Source of Animal Protein

Both in early explorers' reports and in studies of individual tribes by modern anthropologists, references to peccaries in the diet of Indians are common. Although a few reports simply refer to "wild hogs," most differentiate between the collared and white-lipped species. The desirability of the peccaries as food and their importance in the diet of indigenous people can be seen by the many writers who refer to them.

Farabee (1922) lists both species of peccary as important food for the many tribes known as the Central Caribs of tributaries of the Upper Amazon. Lipkind (1948) isolated the peccary as a favored meat animal when he says, "Although the Carajá are passionate hunters, very few of the animals in the region are eaten. Only the peccary is really sought and constitutes a sizeable item in the larder." Gordon (1957) calls the white-lipped peccary one of the most important food animals of the Chocó of Colombia. Speaking of the Gran Chaco region, Steward and Faron (1959) placed the peccaries at the top of the list of foods. "Peccaries and tapirs, which are larger and tend to herd, are perhaps the most important land game and reward the efforts of the skilled hunter." Murphy (1960) listed the peccary as one of the principal meat species hunted by the Mundurucú Indians of Amazonia. In 1906 Orellana (in Denevan 1966) said that among tribes of the Mojos of Bolivia "high prolonged floods were disastrous for they greatly diminished valuable wild game, especially deer and peccary."

Of the Tenetehara Indians of Southeast Brazil, Wagley and Galvão (1959) said: "Paca, peccaries, wild pork, deer, and tapir are the animals whose meat is most appreciated, but they are hard to hunt in the dense forest and rarely do the Tenetehara men bring them back from the hunt." Nietschmann (1972) has done one of the most complete studies of the place of game meat in the diet of the Miskito Indians of eastern Nicaragua. He recorded all of the game killed between October 1968 and September 1969 for the village of Tasbapauni which contained 997 people. He gave the whole weight of an adult collared peccary as 55 pounds and the field dressed weight as 40 pounds. The weights of the white-lipped peccary he gave as 73 and 50 pounds. In the 12 months that he kept records he accounted for 7,245 pounds of meat of the white-lipped peccary, seven percent of the village's total meat consumption. Seventy percent of the meat diet was green turtle. No other single species accounted for as large a percentage. During the year, Nietschmann reported that 133 white-lipped peccaries and two collared peccaries were taken by this village.

The white-lipped peccary not only rated high in volume but also was first choice of all meats available. Nietschmann says that the Miskitos' liking for fatty meat prompts hunting efforts toward white-lipped peccary which made up 70 percent of the meat yield per land hunter. Murphy and Murphy (1974) list both the white-lipped and the collared peccary as major game animals of the Mundurucú Indians of Brazil.

Smole (1976) says the peccary rates very highly among the Yanoama of the headwaters of Rio Orinoco: "Among the manifold species hunted, the most esteemed are certain large mammals, such as the tapir, the agouti and the peccary." Many other writers have listed the peccaries as an important source of animal protein. These include Karsten (1935) for various Ecuadorian tribes; Fejos (1943) for the Yagua of Amazonia; Furneaux (1969) for the tribes of the Upper Amazon; and Meggars (1971) for Kayapó, Sirionó, Warwari, and the Jívaro, all Amazonia tribes. Peccaries have also been listed in the diets of the Tupí-Cawabíb (Levi-Strauss 1948), the tribes of the Uapupes-Caqueta region of the western Amazon basin (Goldman 1948), the tribes of the Guianas and tributaries of the Amazon (Gillin 1948), the Witotoan tribes of the Para-Paraná and upper Caqueta rivers of Brazil (Steward 1948b), the Warrau of the Orinoco delta (Kirchoff 1948), and the Amahuaca of eastern Peru (Carneiro 1974).

Among game killed by residents of agrovilas along the Transamazon highway, the white-lipped peccary rated highest, making up 46.5 percent of the game protein mass taken during a month in 1973–74.

The collared peccary made up 8.1 percent of the weight taken, ranking fourth after the white-lipped peccary, tapir *(Tapirus terrestris)*, and brocket deer *(Mazama americana)* (Smith 1976). Among the Aché Indians of eastern Paraguay, Hawkes et al. (1982) rate the white-lipped peccary the highest in average calories of food taken per consumer per day. In the heavily forested country of northeastern Paraguay the collared peccary rated sixth in average calories per consumer per day, behind the white-lipped peccary, armadillo, monkey, coatimundi and paca. Both bow and arrow and shotguns were used by the Aché.

Kiltie (1980) has quantitatively reviewed the importance of the collared and white-lipped peccaries in the diet of various Neotropical groups. He concluded that white-lipped peccaries are usually taken in equal or greater numbers than collared peccaries and that the species that was killed most often during a sample period contributed more meat to the groups' diet than any other nonaquatic prey species.

Hunting Methods for the Peccary

The literature leaves little doubt that the Indians of Central and South America were expert at obtaining game. They knew the habits of the animals and ingeniously made use of this knowledge in the pursuit and killing of game animals. The noisy feeding of the white-lipped peccary, its close herding tendencies, and its extremely strong odor were highly advantageous to the hunter. The peccary's acute sense of smell was of less importance in the deep tropical forest; when the wind became a factor, the natives approached from downwind.

Weapons and techniques for hunting peccaries vary greatly among tribes. Chagnon (1977) describes the hunting practices of the Yanoama: "Frequently dogs are used to run tapir, wild pigs and deer but most hunting is merely the individual stalking and shooting [of] whatever game is available. As men always carry their weapons with them when they leave, they are, in effect, continuously hunting."

For the peccary, however, especially the white-lipped, most writers give far more elaborate descriptions. To be really effective in hunting the white-lipped peccary, large numbers of men are far more successful. Fejos (1943), speaking of the Yagua of northeastern Peru, says

> Group hunts are organized to kill wild pigs, such as the diverse species of peccary, as well as deer and tapir. The communal hunts are usually under the leadership of the chief, but if the latter is in any way incapacitated the best hunter takes charge. In hunting peccary the men move about in groups, spreading out as much as the vegetation allows. A few men are sent ahead to locate the scent of the pigs. Once the herd is located, the hunters form a circle about the peccaries' feeding ground, and as the animals are extremely noisy, it is comparatively easy to approach them closely without being detected. The hunters climb nearby trees as

noiselessly as possible, and from their vantage point shoot darts into the animals with sufficient force to penetrate their tough hides. Surprisingly large numbers of pigs — as many as thirty or thirty-five — are shot before the herd takes alarm. Usually the pigs emit only a small squeal when a darts hits them, and as they constantly jostle each other during the feeding and give similar grunts and squeals, no attention is paid them by the other animals. Each hunter singles out a pig for himself and shoots five to ten darts into it, so as to kill the animal as speedily as possible. Only about a minute is necessary to kill a pig in this manner, while one dart alone will cause the death of the animal in from ten to thirty-five minutes. After the herd has fled in alarm, the hunters descend from the trees and dispatch with their spears the pigs found paralyzed on the ground — meat is distributed by the chief.

Steward and Métraux (1948) confirm the use of the blowgun by the Yagua for killing peccaries. Steward (1948a) indicates that the Sioni Indians of Colombia also kill most of their game, including peccaries, with a blowgun. Whenever the blowgun is used, poisoned darts, as described by Fejos, were used to kill the white-lipped peccary.

Although Fejos and Steward and Métraux describe the effective use of the blowgun and darts against peccaries, many tribes who use blowguns do not use them against such large land mammals. Gordon (1957) says of the Chocó Indians of Colombia, "Against some of the important food animals the blowgun seems to be unsatisfactory. It is not much used in hunting the white-lipped peccary *(Tayassu pecari)*, the small collared peccary or the tapir — these animals are killed with a lance with a ten foot shaft." According to Harner (1973), the Jívaro, who obtain their blowguns and curare poison by trade with the Achuara but attain great skill in their use, do not use it for large game including peccaries, He says, "The blowgun is not considered satisfactory for hunting ground-dwelling creatures which are instead killed with shotgun and rifle." Even today the long bow is apparently an effective and much used weapon for the white-lipped peccary. Siskind (1973) says that the Sharanahua Indians of the upper Amazon in Peru use the bow and arrow to obtain the white-lipped peccary for meat and hides when they run out of shells. Smole (1976) reports that the Yanoama Indians of Venezuela rely on the long bow to kill the white-lipped peccary. Among the additional tribes which have or are still using the bow and arrow for killing peccaries are the Tapirapé of central Brazil (Wagley and Galvão 1948) and the Carajá of central Brazil as reported by Lipkind (1948). Referring to hunting methods of the Amahuaca Indians of Peru, who use bow and arrows, Carneiro (1974) says

> ... the only occasion when a number of men cooperate in hunting is when a herd of white-lipped peccaries is detected near the settlement. Unlike collared peccaries, which travel singly or in pairs, white-lipped peccaries travel in herds of up to 100. A group

of hunters may be able to kill as many as ten peccaries before the rest take flight. A lone hunter coming upon a herd of feeding peccaries from the downward side approaches them stealthily and attempts to kill one or two before the others discover his presence. Once alerted, the peccaries either flee or charge.

Carneiro also says that clubs are often used against white-lipped peccaries.

An unusual way to bag large numbers of peccaries at one time has been described by Métraux (1946a). Describing the methods used by the early Mbayá of the Chaco he says, "The Mbayá shot white-lipped peccaries *(Tayassu pecari)* with arrows or clubbed them at close range, despite the danger of being attacked by these animals if aroused. Peccaries were also driven into the river, where they were slaughtered, or into a deep ditch covered with twigs where they fell on top of each other."

Another ingenious method used by the Indians in hunting peccaries has been described by Denevan (1966) for several tribes in northeastern Bolivia. He says, "Peccary was sometimes hunted by first capturing a young one and placing it on a tree branch where its cries attracted the herd which was readily dispatched with arrows and spears."

Several writers besides Chagnon and Farabee refer to the use of dogs in hunting peccary. Murphy (1960) describes the use of dogs in hunting peccaries by the Mundurucú Indians of central Brazil. Other writers who have referred to the use of dogs have been Bennett (1962) for the Bayano Cuna Indians of Panama, and Meggars (1971) for the Jívaro of the upper Amazon basin and the Waiwai of North Amazon areas. Smith (1976) describes the use of dogs for hunting both the collared and white-lipped peccaries along the Transamazon Highway. Dogs were used to chase the smaller collared peccaries into holes and hollow trees where they could be sealed off, forced out at ease with a long stick, and then shot. Smith described the use of dogs to allow the hunter to catch up to defensive white-lipped peccaries, allowing more animals to be bagged.

The popularity of bows and arrows and dogs among the Caingang has been described by Métraux (1946b) who says, "An entire band participates in a peccary hunt. Old and young, preceded by dogs, endeavor to drive the animals towards hunters who shoot them with arrows. The Aweikoma-Caingang follow droves of wild pigs for several days, killing all those which come within their reach."

The coming of white man and his modern weapons has definitely had an impact upon the way these animals are hunted and the number of animals killed. There is little doubt that guns have easily, and at a very early date, reached far into the jungles of South and Central America and that they have affected hunting methods for peccaries.

For example, Harner (1973), speaking of the Jívaro of the upper Amazon, says,

> The relative isolation of the interior Jívaro, however, had not prevented them from obtaining increasing quantities of machetes, steel axes, and shotguns. By means of neighborhood-to-neighborhood relays of trading partners, these products of Western civilization passed from the frontier Jívaro into the most remote parts of the tribal territory. All of the interior Jívaro neighborhoods were thus supplied with steel cutting tools, firearms and ammunition without the necessity of coming into direct contact with the white population.

It seems inevitable that modern firearms have increased the kill of peccaries, especially in view of the marketable value of their hides. Nietschmann (1972) describes the increased pressure on the herds due to the market value of their hides and the hunting methods of the Miskito Indians of Nicaragua: "When hunting, the Miskito concentrate on the white-lipped peccary, not only for its esteemed fatty meat but because these animals travel in large droves of 100 to 200 individuals. If attacked, the droves display a 'covered wagon' defense which allows the hunter to be reasonably successful when armed with a shotgun and sufficient shells. Hunters are increasingly feeling the need to have a shotgun so they can make large kills." In some areas the impact of firearms for the killing of peccaries has apparently not led to greatly increased kills. Gordon (1957), for example, says of the Chocó Indians of Colombia, "I met only a few Indians who had guns, all were old weapons, such as Spanish muzzle-loaders." There seems to be a great deal of variation in the degree to which traditional weapons and modern firearms are used among the various tribes hunting peccaries. In the western Chaco of Paraguay, where the Chacoan peccary was the principal species taken for food, I found shotguns with buckshot loads and .22 rifles the most commonly used weapons.

From an examination of all evidence it is apparent that a great mixture of weapons, ranging from the traditional blowgun and long-bow, to ancient muzzle-loading shotguns, to more modern cartridge shotguns, .22 rifles, and the .44 Winchester carbine, is used. As the indigenous people lose their original crafts and have more contact with European man, firearms take the place of the original weapons, especially when a hide trade develops and weapons become an important item of trade for the hides.

Hunting as a Sport or Cultural Activity

Hunting furnishes not only valuable animal protein for the Indian tribes, but it also provides a cherished pastime and has a definite place in the social life of the tribe. According to many writers, hunting seems to dominate the lives of these people.

The social significance of hunting to the Yurucare Indians of the Bolivian Andes is described by Métraux (1948b) who says, "Among the ancient Yurucare, hunting, besides its economic importance, had social significance; it was regarded as a dignified occupation for men and gave prestige to those who were proficient in it."

Of the Tupinamba of southeastern Brazil Métraux (1948a) has said, "The chase was a major masculine occupation; Indians wishing to eulogize their country declared that it abounded in game — deer, wild pigs, monkeys etc."

Speaking of the Kayapó Indians of the lower Amazon basin, Meggars (1971) says

> Hunting is a sport as well as a subsistence activity, and men are experts at tracking and at imitating animal and bird cries. The head of the family may go off hunting for several days alone, but more commonly related men and boys join together. Communal hunts are organized for peccary and tapir, and also when a large quantity of meat is required for a feast.

Of the Sirionó Indians of Bolivia, Meggars says, "The most important male activity is hunting, and a man spends at least 50 percent of his time this way." About the Waiwai Indians, she notes, "Hunting is the favorite pastime of the men who go out with their bows and arrows before dawn in company of a relative... tapir, peccary and deer are usually hunted with dogs. ... Being a good hunter is a way to achieve prestige, and a variety of magical practices is employed to enhance the possibility of success."

Carneiro (1974) says of the Amahuaca of eastern Peru, "Every man is a hunter, and every good hunter enjoys the chase. Such a man may go hunting even when there is still meat at home. Those not so skilled go less often, but because meat is commonly shared among all families in a community no one is without it for long." The self-image of the hunter and his role among the Mundurucú Indians has been described by Murphy and Murphy (1974) who say, "The essential male activity is hunting. The men think of themselves as hunters, not as gardeners or fishermen, the religion is oriented toward hunting and the spirit world is closely associated with the species of game."

The role of the hunter in the social order of the Yanoama Indians has been described by Smole (1976): "Hunting is a prestigious and honorable activity. It involves the chase of wild animals by men armed for the purpose of killing them. This is strictly a masculine pursuit, indispensable to the Yanoama life style."

Cooking Methods

Because peccaries are large animals and move in herds, considerable quantities of meat are available to the tribes following successful hunts. The local chief usually decides how to divide the meat (Fejos 1943 and Steward and Métraux 1948 for the Yagua; Meggars 1973 for the Kayapó; Meggars 1971 for the Jívaro; Murphy and Murphy 1974; Wagley and Galvão 1969 for the Tenetehara). Several writers have commented on the care various tribes take not to waste meat. Murphy and Murphy reported that the Mundurucú of Brazil refrain from taking more game than the villagers can eat because it is considered a grievous offense against the spirit mothers of the animals to commit slaughter or to kill an animal only for its hide." The Yanoama Indians do not kill more than can be eaten because of religious sanctions against needless killing. "They hunt only to meet their requirements, and all the game that is taken is to be eaten. Every digestible part of the animal is eaten. Nothing is wasted." (Smole 1976). Hawkes et al. (1982) also say that the Aché of eastern Paraguay "eat every edible bit of an animal."

In the Chaco of Paraguay I found that Paraguayan workers cut peccary meat into long strips and dry it in the sun. Most tribes in more tropical areas slowly roast large chunks of the meat over a wood fire. Lowie (1946) says of the Bororo of southwestern Brazil, "All animals are roasted in their skins; only the intestines are boiled." Levi-Strauss (1948), speaking of the Tupí-Cawabíb says, "Game is singed and smoked in the skin, either intact or in pieces. . . . Game is smoked for 24 hours; during the night an attendant takes care of the fire." Holmberg (1948) found similar cooking methods among the Sirionó Indians of eastern Bolivia: "Game is not skinned for cooking; the hair is burned off in the fire and the skin eaten. All parts of the animal are consumed." Steward (1948b), speaking of the Witotoan tribes of Brazil, said the meat was smoked on a rack called a *babracot*.

Taboos, Myths, and Magic

So far I have tried to evaluate the importance of meat and especially that of the peccary in the diet of the many Indian tribes of Latin America. Although the evidence of the value of hunting in these societies and the importance of the meat protein is high, there are exceptions that should be mentioned.

A few tribes apparently have complete taboos against eating peccary meat. Métraux (1949) says, "The Mataco never eat peccary lest they get a toothache and their teeth chatter as do those of the animal when it is aroused." He states further, "The Toba fear that meat of the collared peccary and the domesticated pig will give them ulcers of the nose."

In speaking of the Kalapalo Indians of central Brazil, Basso (1973) says

> In contrast with such groups as the Shavante, Kayapo, Nambikwara, and Mundurucú, the residents of the Upper Xingu Basin are settled agriculturists and fishermen, an adaptation which can be ascribed in part to the environmental peculiarities of the region. Equally important are the dietary practices... which restrict the number of hunted species to a very few. In contrast to their Tupí

and Gê-speaking neighbors, who place positive value on eating meat, the pursuit of hunting, and an aggressive masculinity associated with that pursuit, the members of Upper Xingu society reject these values and adopt the opposite moral code: Fishing and agriculture, rather than hunting are the proper male subsistence activities and passivity and generosity are ideals of behavior.

Basso also says, "Whereas many groups surrounding the Upper Xingu Basin prize meat, the Kalapalo and other Upper Xingu villagers regard virtually all land mammals or n,ene as disgusting and refuse to eat them. The two exceptions are monkey and sometimes coati..."

Among the meat-eating tribes, as contrasted to those of the Upper Xingu area, there are many descriptions of taboos against eating certain animals. For example, Webster (1942) says, "The Boro of Brazil think that every tapir, every wild pig and every alligator shelters the soul of a deceased tribesman; hence they will never kill one of these animals unless a magician is within reach to exorcise its soul. They believe if they should eat it they would surely die." Meggars (1971) and Webster (1942) report that neither the deer nor the tapir are eaten by the Jívaro of the upper Amazon. This tribe does, however, eat the meat of the peccary (Meggars 1971; Harner 1973). Ross (1978) discussed food taboos, diet and hunting strategy among Amazon tribes and put forth some interesting new theories on the origin of taboos. He does not, however, disagree with other authors on the importance of the peccaries in the diet or the near absence of taboos on the consumption of peccary meat.

Although few restrictions against eating peccaries can be found in the literature concerning the Indians of Latin America who inhabit the range of these species, those restrictions which do exist are often very complicated. McDonald (1977) studied taboos against eating meat among 11 different societies and found widely varying restrictions on the consumption of meat by various sex and age classes as well as their physical condition. He found that among the Kayapó, pregnant females were not allowed to eat the meat of peccaries; Desana boys could not eat it for 12 months prior to puberty; neither pregnant Yanoama females nor their spouses could eat peccary meat for two years after first menses, and Jívaro parents of newborn young could not eat it for 12 months. McDonald found no taboos against eating peccary meat among the Sirionó, Shavante, Tenetehara, Tapirapé, East Timbira, or the Tukuna.

McDonald's study is interesting because he estimated the percentage of reduction in the utilization of the game resource as a result of food taboos. He noted that in no instance was the meat of any animal completely banned from the diet. No tribe reduced the percentage of harvest of peccary more than 21 percent because of a food taboo. Of the six tribes where the peccary harvest was reduced because of a food taboo, he found that the percentage reduction varied from 0.1 percent for the Shavante to 21 percent for the Desana. Kiltie (1980) discussed the significance of the white-lipped peccary in the diet of Amazonia tribes and concluded that there is almost a complete absence of taboos on white-lipped peccaries. He believes that this is understandable in terms of ecological economics but says that the reasons for taboos on tapir and deer are still problematic from this viewpoint.

Among the Indian tribes of Latin America there are many religious beliefs, myths and magic concerning wild animals. Many of these are about hunting, and especially hunting the peccary, because of its high place in the food list of so many people.

The importance of the peccary to the Campa Indians of Peru is illustrated in their religious beliefs. Weiss (1974) explains,

> Certain game birds are understood to be raised and thus provided by the good spirits who reside on the mountain ridges. The Campa call these birds *ivíra ítomi Pává* or *ivira otishasati*, "creatures raised by the children of the Sun, or the mountain ridge dwellers." ... The mountain ridge dwellers also raise the game animal kapeshi (the coati, *Nasua nasua*) as their equivalent of the dog. The peccary (shintori), an important game animal, is *ivíra Pává*.

Holmberg (1948) says of the Sirionó Indians of eastern Bolivia, "Certain hunters are believed to possess special powers to hunt particular animals. Often when a man of such reputation is dying, hunters will gather around and ask him to pass them some of his luck." He may tell them to go to a certain place after he dies where they will find, for example, a band of peccary.

Game Depletion

The problem of game depletion for a people so heavily dependent on wild game meat is critically important. There are really two kinds of depletion — that which results from an individual tribe's day-to-day hunting, uninfluenced by European man, and second the rapid and lasting depletion of game following influences by European man.

The first kind of game depletion is not new and is associated with settlement patterns. Carneiro (1970) says, "... it is hunting, not fishing, which must be relied on for the bulk of the protein in the diet. This fact is of special significance for settlement patterns, since a heavy reliance on hunting is incompatible with sedentary village life. Even communities as small as 15 people, which are characteristic of the Amahuaca, severely deplete the game in their vicinity in a year or two." Likewise, Siskind (1973) says that "Interfluvial societies such as the Sharanahua, exploiting small streams for fish and depending primarily on hunting as their protein source, tend to be small groups, moving their settlements frequently since these resources are easily exhausted. Game is the factor that determines population density, settlement size, and the duration of time a settlement may remain in the same place." Their subsistence was made up of 60 percent agriculture, 30 percent hunting, five percent fishing, and five percent gathering.

In much of the tropical forested areas, such as Amazonia, the variety of plants and animals is very high but densities are low. Commenting on this fact and its effect on the Jívaro Indians, Harner (1973) says,

> This low density sometimes poses a problem for Indians engaged in collectiing a specific kind of wild fruit or hunting a particular species of game. This situation is aggravated for the hunter by the fact that virtually all of the Jívaro territory has been hunted efficiently for a long period of time, with the result that game is not as abundant as in regions unoccupied by the Indians. This fact was particularly driven home to my Jívaro companions and me in 1969 when, in traveling through an unhunted "no-man's land" between the Jívaro and the Achuara along the lower Rio Canjaimi, which had not been exploited because of the enmity between the two groups, we encountered unprecedented quantities of monkeys and birds.

Harner includes peccary as especially important to the subsistence of the Jívaro.

The second kind of game depletion associated with an increase of European residents and the use of firearms and the hide trade has been described by many writers. Chagnon (1977) says of the Yanoama:

> I remember the incredible herds of Capybara, wild pigs, flocks of ducks and river otters that abounded in the Upper Mavaca River from 1968 through 1971, when I was the only Westerner who ascended it. After the mission personnel, Venezuelan and Brazilian employees began hunting it, it turned into a near desert. Now not a single otter can be seen along its entire course, and many other species of common game animals are almost non-existent. The impact of this intensity of hunting on the local game supply — and the Yanomamö diet — will eventually be catastrophic.

Nietschmann (1972) examined the many factors which influenced hunting and fishing activities among the Miskito Indians of eastern Nicaragua. He concluded that the most important factors were "dietary preferences and prohibitions, costs involved, differential productivity and dependability of particular species, seasonality and scheduling, and the impact of cash market opportunities for faunal resources." He stressed the importance of these new changes by saying, "Under the impetus of population growth and rising aspirations the Miskito's efforts to secure increasing numbers of animals for both subsistence and market are leading to severe pressures on selected species and to cultural and ecological disruptions."

Denevan (1974) gives a similar report about the Campa Indians of eastern Peru: "Most of the large game is seriously depleted in Gran Pajonal, even though the Campa population itself has been greatly reduced in recent years." The rate at which game disappears in settled country has been described by Smole (1976) for the Yanoama Indians.

"In the vicinity of established human settlements, game is extremely scarce, having been effectively hunted or frightened off and hunters quickly dispose of what game there might be found around the Shabano and gardens. It is the remote high forests and old gardens thick with secondary growth that provide the habitats attractive to the bulk of game species."

The sequence of events leading to permanent game depletion as a result of European man's entry in the tropics has been summarized by Wagley (1953):

> The tropical forest Indians who inhabited the Amazon region before the arrival of the European depended, in addition to their gardens, upon hunting and fishing for their subsistence. In the early days of the European era, hunting and fishing were of great importance in feeding the colonists and their slaves. It was the Indian who taught the European newcomers to live in the strange Amazon environment. The Indian was the hunter and fisherman, and the methods of hunting and fishing of Amazon regional culture are therefore mainly of aboriginal origin. Although the modern inhabitant of the Valley hunts with a shotgun or a .44 caliber rifle or fishes with a metal fishhook or European-type net, he does so with the knowledge of the local fauna derived from his Indian cultural heritage. In addition, numerous aboriginal techniques are still used, and many folk beliefs of Indian origin persist in regard to hunting and fishing. Nowadays, however, neither hunting nor fishing is important in the regional economy. Along the main arteries of the Amazon River system, hunting is no longer a lucrative occupation. After centuries of human occupation the country has been hunted out.

While the impact of hunting upon the game supplies around native villages is well documented, the disappearance of game due to habitat destruction has received little attention. The slash-and-burn agriculture in many tropical areas has probably not been extensive enough to take away much habitat. In areas like the Chaco of western Paraguay, habitat destruction is wholesale and disastrous to the wildlife populations. Much of this area is being cleared of native vegetation and planted to African grasses for pasturage. First, long straight roads are put in to separate the blocks of land into square parcels for later removal of the vegetation by bulldozers. These roadways then become avenues for hunters who, traveling by car or motorcycle, find the peccaries and deer along the highways. None of the meat is wasted but is carefully used by local people. The hides are usually dried, bundled, and sold (Fig. 11.1), although many taguá hides are thrown away with the skull. The game is usually depleted in these areas before the forest is cleared. After the pasture land is established, the peccaries are gone and only a few brocket deer remain near the small, low, wet oxbow areas that could not be cleared.

Figure 11.1. Peccary hides awaiting shipment to a large city market. (Photograph by Lyle K. Sowls)

NORTH AMERICA

The white-lipped peccary is present in North America in only a small part of the southern tip of Mexico. The collared peccary was at one time present in nearly all of Mexico except in the mountainous country. In what is now the United States it was at one time present in the southern third of Arizona (Knipe 1957) and in a small part of southwestern New Mexico and in southern Texas (Jennings and Harris 1953). There is a scarcity of published information on both species in Mexico and their role among the Indians of that country.

Of the Seri Indians of northwestern Sonora, Mexico, McGee (1895–96) said, "The individual taking of large game is effected either by stealthily stalking or by patient ambuscade ended by a sudden rush; when, if the chase is successful, the quarry is rent and consumed as at the finish of the semi-ceremonial collective chase. The fleet but wary antelope, the perquasious peccary, the wandering puma and jaguar."

Today, with human overpopulations and food scarcities, the peccaries are hunted for their meat and hides by all the country people in Mexico. The collared peccary has proven itself able to withstand heavy hunting pressure. Summarizing its situation in Mexico, Leopold (1959) says, "Javelinas are still overhunted in much of Mexico but, like the white-tailed deer, they have shown a remarkable capacity to persist, at least in low numbers, on suitable ranges. With a minimum of protection the javelina can be expected to hold its own indefinitely." Of the white-lipped peccary, however, Leopold (1959) says it "is disappearing from Mexico as settlement is extending into the wet tropics. Overhunting is the most immediate cause of the decrease, but even if hunting were brought under rigid control the loss of suitable habitat eventually would eliminate the species."

North of Mexico the collared peccary, before the arrival of European man, occupied about 225,000 square miles of country. In this area of mixed desert and high mountain ranges, populations were spotty. The land was occupied by the Papago and Pima Indians and various Apache tribes. Little information on the role of the collared peccary in the life of these tribes is available.

According to Opler (1941), the peccary did not hold a high position in the mind of the Chiricahua Apache: "He believes his dreams are true. When he dreams about the peccary it means something bad. When he dreams about deer it means something good. It is interesting that the good omen, deer, an animal much sought by the hunter, should be contrasted with peccary, an animal that most Chiricahua Apaches will not taste." He states further that "although peccaries are found in some parts of the tribal range, the members of at least two of the bands — the Eastern and Central — will not eat this meat because the peccary eats snakes." A southern Chiricahua man, however, told of hunts in which wild hogs were rounded up like rabbits and shot down with arrows. The hunters would surround a brushy place, for the "peccaries are found where there is a lot of brush; when on the flats they always make for the brush." The same informant told Opler that "the unborn of the peccary is eaten also."

Thus there seems to be some confusion in the literature concerning the use of peccaries by the Apache tribes. Bourke (1891) describes Apaches killing peccaries but does not say whether they ate them. It may be significant that the early writings on the Apache abound with descriptions of hunting and use of deer and antelope, yet hardly mention the peccary. The same can be said for the early writings about the Papago who also occupy land within the range of the peccary. According to Papago authority Bernard Fontana (pers. comm.), "In early writings on the Papagos the peccary is conspicuous by its absence." For the closely related Pima Indians, however, Russell (1975), who studied them in 1901–02, lists peccaries as a food item for that tribe. He said, "*Kâ-âtci*, or *tâsi-ikâlt*, *Tayassu angulatum sonorience*, the peccary, is yet found in the larger mountain chains that were formerly reached by the hunters of Pimeria, though the Gila River is about the northern limit of the range of this animal in the west. It could never have been an important article of the diet, and is practically unknown to the younger generation."

A review of the role of peccaries in the life of indigenous man shows that these animals have been very important over a vast area of land. As the various tribes evolved and filled particular niches in the environment, their relationship to wildlife, including peccaries, evolved also. Thus, for millennia native people depended on peccaries for food and developed a mythology concerning them. To them game depletion was only temporary, and they could remedy it by moving their camp. The role of wildlife, however, including peccaries, has been constantly changing since the arrival of Europeans. These changes, especially since World War II, have been dramatic over a vast area. The destruction of habitat, which affects both the indigenous people and the wildlife, is the issue of importance to peccary populations today.

12 | Peccaries and European Man

WHILE INDIGENOUS MAN LIVED IN HARMONY with his environment and had relatively little lasting influence on wildlife populations, European man brought many disruptive influences because of the wholesale destruction of wildlife habitat. While indigenous man hunted wildlife for food, European man hunts for sport. It is his interest in hunting which, in many instances, has led to management practices or conservation measures that help wildlife. It is European man who has introduced the hide trade to the new world and furnishes weapons to the natives. European man has been the buyer of the hides which come from the forests of the New World.

HABITAT DESTRUCTION

During the past few years a great deal has been written about deforestation of the tropical forests (Richards 1975; Davis 1977; Barrett 1980; Myers 1980, 1981; Caufield 1981; Denevan 1981; Hecht 1981; Raven 1981; and Teixeira 1982; Salati and Vose 1983). The causes for this have been many, but the principal ones are logging for commercial timber and the conversion of forest lands to artificial pasture for cattle.

Lumbering operations in the tropical forests and road building in the wilderness undoubtedly have greatly affected the herds of wild peccaries. Lumbering camps bring guns and hunters, and alteration of the environment eliminates suitable habitat as the great trees are cut down and taken out. Richards (1975) comments on the effects of clearing land for the Transamazon Highway: "During the construction of the highway, running 5,400 km from the north-east Brazil to the Peruvian frontier, over 130,000 km² of forest (an area four times the size of Belgium) were cut down and burned." Commenting on the ecologically vulnerable forest ecosystem, Richards also says:

> The soils on which tropical forests grow are for the most part remarkably poor in nitrogen, phosphorus, and other elements necessary for plant growth, a fact which is concealed by the luxuriant appearance of the vegetation.
>
> The poverty of the soils is partly due to the long-continued effects of heavy rainfall and partly to the geological history. The explanation of the paradoxical vigour of the vegetation is that a large part of the nutrient capital of the ecosystem is contained in the trees themselves and is rapidly recycled. When the leaves and dead wood fall to the ground fungi and other decomposer organisms quickly break them down and the nutrients released in this way are very quickly absorbed by roots and re-used.
>
> In tropical forests this recycling process seems to be extremely efficient and so little nutrient is lost in the drainage water that the streams flowing from undisturbed forest areas, such as parts of Amazonia, carry water little different in composition from pure rain water. When cultivated land is abandoned, tangles of bushes and climbers soon invade and a new secondary forest results.

Following lumbering operations, even a poor quality forest may not grow, as Richards points out: "When forest clearance is on a very large scale, as in modern lumber undertakings, it is often doubtful if enough forest is left to ensure recolonization, even if this is the intention. If deforested land is repeatedly disturbed, and especially when it is also subject to fires, it is often invaded by *Imperata* and other coarse grasses which convert the forest into a kind of savanna."

This rapid wholesale destruction of the tropical forests also means destruction of native wildlife. The white-lipped peccary, a wilderness animal requiring large quantities of food and large tracts of land for its circuit pattern of movement, is no longer able to survive. The Chacoan peccary is also a wilderness animal unable to survive when the forest is removed. The collared peccary, with a small home range and the ability to adapt to changing conditions, may survive in scattered places.

THE HIDE TRADE

Hides of the collared and white-lipped peccaries make fine leather and are in great demand in European countries, the United States, and some Asian countries. Numerous writers have described the place of peccaries in the international hide trade. Evidence indicates that in recent years trade in these skins has been increasing. Grimwood (1968) reported that during the period 1946 to 1966, over two million collared peccary hides and 848,000 white-lipped peccary hides were exported from Iquitos, Peru. Hvidberg-Hansen (1970a, 1970b) described the taking and export of peccary hides from Peru. He noted that some hunters have been forced to hunt longer to obtain peccaries than they had five years earlier. However, he pointed out that the high number of peccaries killed and the number of skins exported indicates that these species are common. Hvidberg-Hansen found that the peccaries are hunted primarily for meat and that stories about killing peccaries only for the hides were generally not true. He found that prices paid to the hunters by dealers varied from 15 to 55 soles (0.30 to 1.30 U.S. $ eq.) for the collared peccary and from 10 to 35 soles (0.20 to 0.80 U.S. $ eq.) for the hide of a white-lipped peccary.

Doughty and Myers (1971) report that between 1960 and 1966 exports from Belém in Brazil increased fivefold to 587,000 kg. Ojeda and Mares (1982) gave a figure of 312,115 peccary hides of three species being exported from Argentina between 1972 and 1979. According to the World Wildlife Fund, which obtains records on the international trade in wildlife, peccary hides have been widely available for wallets, shoes, gloves and belts. In 1981 equestrian gloves made of peccary in West Germany sold in Japan for $100 to $140 per pair; peccary shoes from Italy for $345 per pair; belts for $150; and wallets for $55 to $85. West Germany, Italy, France and Japan are the principal nations importing peccary hides. Numerous writers have described the sale of hides and their transport to the cities. Harner (1973) describes the preparation of peccary skins for market by the Jívaro and the great increase in market hunting for hides with the increased use of firearms. Nietschmann (1972) discusses the increased pressure upon the two species of peccary in Nicaragua because of the relatively new hide market available to the Miskito Indians.

For hides sold at Esperanza, Peru, a Sharanahua hunter received 20 soles ($0.80 U.S.) for collared peccary and 1,200 and 1,600 soles ($48 to $64) for jaguar (Siskind 1973). In comparison, Siskind quotes 25 soles ($1 U.S.) per day as the wages of the native laborer. She describes "the stinking rolls of peccary skins, jaguars and ocelot as they are thrown out at the plane's destination."

In the Chaco of western Paraguay in 1976 I found that taguá hides only occasionally were saved. They were usually thrown away with the head where the animals were shot (Fig. 12.1). Hides from the other two species were being sold to local dealers. The hunters told me they were receiving 350 Guaranis (approximately $2.70 U.S.) for a hide from any of the three peccary species.

When I returned to the Chaco in 1979, I found that the prices of some hides in the same area had risen. The native consultant who gave me price information in 1976 gave these figures in 1979: collared peccary, G 650 ($5.00 U.S.); white-lipped peccary, G 350 ($2.70 U.S.); Chacoan peccary, G 250 ($1.95 U.S.).

Figure 12.1. Head and hide of two Chacoan peccaries thrown away on road where the animals were shot. (Photograph by Lyle K. Sowls)

COMPETITION AND CONFLICT WITH MAN

Damage to crops by peccaries affects both the fields of European man and gardens of Latin American Indians. Green corn, melons, manioc, sugar beets, squash, beans and sorghum have been the crops I have known to be raided by peccaries.

Basso (pers. comm.) says the Kalapolo Indians of Brazil build elaborate fences and moats around some of their fields to protect them from the peccaries. She also pointed out that the collared peccary became easier to kill when it invaded the gardens and came near the villages.

Knipe (1957) has discussed competition between livestock and collared peccaries on Arizona grasslands. He described the digging for roots that is common in areas of filaree (*Erodium cicutarium*), but refuted the contention that peccaries root up grasses. He concluded that the requirements of the peccary on a normally grazed grass-browse range should not constitute a competitive factor with livestock, unless the herds are excessively large.

In the cacti desert where production of grasses and succulent forbs is extremely low, especially during drought, competition for cacti fruits, succulent forbs, and, in extreme cases, even cacti may result. On year-round cattle ranges where green succulent annual growth of forbs is evident early in the spring and summer, competition between cattle and the collared peccary may occur. Eddy (1959) observed a herd of nine peccaries in the Santa Rita Experimental Range study area on the flats of the semidesert feeding intensively on forbs and rooting out and destroying some young plants. A ten-square-yard bed of forbs was almost completely destroyed.

To a certain degree cattle compete with peccaries in some areas by eating out the young flower stalks of century plants (agaves), thus lowering the value of the plant to peccaries. This often occurs on year-round ranges in late spring when succulent forbs and green grasses are scarce and the dry grass is tough and unpalatable. This kind of damage was evident in the Canelo Pass area in Arizona in the spring of 1958. Ninety-three plants were damaged in a quarter-mile-square area, thus reducing the value of the range to peccaries.

Throughout much of its range, the peccary eats foods not ordinarily taken by cattle. Cacti, fruits, tubers, bulbs, beans, nuts, and century plants are seldom used by cattle, yet these foods make up the bulk of the peccary's diet.

Significant competition probably does not exist except where the supply of important food plants is low and peccary numbers are great, resulting in direct conflict with cattle for food plants. A study similar to Eddy's on the damage to the Texas rangeland was done by Jennings and Harris (1953). They found in Texas no evidence of damage to range plants, nor had there been any reports of peccaries killing young sheep and goats, especially in the Trans-Pecos area.

Unlike the attitude toward this animal in Arizona and New Mexico, a great deal of prejudice is found against the collared peccary in Texas where it is sometimes considered a pest and a menace to sheep and goats (Ellisor and Harwell 1979). As demand for animals to hunt increases, however, ranchers probably will become more interested in the collared peccary as a possible source of income from hunters' fees (Everitt et al. 1981).

SPORT HUNTING

The concept of sport hunting in the United States differs from the hunting in Central and South America. The collared peccary is the only one of the three peccaries that lives in the United States. In Arizona, Texas, and New Mexico it is legally classified as a game animal and there are annual open seasons and bag limits for its taking. The most satisfactory and most common procedure used by experienced hunters in the American Southwest involves more searching than shooting. Inasmuch as the peccary is a social animal which travels in herds and has a definite home range, advance knowledge of certain herds can be obtained by scouting potential hunting areas before the open hunting season.

Equipped with an idea of the approximate location of a herd, the hunter is found on opening morning on a high place with binoculars ready as the first light of day appears. From such a vantage point the hunter is able to locate the herd and plan his attack. A good hunter considers wind direction and never approaches upwind from the herd. By quietly approaching from a downwind direction, the hunter generally is able to get close enough to the herd to use the weapon of his choice. Most hunters in the American Southwest use conventional big game rifles to hunt the collared peccary. The Arizona Game and Fish Department, however, has been conducting research on the designation of certain hunt areas for handguns only. Arizona law requires that the hunter use either a centerfire rifle or a .22 magnum cartridge in a rifle and only centerfire cartridges in handguns.

In addition to rifles and handguns, muzzle-loading weapons and bow and arrow are becoming popular in the three states where regulated hunting is permitted. In Arizona, for example, separate early seasons have been authorized for archery hunts. In 1982, 8,869 archery hunters took 1,583 animals for a success rate of 18 percent. The effectiveness of the bow and arrow is obvious when compared to the 22.6 percent success for hunters who used firearms in 1982 (Arizona Game and Fish Department 1982).

Care of Meat and Hides

Although many sport hunters take good care of the carcasses of the peccaries, some do not. Evidence of this was always present at the hunter-checking stations that the wildlife research unit operated between 1957 and 1973. It did not appear that hunters cared for peccary meat as well as they did deer meat. Almost none made use of the hides. Many hides were destroyed when hunters removed the scent gland. There seems to be a fear among hunters that as soon as the animal is killed the scent permeates the meat. It is easy to see how this belief originated in a hot country if the hide and the carcass are placed in a confined area like the trunk of a car on a very hot day.

Among early explorer reports, advice to remove the scent gland is common. Cutright (1940) says "The South American naturalists are one in saying that if the meat of the peccary is to be eaten, the musk gland must be removed on the spot or the flesh will be tainted." However, I have been unable to find any suggestion that the indigenous people of Latin America remove the scent gland immediately after a kill. The answer is that they probably never do because it would spoil the hide as a marketable item. In all the hides I have seen prepared for market, the scent gland is removed from the inside and the hide is simply dried without being cut.

At the San Francisco Hotel at Copogro, in the Paraguayan Chaco, I have eaten peccary meat of all three species from which the scent gland was not immediately removed. All the meat was excellent.

One old female white-lipped peccary which I shot in the Chaco in 1976 was skinned about six hours after collection. When roasted over an open fire, there was no trace of the scent. The animal, which must have been at least 10 years old according to the teeth, was tasty but very tough.

In 1977 the wildlife research unit kept a record of the percentage of hunters who removed the scent gland from the animals they had shot. Of 67 specimens examined at the checking station that year, 43, or 64 percent, had had the scent gland cut away and 24, or 36 percent, still had the scent gland on the hide. Twenty-four hunters volunteered the information that they intended to discard the hide. Five said they planned to have it tanned. Ten hunters were going to have the head mounted, and 11 were going to save the skull. Of those that had not removed the scent gland, all said they did not believe that it mattered.

Most hides from animals killed in the United states presently are wasted because the cost of tanning is too high. As they have done with deer hides, buyers could collect more hides and have more of them to tan, thus saving this valuable resource. To realize this saving with peccary hides, hunters must be taught not to destroy the hide by removing the scent gland.

For those afraid of the scent gland permeating the meat when the gland and meat are kept together, a simple solution is available. The hunter could completely skin the animal in the field and place the skin in a large plastic bag away from the meat. The meat could be put in a separate game bag or cheesecloth and preferably cooled as much as possible in the field. As hunting permits for peccaries become harder to obtain because of the increased number of applicants, perhaps hunters will better care for the meat and the valuable hides.

MANAGEMENT PRACTICES

It has been shown that no serious effects have resulted from long-term, continuous hunting of peccaries in Arizona. However, individual herds in certain local areas can be depleted if accessibility leads to over-hunting. This problem has been studied by Day (1976) who says that "even with a limited number of hunters and a short season, rifle hunters on the Three Bar unit apparently reduced two herds by more than 65 percent. Other herds were essentially unaffected by hunting. Interestingly, no single herd was completely eliminated but one may have been reduced to a level from which it may have trouble recovering... the problem for the javelina manager is how to get the necessary distribution of rifle hunters over most of the animal's habitat so as to avoid the likelihood of overharvesting any one herd." Among the suggestions offered by Day to reduce the kill in local areas is to designate more accessible areas for handgun-only or "primitive" weapons such as the muzzle-loading rifle and bow and arrow. Detailed experiments on these

Table 12.1. Number of Peccary Hunters and Animals Killed in Arizona from 1950–1980

Year	Number of Tags Sold	Hunters Afield	Total Harvest	Percent Success	Season Dates
1950	9,294	7,788	1,344	17.3	3/01–3/31
1951	9,995	8,625	1,851	21.5	3/01–3/31 & 2/15–3/31
1952	12,581	10,496	1,762	16.8	3/01–3/31 & 2/15–3/31
1953	15,095	13,320	2,510	18.9	3/01–3/31
1954	15,299	14,829	2,661	18.5	2/14–2/28
1955	16,832	14,778	3,142	21.3	2/12–2/28
1956	17,644	14,851	2,930	19.7	3/11–2/27
1957	18,724	16,672	2,236	13.4	2/08–2/24
1958	17,156	14,340	2,511	16.4	2/07–2/16
1959	14,279	13,110	3,010	23.0	2/06–2/15
1960	16,070	15,082	3,098	20.5	2/05–2/15
1961	19,817	18,640	4,191	22.5	2/03–2/13
1962	22,678	20,697	4,343	21.0	2/22–3/04
1963	24,940	23,202	4,867	21.0	3/01–3/10
1964	24,653	22,704	5,898	26.0	2/21–3/08 & 2/28–3/08
1965	24,393	22,461	5,231	23.3	2/20–3/07 & 2/27–3/07
1966	25,796	23,446	5,267	22.5	2/26–3/06 & 2/28–3/06
1967	28,386	26,076	5,310	20.4	2/25–3/05 & 2/27–3/05
1968	29,793	27,874	5,082	18.2	2/24–3/06 & 2/26–3/06
1969	32,400	30,226	5,903	19.5	2/22–2/28 & 2/22–3/02
1970	33,062	32,118	6,602	20.6	2/21–2/27
1971	31,208	28,541	5,959	21.1	2/20–2/26
1972	*25,830	21,842	3,966	18.2	2/19–2/25
1973	*25,025	24,983	4,746	23.0	2/17–2/23
1974	*23,645	19,696	5,195	26.4	3/02–3/08
1975	*23,131	19,534	4,793	24.5	3/01–3/07
1976	*22,425	18,758	4,522	24.1	2/28–3/05
1977	*22,050	18,290	4,576	25.0	2/26–3/04
1978	*21,650	17,365	3,594	20.7	2/25–3/03 & 3/04–3/10
1979	*21,884	17,906	4,006	22.4	3/10–3/16 & 3/17–3/23
1980	*20,460	16,604	4,039	24.3	2/28–3/06 3/08–3/14 & 3/14–3/20

*Hunting by permit only according to set number.
SOURCE: Arizona Game and Fish Department, 1968, 1971, 1975, 1976, 1979.

practices now are underway. Day also suggested a "rest-rotation" system of hunting as an alternative for some areas.

The figures in Table 12.1 show good populations of peccaries being maintained rather consistently where the habitat is not being destroyed. They also seem to furnish adequate proof that the game and fish department's management practices are working.

From 1950 through 1980 Arizona's population has increased from 749,587 to 2,717,866.

This rising number of people and the resulting increase in people who want to hunt the collared peccary, led to the department's move in 1972 to assign a certain number of permits to each management unit. The system of inventory and the establishment of hunting season regulations has reached a sophisticated level, and since 1972 the number of hunters has been restricted by a permit system designed to decrease the kill in some areas. The number of tags sold, hunters afield, total harvest, and percent success for Arizona are given in Table 12.1.

The range of the collared peccary in New Mexico is small, and the total number of animals killed by hunters has been low, less than 100 each year between 1973 and 1975 (Pursley 1976). The status of the animal in Texas, the state with the largest populations and largest area of occupied range, is not well defined. This is primarily because of the large amount of private land and the many regulations determined on a county basis; the Texas Parks and Wildlife Department has less control over hunting than do comparable agencies in Arizona and New Mexico. With some local exceptions, in all three states management of the collared peccary has become so refined that legal hunting removes only the number that is not harmful or that can be compensated for by recruitment into the population. The threat to this animal in these states is destruction of habitat.

In 1980 the Arizona Game and Fish Department published a Big Game Strategic Plan for the period 1980 to 1985 (Arizona Game and Fish Department 1980). In this plan the department put forth its goals for management of the herds of collared peccary. It recognized the decline of herds in accessible areas, the influence of development in reducing habitat, the possible effect of unlawful hunting, the clearing of perennial vegetation on some state land, the lack of water, and the effect of range deterioration from livestock grazing as possible influences on collared peccary populations. Its recommendations were aimed at increasing the average herd size to 10 from the 1980 level of 7.5, allowing a maximum annual harvest of 5,000 animals, and increasing hunting with primitive weapons. It also recommended research on several aspects of peccary management.

EPILOGUE

What does the future hold for the peccaries? Over much of their range their habitat is disappearing at a rapid rate; their pelts have become prizes on the world markets, and pursuit by hunters over the majority of their range is uncontrolled. Few inviolate sanctuaries for their perpetuation have been set aside.

Of the three species, the Chacoan peccary or taguá seems to be, by far, the most vulnerable. Comparing the ranges of the three species, we note that the Chacoan peccary occupies an area no larger than the state of North Carolina. It is a wilderness animal that does not appear to be able to survive when roads and trails are cut into the scrub forest.

Its livable environment has narrow temperature and rainfall limits. Its fearless habit of walking into newly built roads to investigate a passing vehicle has been described by Wetzel (1981a) and Sowls (in press). Wetzel (1981a), who first described the Chacoan peccary in 1975, has this to say about the future welfare of the Chacoan peccary:

> Unfortunately for this interesting beast, the native vegetation is being cleared by bulldozers and replaced by Texas-style pasture grass for the modern symbol of prosperity, beef cattle. Thousands of acres of Chaco are now being transformed into pasture which will eventually cause the loss of most of the native mammals. One hope for the Chacoan peccary's survival is that the ranches are huge size and not all ranches can maintain a monoculture of grass at any one time because of the constant pressure of encroaching thorn brush. Another is that at least one nation, Paraguay, has established a national park of more than one million acres in its northern Chaco. If properly patrolled and protected against grazing and poaching, the Parque Nacional de Defensores del Chaco will be a refuge of last resort for the Chacoan peccary and its cohorts. If none of these measures is effective, the Chacoan peccary may disappear within two decades of its discovery.

In spite of its wide range and abundance, the white-lipped peccary has almost escaped any type of biological investigation. Not until Kiltie's (1979) work in Peru had any research been carried out on this interesting animal. Anthropologists studying remote Indian tribes had, for years, more to say about this animal than did biologists. The lack of studies of the white-lipped peccaries can be attributed to the remoteness of the country they inhabit and the difficulty European man had reaching them. In the wholesale destruction of the tropical forests, which are the home of the white-lipped peccary, we may hope that the remoteness that made study so difficult may also make the animals' exploitation and destruction equally difficult.

One of the problems facing the white-lipped peccary is the large amount of land that a herd requires. They apparently follow a circuit pattern of movement, spending less time in one place than does the collared peccary. They have not been known to thrive in second-growth timber areas but only in wilderness areas (Leopold 1966). Large areas of near-primitive forest are required for the white-lipped peccary. Although studies of their reproductive cycle and population dynamics have not been made, it is logical to assume that, like the collared peccary, they have a high reproductive rate if they have sufficient habitat.

Hunting by indigenous people would probably not harm the peccary populations if the habitat was not destroyed. In some areas large blocks of land, which escape conversion for various reasons, could furnish adequate habitat. In Surinam, Schulz et al. (1977) describe the creation of large nature reserves where all wildlife, including peccaries, thrive. Native reserves too could, if large enough and well protected enough, serve as wildlife refuges. For example, in projected land-use patterns for the Brazilian Amazon, Davis (1977) includes an estimated 20,000,000 hectares or 7.7 percent of the total area of land as adequate reserve. Another place where native wildlife, including peccaries, could find a permanent home are biological reserves. Pádua and Quintão (1982) discuss the role of parks and biological preserves in the Brazilian Amazon, pointing out that in 1972 Brazil had 16 national parks and four biological reserves totaling 1.4 million hectares; in 1982 the number had increased to 34 with a total area of 10 million hectares.

Although many Latin American countries have laws to protect wildlife, they are generally not enforced because of the vastness of the country and the scarcity of law enforcement officers. Through the efforts of the World Wildlife Fund, the International Union for the Conservation of Nature, and member nations of the International Convention of International Trade in Endangered Species (CITES), some progress in the reduction of the hide trade has been made. Barrett (1980) and Smith (1976) both believe that hunting pressures on Amazonian wildlife have declined as a result of national and international measures.

While the fate of the Chacoan and white-lipped peccaries depends almost entirely on whether suitable pristine habitat can be saved, the collared peccary has shown that it can survive in a great variety of habitats including cut-over land of regrowth forest. It has demonstrated a wide tolerance for variation in temperature and rainfall patterns and choices of foods. It has a high reproductive rate, and the long continuous record of the annual hunter-kill in Arizona has demonstrated a population vigor that makes it a huntable animal. In the few places where ranchers look at it as a pest, its value in hunter's fees is rapidly changing this attitude. Its future in the American Southwest seems secure.

In the tropical forests of Central and South America there seems no reason why the hardy collared peccary cannot fit into the converted landscapes for many years to come.

In nearly all Latin American countries a few people, through some type of nature organization, are slowly making known the desire to save some of the environment. One hopes that these organizations and individuals will succeed to save a place in the hemisphere for peccaries.

Bibliography

Acosta-Solis, M.
1966. Los Recursos naturales de Ecuador y su conservación. La Porte Tomo II. Los Principales recursos naturales. Instituto Panamericano de Geographia e Historia. Ex-Arzobispo 29, México 18, D.F.

Alicata, J. E.
1931. The occurrence of *Moniezia benedeni* in a peccary. *J. Parasitol.* 19 (1):83.

Alston, E. R.
1879. *Biologia Centrali-Americana.* Taylor and Francis, London. 220 pp.

Altman, M.
1941. The interrelations of the sex cycle and the behavior of the sow. *J. Comp. Phys.* 31:481–98.

Alvarez del Toro, M.
1952. *Los animales silvestres de Chiapas.* Ediciones del Gobierno del Estado, Tuxtla Gutiérrez, Chiapas. 247 pp.

Anon.
1763. *Rudo Ensayo.* By an unknown Jesuit padre. Translated from Spanish by Eusebio Guitéras and published by Amer. Cath. Hist. Soc. Republished by Arizona Silhouettes, 1951.

_____. 1849. *Sketches in natural history of the Mammalia.* Vol. 3. C. Cox. London.

Arizona Game and Fish Department.
1955. Information supporting the 1955 hunting seasons. Phoenix.

_____. 1956–57, 1959–64. Data supporting hunt recommendations. Phoenix.

_____. 1965–66. Information supporting recommendations to the commission for hunting seasons. Phoenix.

————. 1970–71, 1974–76, 1979, 1981. Arizona game management data summary. Phoenix.

————. 1980. Big game strategic plans. Phoenix.

————. 1982. Arizona game survey and harvest data summary. Phoenix. 109 pp.

Armstrong, E. A.
   1947. *Bird display and behavior: an introduction to the study of bird psychology.* Oxford Univ. Press, New York and London. 430 pp.

Asdell, S. A.
   1964. *Patterns of mammalian reproduction.* 2nd Ed. Comstock, Ithaca, N.Y. 670 pp.

Babcock, O. G. and H. E. Ewing.
   1938. A new genus and species of *Anoplura* from the peccary. *Proc. Ent. Soc. Wash.* 40:197–201. [*Pecaroecus javellii*, new species figured and described].

Bailey, V.
   1931. *Mammals of New Mexico.* N. Amer. Fauna No. 53. U.S.D.A. Bur. of Biol. Sur. Wash., D.C. 412 pp.

Baker, R. H. and J. K. Greer.
   1962. *Mammals of the Mexican state of Durango.* Biol. Ser., Mich. State Univ., 2(2):25–154.

Baker, L. N., H. L. Woehling, L. E. Casida, and R. H. Grummer.
   1953. Occurrence of estrus in sows following parturition. *J. Anim. Sci.* 12:33–38.

Balch, D. A. and S. J. Rowland.
   1957. Volatile fatty acids and lactic acid in the rumen of dairy cows receiving a variety of diets. *Br. J. of Nutr.* 11:288–98.

Barrett, R. H.
   1978. The feral hog on the Dye Creek Ranch, California. *Hilgardia* 49:283–355.

Barrett, S. W.
   1980. Conservation in Amazonia. *Biol. Cons.* 18:209–35.

Basso, E. B.
   1973. *The Kalapalo Indians of central Brazil: case studies in cultural anthropology.* Holt, Rinehart and Winston, New York. 157 pp.

Bath, I. H. and J. A. F. Rook.
   1965. The evaluation of cattle foods and diets in terms of the ruminal concentration of volatile fatty acids. II. Roughages and succulents. *J. Agric. Sci.* 64:67–75.

Bauchop, T. and R. W. Martucci.
   1968. Ruminant-like digestion of the langur monkey. *Science* 161:698–99.

Beebe, B. F.
   1980. Pleistocene peccary, *Platygonus compressus* Le Conte,

from Yukon Territory, Canada. *Can. J. Earth Sci.* 17:1204–09.

Beilharz, R. G. and D. F. Cox.
1967. Social dominance in swine. *Anim. Behav.* 15:117–22.

Bennett, C. F., Jr.
1962. *The Bayano Cuna Indians, Panama: an ecological study of livelihood and diet.* Assoc. Amer. Geographers, Annals, 52(1):32–50. Lawrence, Kansas.

Benson, D. A.
1957. Abnormal dentition in white-tailed deer. *J. Mamm.* 38:140.

Bigler, W. J.
1964. The seasonal movements and herd activities of the collared peccary *(Pecari tajacu)* in the Tortolita Mountains. M. S. Thesis, Univ. Arizona, Tucson. 52 pp.

———. 1974. Seasonal movements and activity patterns of the collared peccary. *J. Mamm.* 55:851–55.

Bissonette, J. A.
1976. The relationship of resource quality and availability to social behavior and organization in the collared peccary. Doctoral Dissertation, Univ. Mich. 137 pp.

———. 1978. The influence of extremes of temperatures on activity patterns of peccaries. *The South. Natur.* 23:339–46.

———. 1982. *Ecology and social behavior of the collared peccary in Big Bend National Park.* Serv. Mono. Series. No. 16. U.S. Natl. Park Service. Wash., D. C. 85 pp.

Borrero, J. I.
1967. *Mamiferos neotropicales Universidad del Valle,* Departamento de biologia. 110 pp.

Bourke, J. G.
1891. *On the border with Crook.* Charles Scribner's Sons. 1950 edition by Longe College Book Co., Columbus, Ohio. 491 pp.

Bourliére, F.
1973. The comparative ecology of rain forest mammals in Africa and tropical America: some introductory remarks. *In* Meggars, B. J., E. S. Ayensu, and W. D. Duckworth, Eds. *Tropical forest ecosystems in Africa and South America, a comparative review.* Smith. Inst. Press. Wash. pp. 279–92.

Brennan, J. M. and C. E. Yunker.
1966. The chiggers (Acarina: Trembiculidae) of Panama. *In* Wenzel, R. L. and V. J. Tipton, Eds. *Ectoparasites of Panama.* Field Mus. Nat. Hist., Chicago. pp. 221–66.

Bromley, P. T. and D. W. Kitchen.
1974. Courtship in the pronghorn *(Antilocapra americana). In* Walther, F. and V. Geist, Eds. *The behavior of ungulates and its relation to management.* IUCN. Morges, Switzerland. pp. 356–81.

Brown, W. H., J. W. Stull, and L. K. Sowls.
    1963.   Chemical composition of the milk fat of the collared peccary. *J. Mamm.* 44:112–13.
Brownlee, R. G., R. M. Silverstein, D. Müller-Schwarze, and A. G. Singer.
    1969.   Isolation, identification, and function of the chief component of the male tarsal scent of black-tailed deer. *Nature* 221:284–85.
Buffon, LeConte de.
    1787.   *Historie naturelle. Quadrupedes.* Vol. 8. Aux Deux-Ponts. Chez Sanson and Compagnie.
Byers, J. A.
    1978.   Probable involvement of the preorbital glands in two social behavior patterns of the collared peccary *Dicotyles tajacu*. *J. Mamm.* 59:855–56.
    _____.   1980. Social behavior and its development in the collared peccary, *Tayassu tajacu*. Doctoral Dissertation. Univ. Colorado, Boulder, 185 pp.
Byers, J. A. and M. Bekoff.
    1981.   Social spacing and cooperative behavior of collared peccary, *Tayassu tajacu*. *J. Mamm.* 62:767–85.
Cabrera, A. and J. Yepes.
    1940.   *Historia natural ediar: mamiferos sud-americanos,* Cia. Argentina de Editores, Buenos Aires. 370 pp.
Cardim, F.
    1939.   *Tratados da terra e gente do Brasil.* Serie 5. Brasiliana. Vol. 168. Bibliotheca Pedagogica Brasileira. Companhia. Editoria Nacional. São Paulo, Rio, Recife, Porte Alegre.
Carneiro, R. L.
    1970.   The transition from hunting to horticulture in the Amazon Basin. Proceedings, VIII International Congress of Anthropological and Ethnological Sciences, Tokyo, 1968. Vol. 3, pp. 224–84. Science Council of Japan, Tokyo.
    _____.   1974. Hunting and hunting magic among the Amahuaca of the Peruvian montana. *In* Lyon, P. J., Ed. *Native South Americans, ethnology of the least known continent.* Little, Brown, New York. pp. 122–33.
Carpenter, C. R.
    1964.   *Naturalistic behavior of non-human primates.* Penn. State Univ. Press, Univ. Park. 454 pp.
Carr, W. H.
    1946.   Wild pigs of the desert. *Nat. Hist.* 55:352.
Carroll, E. J. and R. E. Hungate.
    1954.   The magnitude of the microbiological fermentation in the bovine rumen. *Appl. Microbiol.* 2:205–14.

Castellanos, A. H. G.
    1982. Resumen: patrones de movimiento uso de habitat del baquiro de collar, *Tayassu tajacu* L., en los llanos Centrales de Venezuela. Thesis. Faculad de Ciencias, Instituto de Zoología Tropical. U.C.V. Caracas, Venezuela.
Caufield, C.
    1981. How hamburgers destroy forests. *Bus. and Soc. Rev. 39:29–32.*
Caughley, G.
    1966. Mortality patterns in mammals. *Ecology* 47:906–18.
    _____. 1977. *Analysis of vertebrate populations.* John Wiley & Sons, New York. 234 pp.
Chagnon, N. A.
    1977. *The fierce people: case histories in cultural anthropology.* 2nd Ed. Holt, Rinehart and Winston, New York. 174 pp.
Chapman, F. M.
    1936. White-lipped peccary. *Nat. Hist.* 38:408.
Chealum, E. L. and Morton, G. H.
    1942. Techniques used in determining the period of the rut among white-tailed deer in New York state. *Trans. 7th N. Amer. Wildl. Conf.* pp. 334–42.
Chitwood, M. B. and M. Cordero de Campillo.
    1966. *Texicospirura turki* gen. and sp. n. (Nematoda: Spiruroidea) from the stomach of the peccary in the United States, and a key to the genera of Ascaropsinae. *J. Parasitol.* 52(2):307–10.
Church, D. C.
    1969. *Digestive physiology and nutrition of ruminants.* Vol. 1. Dept. An. Sc. Oreg. State Univ., Corvallis. 316 pp.
Church, C. F. and H. N. Church.
    1975. *Bowes' and Church's food values of portions commonly used.* J. B. Lippincott Co. Philadelphia. 197 pp.
Colbert, E. H.
    1933. *An Upper Tertiary peccary from India.* Amer. Mus. Nov. No. 635. 9 pp.
    _____. 1938. *Pliocene peccaries from the Pacific coast region of North America.* Carneg. Inst. Wash. Pub. No. 487. pp. 240–69, pls. 1–6.
    _____. 1980. *Evolution of the vertebrates, a history of the backboned animals through time.* 3rd Ed. John Wiley & Sons, New York. 510 pp.
Cook, W. A.
    1909. *Through the wilderness of Brazil.* Amer. Tract Soc. New York. 487 pp.

Corner, G. W.
    1921.   Cyclic changes in the ovaries and uterus of the sow and
    their relation to the mechanism of implantation. *Contr. Embryol.*
    13:117–46. Carneg. Inst., Wash.
Cowan, I. M.
    1946.   Parasites, diseases, injuries and anomalies of the Colum-
    bian black-tailed deer, *Odocoileus hemionus columbianus*
    (Richardson) in British Columbia. *Can. J. Res.* 24:D:71–103.
————.   1950. Some vital statistics of big game on overstocked
    mountain range. *Trans. 15th N. Amer. Wildl. Conf.* pp. 581–88.
Cumming, D. H. M.
    1975.   *A field study of the ecology and behavior of warthog.*
    Museum Memoir No. 7. Nat. Mus. and Mon. of Rhodesia. Salis-
    bury, Rhodesia. 179 pp.
Cutright, P. R.
    1940.   *The great naturalists explore South America.* The Mac-
    millan Company, New York. 340 pp.
Dalquest, W. W.
    1949.   *The white-lipped peccary in the state of Veracruz, Mexico.*
    Sobretiro de los Anales del Instituto de Biologia, Vol. 20. Mexico. 3 pp.
Dardiri, A. H., R. J. Yedloutschnig, and W. D. Taylor.
    1969.   Clinical and serologic response of American white-collared
    peccaries to African swine fever, foot and mouth disease,
    vesicular stomatitis, vesicular exanthema or swine hog cholera,
    and rinderpest viruses. *Proc. U.S. Animal Health Assoc.* 73:437–52.
Darling, F. F.
    1937.   *A herd of red deer.* Oxford Univ. Press, London. 215 pp.
Davis, Goode P., Jr.
    1982.   *Man and wildlife in Arizona: the American exploration
    period 1824–1865.* Brown, David E. and Neil B. Carmony, Eds.
    Ariz. Game and Fish Dept., Phoenix. 232 pp.
Davis, S. H.
    1977.   *Victims of the miracle.* Cambridge Univ. Press. London.
    169 pp.
Day, G. I.
    1967.   Investigations of factors influencing javelina populations.
    Job. Compl. Rpt. W-78-R-11, WP-4, J-6. Ariz. Game and Fish Dept.,
    Phoenix. 7 pp.
————.   1972. Effect of hunting on javelina populations. Job Compl.
    Rpt. W-78-R-17, WP-2, J-7. Ariz. Game and Fish Dept., Phoenix. 8 pp.
————.   1976. The effect of hunting on a javelina population. Final Rpt.
    Ariz. Game and Fish Dept., Phoenix. Fed. Aid Proj. W-78-R, Work
    Plan 2, Job 7. 16 pp.
————.   1977a. Climate and its relationship to survival of young
    javelina. Final Rpt. W-78-R, WP-2, J-8. Ariz. Game and Fish Dept.,
    Phoenix. 12 pp.

_____. 1977b. Javelina activity patterns. Final Rpt. Ariz. Game and Fish Dept., Phoenix. Fed. Aid Proj. W-78-R. Work Plan 2. Job 9. 13 pp.

_____. 1980. Javelina trapping method. Compl. Rpt. Fed. Aid to Wildl. Rest. Proj. W-78-R. Ariz. Game and Fish Dept., Phoenix. 9 pp.

Deevey, E. S.
1947.   Life tables for natural populations of animals. *Quart. Rev. Biol.* 22:283–314.

De La Tour, G. D.
1949.   *El Desquilibrio de la fauna, retrocesion general, desmucion pronunciada de ciertas especie extincion de algunos, aumento desproporcionado de olran.* Separatum de la revista "Diana." No. 118. 18 pp.

Denevan, W. M.
1966.   The aboriginal cultural geography of the llanos de majos of Bolivia. *Ibero-Americana* 48:1–185.

_____. 1974. Campa subsistence in the Gran Pajonal, Eastern Peru. *In* Lyon, P. J., Ed. *Native South Americans, ethnology of the least known continent.* Little, Brown, New York. pp. 92–110.

_____. 1981. Swiddens and cattle versus forests: the imminent demise of the Amazon rain forest reexamined. *In* Sutlive, V. H., N. Altshuler and M. D. Zamora, Eds. *Where have all the flowers gone? Deforestation in the Third World.* College of William and Mary, Williamsburg, Virginia. pp. 25–44.

Diaz, G. A. C.
1978.   *Social behavior of the collared peccary in captivity.* Ceiba. Escuela Agricola Panamericana. Depto. de Vida Silvestre y Recursos. Tegucigalpa, Honduras. pp. 75–125.

Dobroruka, L. J. and R. Horbowyjova.
1972.   Notes on ethology of collared peccary, *Dicotyles tajacu* (Linnaeus, 1766) in the Prague Zoological Garden. *Lynx, Mus. Nat. Praha* (Series Nova) 13:85–94.

Dominguez G. P., P. Huerta M., and M. Baez R.
1972.   Faunistic study program of Chihuahua, 1972 report. Direccíon general de la fauna silvestre. Subsecretaria forestal y de la fauna. S.A.G.

Donaldson, B.
1967.   Javelina. *In New Mexico wildlife management.* New Mexico Dept. of Game and Fish. pp. 88–94.

Doughty, R. W. and N. Myers.
1971.   Notes on the Amazon wildlife trade. *Biol. Conser.* 3:293–97.

Driesch, A. Von Den.
1976.   *A guide to the measurement of animal bones from archeological sites.* Peabody Mus. Arch. and Ethn. Bull. No. 1. Harvard Univ. Press, Cambridge. 136 pp.

Dyson, R. F.
    1969.   Nutritional investigations with the collared peccary
    (Pecari tajacu). M.S. Thesis, Univ. Ariz., Tucson. 52 pp.
Eads, R. B.
    1951.   A note on the ectoparasites of the javelina, or wild pig,
    Tayassu angulatus (Cope). *J. Parasitol.* 37:317.
Eckstein, P. and S. Zuckerman.
    1956.   The oestrous cycle in the mammalia. *In* Parke, A. S., Ed.
    Marshall's Physiology of Reproduction. Vol. 1, Pt. 1, Chap. 4.
    Longman, Green, London.
Eddy, T. A.
    1959.   Foods of the collared peccary *Pecari tajacu sonoriensis*
    (Mearns) in southern Arizona. M. S. Thesis. Univ. Ariz. Tucson.
    102 pp.
————.   1961. Food and feeding patterns of the collared peccary
    in southern Arizona. *J. Wildl. Manage.* 25:248–57.
Eibl-Eibesfeldt, I.
    1967.   Odour signals as a means of demarcating territory. *In*
    Burkhardt, D., W. Scheidt, and H. Altner, Eds. *Signals in the
    animal world.* George Allen and Unwin, London. pp. 143–44.
Eisenberg, J. F. and M. C. Lockhart.
    1972.   *An ecological reconnaissance of Wilpattu National Park,
    Ceylon.* Smith. Contrib. to Zoo. No. 101.
Eisenberg, J. F. and G. M. McKay.
    1974.   Comparison of ungulate adaptations in the New World
    and the Old World tropical forests with special reference to
    Ceylon and the rain forests of Central America. *In* Geist, W. and
    F. Walther, Eds. *The behaviour of ungulates and its relation to
    management.* IUCN. Morges, Switzerland. pp. 585–602.
Elder, J. B.
    1953.   Utilization of man-made waterholes by wildlife in southern
    Arizona. M.S. Thesis. Univ. Ariz., Tucson. 114 pp.
————.   1956. Watering patterns of some desert game animals. *J.
    Wildl. Manage.* 20:368–78.
Elliott, D. G.
    1905.   *A check list of mammals of the North American continent,
    the West Indies, and neighboring islands.* Field Columbian Mus.
    Pub. No. 105, Zoo. Ser. Vol. 6.
Ellisor, J. E. and W. F. Harwell.
    1969.   Mobility and home range of collared peccary in southern
    Texas. *J. Wildl. Manage.* 33:425–27.
————.   1979. *Ecology and management of javelina in south Texas.*
    F. A. Report Series No. 16. Texas Parks and Wildlife Dept., Austin.
    25 pp.
Emerson, K. C.
    1966.   Mallophaga of the mammals of Panama. *In* Wenzel, R.

L. and V. J. Tipton, Eds. *Ecotoparasites of Panama.* Field Mus. Nat. Hist., Chicago. pp. 267–72.

Enders, R. K.
1930.   Notes on some mammals from Barro Colorado Island, Canal Zone. *J. Mamm.* 11:284–85.
————. 1935. Mammalian life histories from Barro Colorado Island Panama. *Bull. Mus. of Comp. Zoo.* Harvard College 78:383–502.

Epling, G. P.
1956.   Morphology of the scent gland of the javelina. *J. Mamm.* 37:246–48.

Erwin, E. S., G. J. Marco, and E. M. Emery.
1961.   Volatile fatty acids analysis of blood and rumen fluid by gas chromatography. *J. Dairy Sci.* 44:1768.

Eshelman, R. E., E. B. Evenson, and C. W. Hibbard.
1972.   The peccary *Platygonus compressus,* Le Conte, from beneath late Wisconsinan till, Washtenaw County, Michigan. *The Mich. Acad.* 5:243–56.

Espe, D. and V. R. Smith.
1952.   *Secretion of milk.* Iowa State College Press, Ames, Iowa. 291 pp.

Estes, R. D.
1974.   Social organization of the African Bovidae. *In* Geist, V. and F. Walther, Eds. *The behaviour of ungulates and its relation to management.* IUCN. Morges, Switzerland. pp. 166–205.

Etkin, W. T.
1963.   Cooperation and competition in social behavior. *In* Etkin, W. T., Ed. *Social behavior and organization among vertebrates.* Univ. Chicago Press, Chicago. 307 pp.

Everitt, J. H., C. L. Gonzalez, M. A. Alaniz, and G. V. Latigo.
1981.   Food habits of the collared peccary on south Texas rangelands. *J. Range Manage.* 34:141–44.

Ewer, R. F.
1958.   Adaptive features in the skulls of African Suidae. *Proc. Zoo. Soc. Lond.* 131:135–55.
————. 1968. *Ethology of mammals.* New York, Plenum Press. London, Logos Press. 418 pp.

Ewing, H. E.
1924.   On the taxonomy, biology, and distribution of the biting lice of the family Gyropidae. *Proc. U.S. Nat. Mus.* 63 20:1–42.

Fairchild, G. B., G. M. Kohls, and V. J. Tipton.
1966.   The ticks of Panama (Acarina: Ixodoidea). *In* Wenzel, R. L. and V. J. Tipton, Eds. *Ectoparasites of Panama.* Field Mus. Nat. Hist., Chicago. pp. 167–219.

Farabee, W. C.
1922.   *Indian tribes of eastern Peru.* Papers, Peabody Mus. Amer. Arch. and Ethn., Vol. 10. Harvard Univ., Cambridge. 194 pp.

Fejos, Paul.
    1943.   *Ethnology of the Yagua*. Viking Fund, New York. 144 pp.
Field, C. R.
    1968.   A comparative study of the food habits of some wild
    ungulates in the Queen Elizabeth National Park, Uganda. Prel.
    Rpt. *In* Crawford, M. A., Ed. *Comparative nutrition of wild animals*.
    Symp. Zool. Soc. Hand. No. 21:135–51.
    ———. 1970. Observations on the food habits of tame warthog and
    antelope in Uganda. *E. Afr. Wildl. J.* 8:1–17.
    ———. 1972. The food habits of wild ungulates in Uganda by analyses
    of stomach contents. *E. Afr. Wildl. J.* 10:17–42.
Findley, J. S., A. H. Harris, D. E. Wilson, and C. Jones.
    1975.   *Mammals of New Mexico*. Univ. New Mexico Press,
    Albuquerque. 360 pp.
Finley, I.
    1947.   A fierce little pig. *Nature* 4:358.
Frädrich, H.
    1965.   Zur Biologie und Ethologie des Warzenschweines (*Phaco-
    choerus aethiopicus*, Pallas), unter Berücksichtigung des Ver-
    haltens anderer Suiden. *Zeit. Tierpsychol.* 22:328–93.
    ———. 1967. Das Verhalten der Schweine (Suidae, Tayassuidae)
    und Flusspferde (Hippopotamidae). *Hdb. d. Zool.* 10(26):1–44.
Franklin, W. L.
    1974.   The social behavior of the vicuña. *In* Geist, V. and F.
    Walther, Eds. *The behaviour of ungulates and its relation to
    management*. IUCN. Morges, Switzerland. pp. 477–87.
French, C. E., L. C. McEwen, N. D. Magruder, R. H. Ingram,
and R. W. Swift.
    1956.   Nutrient requirements for growth and antler development
    in the white-tailed deer. *J. Wildl. Manage.* 20:221–32.
Furneaux, R.
    1969.   *The Amazon, the story of a great river*. G. P. Putnam's
    Sons, New York. 258 pp.
Gasaway, W. C.
    1976a.   Volatile fatty acid and metabolizable energy derived from
    cecal fermentation in the willow ptarmigan. *Comp. Biochem.
    Physiol.* 53A:115–21.
    ———. 1976b. Seasonal variation in diet, volatile fatty acid produc-
    tion and size of the cecum in rock ptarmigan. *Comp. Biochem.
    Physiol.* 53A:109–14.
Gaumer, G. F.
    1917.   *Monographia de los mammiferos de Yucatán*. Secretaria
    de Fomento, Departamento de talleres Fomento, Graficos, Mexico.
    331 pp.
Geist, V.
    1964.   On the rutting behavior of the mountain goat. *J. Mamm.*

45:551–67.

―――. 1966. The evolution of horn-like organs. *Behaviour* 27:12–213.

―――. 1971. *Mountain sheep: a study in behavior and evolution.* Univ. of Chicago Press, Chicago. 383 pp.

―――. 1974. On the relationship of social evolution and ecology in ungulates. *Amer. Zool.* 14:205–20.

Geist, V., and F. Walther.
1974. General introduction. *In* Geist, V., and F. Walther, Eds. *The behaviour of ungulates and its relation to management.* IUCN. Morges, Switzerland.

Getty, R.
1975. Sisson and Grossman's *The anatomy of domestic animals.* 5th Ed., with ed. coord. by C. E. Rosenbaum, N. G. Ghoshal and D. Hillman. Saunders, Philadelphia. 209 pp.

Gillin, J.
1948. Tribes of the Guianas and the left Amazon tributaries. *In* Steward, J. H., Ed. *Handbook of South American Indians.* Smith. Inst. Bur. Amer. Ethn. Bull. 143. pp. 799–860.

Giannoni, M. A. and I. Ferrari.
1976. Estudo biométrico do cariótipo da espécie *Tayassu albirostris. Rev. Ciênc. Cult.* 28(4):432–35.

Goldman, F. A.
1920. *Mammals of Panama.* Misc. Coll., Vol. 69, No. 5. 309 pp.

Goldman, I.
1948. Tribes of the Uapupes-Caqueta region. *In* Steward, J. H., Ed. *Handbook of South American Indians.* Smith. Inst. Bur. Amer. Ethn. Bull. 143. pp. 763–98.

Goodwin, G. G.
1946. Mammals of Costa Rica. *Bull. Amer. Mus. Nat. Hist.* 87(5):271–474.

Gordon, L.
1957. Human geography and ecology in the Sinú country of Columbia. *Ibero-Americana* 39:1–136.

Gorham, J. R.
1973. The Paraguayan Chaco and its rainfall. *In* Gorham, J. R., Ed. *Paraguay: ecological essays.* Acad. of Arts and Sciences, Miami. pp. 39–60.

Grant, C.
1916. Big game of the Texas border. *N.Y. Zool. Soc. Bull.* pp. 1386–87.

Grimwood, I. R.
1968. *Notes on the distribution and status of some Peruvian mammals.* IUCN. 1110, Morges, Switzerland. 85 pp.

Grubb, W. B.
1911. *An unknown people in an unknown land.* Seeley and Co., London. 330 pp.

Guilday, J. E., H. W. Hamilton, and A. D. McCrady.
  1971.   The Welsh cave peccaries *(Platygonus)* and associated fauna, Kentucky Pleistocene. *Annals of Carneg. Mus.,* Vol. 43, Art. 9, pp. 249–320.
Grzimek, B.
  1968.   *Grzimek's Tierleben, Enzyklopädie des Tierreiches,* Vol. 13. Kindler Verlag, Zurich.
Hafez, E. S. E. and I P. Signoret.
  1969.   The behavior of swine. *In* Hafez, E. S. E., Ed. *The behavior of domestic animals.* 2nd. Ed. Williams and Wilkins, Baltimore. pp. 349–90.
Hagen, H. L.
  1951.   Composition of deer milk. *Calif. Fish and Game* 37: 217–18.
Hall, E. R.
  1981.   *The mammals of North America.* 2nd. Ed., Vol. 2. John Wiley and Sons. New York. 1181 pp.
Halloran, A.
  1945.   Five fetuses for *Pecari angulatus* from Arizona. *J. Mamm.* 26:434.
Hamblin, N. L.
  1980.   Animal utilization by the Cozumel Maya: interpretation through faunal analysis. Doctoral Dissertation. Univ. Ariz., Tucson. 349 pp.
Handley, C. O., Jr.
  1950.   Game mammals of Guatemala. *In* Saunders, G. B., A. D. Holloway, and C. O. Handley. *A fish and wildlife survey of Guatemala.* Spec. Rpt. Wildl. U.S. Fish and Wildl. Serv. Wash., D.C. pp. 141–62.
Harner, M. J.
  1973.   *The Jivaro: people of the sacred waterfalls.* 1973 edition by Anchor Books. Anchor Press/Doubleday, Garden City, New York. 233 pp.
Hauge, T. M. and L. B. Keith.
  1981.   Dynamics of moose populations in northeastern Alberta. *J. Wildl. Manage.* 45:573–97.
Hawkes, K., K. Hill, and J. F. O'Connell.
  1982.   Why hunters gather: optimal foraging and the Aché of eastern Paraguay. *Amer. Ethologist* 9:379–98.
Hay, O. P.
  1923.   *The Pleistocene of North America and its vertebrated animals from the states east of the Mississippi River and from the Canadian Provinces east of longitude 95°.* Carneg. Inst. Wash. Pub. No. 322. 499 pp.
———.   1924. *The Pleistocene of the middle region of North America*

and its vertebrated animals. Carneg. Inst. Wash. Pub. No. 322A. 385 pp.

———. 1927. *The Pleistocene of the western region of North America and its vertebrated animals.* Carneg. Inst. Wash. Pub. No. 322B. 346 pp.

Hayer, W. T
1961. Cellulose digestion in the javelina. Unpub. Ms. Dept. Zoo., Univ. Ariz., Tucson. 6 pp.

Hecht, S. B.
1980. Deforestation in the Amazon basin: magnitude, dynamics and soil resource effects. *In* Sutlive, V. H., N. Altshuler, and M. D. Zamora. *Where have all the flowers gone? Deforestation in the Third World.* College of William and Mary, Williamsburg, Virginia. pp. 61–108.

Hediger, H.
1949. Säugetier-Territorien und ihre Markierung Bijdr. *Dierkunde* 28:172–84.

———. 1950. *Wild animals in captivity.* Butterworth Scient. Publ., London. 207 pp.

Hendey, Q. B.
1976. Fossil peccary from the Pliocene of South Africa. *Science* 192:787–89.

Herring, S. W.
1972. The role of canine morphology in the evolutionary divergence of pigs and peccaries. *J. Mamm.* 53:500–12.

Hershkovitz, P.
1972. The recent mammals of the Neotropical region: a zoogeographic and ecological review. *In* Keast, A., F. C. Erk, and B. Glass, Eds. *Evolution, mammals and southern continents.* State Univ. of New York Press, Albany. pp. 311–41.

Hibbard, C. W.
1941. Mammals of the Rexroad fauna from the Upper Pliocene of southwestern Kansas. *Ibid.* 44:265–313, pls. 1–4.

Hickey, J. J.
1952. *Survival studies of banded birds.* Spec. Sci. Rpt. Wildl. No. 15. U.S. Fish and Wildl. Serv. Wash., D.C. 177 pp.

Hildebrand, M.
1960. How animals run. *Sci. Amer.* 202(May):148–57.

———. 1962. Walking, running, and jumping. *Amer. Zoo.* 2:151–55.

Hill, C. A.
1970. The great peccary headache. *Zoonooz* 43:11:12–18.

Hochbaum, H. A.
1944. *The canvasback on a prairie marsh.* Amer. Wildl. Inst., Wash., D.C. 201 pp.

Hodgkinson, A.
  1977. *Oxalic acid in biology and medicine.* Academic Press,
  New York. 325 pp.
Holman, J. A.
  1975. *Michigan's fossil vertebrates.* Educ. Bull. No. 2. Michigan
  State Univ., East Lansing. 54 pp.
Holmberg, A.
  1948. The Sirionó. *In* Steward, J. H., Ed. *Handbook of South
  American Indians.* Smith. Inst. Bur. Amer. Ethn. Bull. 143. pp.
  455–63.
Hornaday, W. T.
  1908. *Camp-fires on desert and lava.* Scribner's Sons. 362 pp.
Hsu, T. C. and K. Benirschke.
  1969. *An atlas of mammalian chromosomes.* Vol. 8, Folio 388.
  Springer-Verlag, New York.
Hungate, R. D.
  1966. *The rumen and its microbes.* Academic Press, New York.
  533 pp.
Hunter, W. P. (Ed.).
  1838. *Natural history of the quadrupeds of Paraguay and the
  River La Plata.* Translated from Spanish of Don Felix de Azara.
  A. and C. Black, Edinburgh. 340 pp.
Husson, A. M.
  1978. *The mammals of Surinam.* Brill, Leiden. 729 pp.
Hvidberg-Hansen, H.
  1970A. Utilization of the collared peccary (*Tayassu tajacu* Linn.)
  in Peru. FAO Forestry Research and Training Project. UNDP/SF.
  No. 116. La Molina, Peru. 9 pp.
  _____. 1970b. Utilization of the white-lipped peccary (*Tayassu
  albirostis* Illinger) in Peru. FAO Forestry Research and Training
  Project. UNDP/SF. No. 116. La Molina, Peru. 9 pp.
Ibarra, J. A.
  1959. *Apuntes de historia natural y mamiferos de Guatemala.*
  Editorial del Ministerio de Educacíon Publica. Jose de Pineda
  Ibarra, Guatemala, Central America. 201 pp.
Ichponani, J. S. and G. S. Sidhv.
  1965. *Indian J. Vet. Sci.* 35:316.
Ihering, R. von.
  1968. *Dicionario dos animais do Brasil.* Pref. de Zeferino Vaz.
  Brasilia, Ed. Universidade. 790 pp.
Inglis, J. M.
  1964. *A history of vegetation on the Rio Grande Plain.* Bull.
  No. 45, Texas Parks and Wildlife Department. Austin. 122 pp.
Institute Nutrition of Central America and Panama.
  1961. Food comparison table for Latin American countries,
  Sponsored by the I.N.C.A.P. Guatemala City.

International Zoo Yearbook. 1959–1962, 1965–1980. Vols. 1–20. Zoological Society London, London.

Jacobsen, N. A.
1941. Occurrence of the genus *Balantidium* in javelina. Arizona P-R, 9-R. Transcript in files of Arizona Game and Fish Dept. Phoenix.

Jamieson, N. D.
1959. Rumen nitrate metabolism and the changes occurring in the composition of the rumen volatile fatty acids of grazing sheep. *New Zealand J. Agric. Res.* 2:314–28.

Jennings, W. S. and J. T. Harris.
1953. The collared peccary in Texas. FA Report Series No. 12. Texas Game and Fish Commission. 31 pp.

Jewell, P. A.
1966. The concept of home range in mammals. *In* Jewell, P. A. and C. Loizos, Eds. *Play, exploration and territory in mammals.* Zoo. Soc. London, Symp. No. 18. London. pp. 85–109.

Jordan, K. and N. C. Rothschild.
1923. New American Siphonaptera. (Description of *Pulex procinus* from *Pecari* in Texas.) *Ectoparasites* 1:309–19.

Joseph, E. L.
1970. *History of Trinidad.* Frank Cass & Co. Ltd., London. 272 pp.

Karsten, R.
1935. *Head hunters of the Amazon.* Socictas Scientiarum Fermica. Comm. Humanarium. Litt. VII 1. Helsinki. 598 pp.

Kaufman, J. H.
1962. Ecology and social behavior of the coati, *Nasua narica*, on Barro Colorado Island, Panama. *Univ. Calif. Publ. Zoo.* 60:95–222.

Kelsall, J. P.
1968. *The migratory barren-ground caribou of Canada.* Canad. Wildl. Serv., Ottawa. 340 pp.

Kerr, M. A.
1965. The age of sexual maturity in male impala. *Arnoldia* 24:1–6.

Kiltie, R. A.
1979. Seed predation and group size in rain forest peccaries. Doctoral Dissertation. Princeton Univ., Princeton.
————. 1980. More on Amazon cultural ecology. *Current Anthropology* 21:541–46.
————. 1981a. Distribution of palm fruits on a rain forest floor: why white-lipped peccaries forage near objects. *Biotropica* 13:141–45.
————. 1981b. The function of interlocking canines in rain forest peccaries (Tayassuidae). *J. Mamm.* 62:459–69.

Kirchoff, P.
1948. The Warrau. *In* Steward, J. H., Ed. *Handbook of South American Indians.* Smith. Inst. Bur. Amer. Ethn. Bull. 143. pp. 869–81.

Kirkpatrick, R. D. and L. K. Sowls.
    1962.   Age determination of the collared peccary by the tooth-replacement pattern. *J. Wildl. Manage.* 26:214–17.
Kitts, W. D., I. Mct. Cowan, J. Bandy, and A. J. Wood.
    1956.   The immediate post-natal growth in the Columbian black-tailed deer in relation to the composition of the milk of the doe. *J. Wildl. Manage.* 20:212–14.
Kleiman, D.
    1966.   Scent marking in the Canidae. *In* Jewell, P. A. and C. Loizos, Eds. *Play, exploration and territory in mammals.* Zoo. Soc. London. Symp. No. 18. London. pp. 167–78.
Klein, E. H. and A. M. Fujino.
    1977.   *Mamiferos de Honduras.* Dept. de Vida Silvestre, Comayaguela, D. C. 91 pp.
Knight, M. A., B. L. Reid, J. I. Forcier, C. M. Donisi, and M. Cooper.
    1969.   Nutritional influences of Mexican-American foods in Arizona. *J. Amer. Diet. Assoc.* 55:557–61.
Knipe, T.
    1957.   *The javelina in Arizona.* Wildl. Bull. No. 2. Ariz. Game and Fish Department. 96 pp.
Koford, C. B.
    1957.   The vicuña and the puña. *Ecol. Mono.* 27:153–219.
Krausman, P. R.
    1980.   *Ecology of the Carmen Mountains white-tailed deer.* Natl. Park. Serv. Wildl. Mono. Ser. No. 15. 162 pp.
Lamprey, H. F.
    1963.   Ecological separation of the large mammal species in the Tarangire Game Reserve, Tanganyika. *E. Afr. Wildl. J.* 1:63–92.
Langer, P.
    1973.   Vergleichend-anatomische Untersuchungen am Magen der Artiodactyla (Owen, 1848). *Gegenbaurs Morph. Jahrb.* 119: 514–561 and 633–95.
_____.   1974. Stomach evolution in the Artiodactyla. *Mammalia* 38:(2): pp. 295–314.
_____.   1978. Anatomy of the stomach of the collared peccary *Dicotyles tajacu* (L. 1758) (Artiodactyla: Mammalia). *Sonderdruck aus Z. f. Saügetierkunde* Bd 43 H. 1, S. 42–59.
_____.   1979. Adaptational significance of the forestomach of the collared peccary, *Dicotyles tajacu* (L. 1758) (Mammalia: Artiodactyla). *Mammalia* 43:235–45.
Lathrop, D. W.
    1970.   *The Upper Amazon.* Praeger, New York. 256 pp.
Laws, R. M.
    1952.   The new method of age determination for mammals. *Nature* 169(4310):972–73.

———. 1953. A new method of age determination in mammals, with special reference to the elephant seal *(Mirounga leonina* Linn.) Falkland Isls. *Dependencies Surv. Sci. Report.* 11 pp.

Leidy, J.
1889.   *On Platygonus, an extinct genus allied to the peccaries.* Trans. Wagner Free Inst. Sci. Philadephia, Vol. 2, pp. 41–50, pl. 8.

Leopold, A.
1933.   *Game management.* Charles Scribner's Sons, New York and London. 481 pp.

Leopold, A. S.
1959.   *Wildlife of Mexico, the game birds and mammals.* Univ. of Calif. Press, Berkeley and Los Angeles. 568 pp.

———. 1966. Adaptability of animals to habitat change. *In* F. F. Darling and J. P. Milton, Eds. *Future environments of North America.* The Conservation Foundation and Doubleday. pp. 69–81.

Leuthold, W.
1977.   *African ungulates: a comparative review of their ethology and behavioral ecology.* Springer-Verlag, Berlin, New York. 307 pp.

Levi-Strauss, C.
1948.   The Tupi-Cawabib. *In* Steward, J. H., Ed. *Handbook of South American Indians.* Smith. Inst. Bur. Amer. Ethn. Bull. 143. pp. 299–305.

Lewis, G. E.
1970.   New discoveries of Pleistocene bison and peccaries in Colorado. *U.S. Geol. Surv. Prof. Paper* 700 B. 137–40.

Ligon, J. S.
1927.   *Wildlife of New Mexico: its conservation and management.* New Mexico Game and Fish Department, Sante Fe. 212 pp.

Lindsay, E. H. and N. T. Tessman.
1974.   Cenozoic vertebrate localities and faunas of Arizona. *J. Ariz. Acad. Sci.* 9:3–24.

Lipkind, W.
1948.   The Caraja. *In* Steward, J. H., Ed. *Handbook of South American Indians.* Smith. Inst. Bur. Amer. Ethn. Bull. 143. pp. 179–91.

Loizos, C.
1966.   Play in mammals. *In* Jewell, P. A. and C. Loizos, Eds. *Play, exploration and territory in mammals.* Zoo. Soc. London. Symp. No. 18. London. pp. 1–9.

Lorenz, K.
1945.   *Man meets dog.* Methuen, London.

———. 1970. *Studies in animal and human behavior.* Vol. 1. Translated by R. Martin. Harvard Univ. Press, Cambridge. 403 pp.

———. 1971. *Studies in animal and human behavior.* Vol. 2. Translated by R. Martin. Harvard Univ. Press, Cambridge. 403 pp.

Lott, D. F.
———. 1974.   Sexual and aggressive behavior of adult male American
bison *(Bison bison). In* Geist, V. and F. Walther, Eds. *The behaviour
of ungulates and its relation to management.* IUCN. Morges,
Switzerland. pp. 382–94.

Low, W. A.
1970.   The influence of aridity on reproduction of the collared
peccary [*Dicotyles tajacu* (Linn)] in Texas. Doctoral Dissertation,
Univ. of British Columbia, Vancouver. 170 pp.

Low, W. A. and I. M. Cowan.
1963.   Age determination of deer by annular structure of dental
cementum. *J. Wildl. Manage.* 27:466–71.

Lowe, V. P. W.
1967.   Teeth as indicators of age with special reference to red
deer. *(Cervus elaphus)* of known age from Rhum. *J. Zool., London.*
152:137–53.

Lowie, R. H.
1946.   The Bororo. *In* Steward, J. H., Ed. *Handbook of South
American Indians.* The Marginal Tribes. Smith. Inst. Bur. Amer.
Ethn. Bull. 143. pp. 419–34.

Lundelius, E. L., Jr.
1967.   Late-Pleistocene and Holocene faunal history of central
Texas. *In* Martin, P. S. and H. E. Wright, Jr. *Pleistocene extinc-
tions, the search for a cause.* Yale Univ. Press, New Haven and
London. pp. 287–319.

Lutwak-Mann, C.
1962.   The influence of nutrition on the ovary. *In* Zuckerman,
S., P. Eckstein, and A. M. Mandl, Eds. *The ovary.* Vol. 2. Academic
Press, London and New York. pp. 291–315.

McCabe, R. A., and A. S. Leopold.
1951.   Breeding season of the Sonora white-tailed deer. *J. Wildl.
Manage.* 15:433–34.

McCullough, C. Y.
1955.   Breeding record of javelina, *Tayassu angulatus,* in Arizona.
J. Mamm. 36:146.

McDaniel, B., R. D. Barnes, and W. Low.
1966.   Recent collections of the giant sucking louse, *Pecaroecus
javalli* Babcock and Ewing, from the type locality. *Ent. Soc. Wash.
Proc.* 68(4):330–31.

McDonald, D. R.
1977.   Food taboos: A primitive environmental protection agency
(South America). *Anthropos* 72:734–48.

McDonald, L. E. and B. L. Lasley.
1978.   Infertility in a captive group of white-lipped peccaries.
J. Zoo. An. Med. 9:90–95.

McDowell, L. R., J. H. Conrad. J. Thomas, and L. Harris.
 1974. *Latin American tables of feed composition.* Univ. Presses of Fla., Gainesville.

McGee, W. J.
 1895-1896. *The Seri Indians.* Bur. Amer. Ethn. Rept. No. 17.

McHugh, T.
 1958. Social behavior of the American buffalo. *Zoologica* 43:1-40
 _____. 1972. *The time of the buffalo.* Alfred A. Knopf. 339 pp.

McIntosh, A.
 1931. A new species of tick from the Texas peccary. *J. Parasitol.* 18:124.
 _____. 1932. Description of a tick, *Dermacentor halli,* from the Texas peccary, with a key to the North American species of *Dermacentor. Proc. U.S. Natl. Mus.* 82(4):1-8.

Mansell, D. W.
 1974. Productivity of white-tailed deer on the Bruce Peninsula. *J. Wildl. Manage.* 38:808-14.

Martin, R. A. and S. D. Webb.
 1974. Late Pleistocene mammals from the Devil's Den fauna, Levy County. *In* Webb. S. D., Ed. *Pleistocene mammals of Florida.* Univ. Presses of Fla., Gainesville. pp. 140-45.

Mayer, J. J. and P. N. Brandt.
 1982. Identity, distribution, and natural history of the peccaries, Tayassuidae. *In* Mares, M. A. and H. H. Genoways, Eds. *Mammalian biology in South America.* Univ. of Pittsburgh Press, Pittsburgh. pp. 547-84.

Mearns, E. A.
 1907. Mammals of the Mexican boundary of the United States. *U.S. Natl. Mus. Bull.* 56, Part 1. Smith. Inst. pp. 1-530.

Mech, L. D.
 1966. *The wolves of Isle Royale.* Fauna Series. U.S. Natl. Park Serv. 210 pp.

Meggars, B. J.
 1971. *Amazonia, man and culture in a counterfeit paradise.* Aldine-Atherton, Chicago and New York. 182 pp.
 _____. 1973. Some problems of cultural adaptation in Amazonia, with emphasis on the pre-European period. *In* Meggars, B. J., E. Ayensu, and W. D. Duckworth, Eds. *Tropical forest ecosystems in Africa and South America, a comparative review.* Smith. Inst. pp. 311-20.

Mendez, E.
 1970. *Los principales mamiferos silvestres de Panama.* Zoologío de laboratorio commemorativo gorgas; miembros de la Comission Nacional de Protecíon de la Fauna Silvestres Panama. 283 pp.

Métraux, A.

1946a.   Indians of the Gran Chaco. *In* Steward, J. H., Ed. *Handbook of South American Indians.* Smith. Inst. Bur. Amer. Ethn. Bull. 143. pp. 197–380.

————.   1946b. Indians of the Gran Chaco. The Caingang. *In* Steward, J. H., Ed. *Handbook of South American Indians.* Smith. Inst. Bur. Ethn. Bull. 143. pp. 445–75.

————.   1948a. The Guaraní. *In* Steward, J. H., Ed. *Handbook of South American Indians.* Smith. Inst. Bur. Amer. Ethn. Bull. 143, pp. 69–94.

————.   1948b. The Yucucare. Tribes of the eastern slopes of the Bolivian Andes. *In* Steward, J. H., Ed. *Handbook of South American Indians.* Smith. Inst. Bur. Amer. Ethn. Bull. 143, pp. 465–506.

————.   1948c. Tribes of the Jura-Purus Basins. Tribes of the Western Amazon Basin. *In* Steward, J. H., Ed. *Handbook of South American Indians.* Smith. Inst. Bur. Amer. Ethn. Bull. 143, pp. 657–86.

Miller, D. F.

1958.   *Composition of cereal grains and forages.* Natl. Acad. Sci. Nat. Res. Council. Wash., D. C. 663 pp.

Miller, F. W.

1930.   Notes on some mammals of southern Matto Grosso, Brazil. *J. Mamm.* 11:18.

Miller, G. S. and R. Kellogg.

1955.   *List of North American recent mammals.* Bull. 205. Smith. Inst. Wash., D. C. 954 pp.

Minnamon, P. J.

1962.   The home range of the collared peccary, *Pecari tajacu* (Mearns), in the Tucson Mountains. M.S. Thesis, Univ. Ariz., Tucson. 42 pp.

Mohr, E.

1961.   Willkurlich Betatigung der Ruchendruse beim Halsband-Pekari. *Zeit. Säugetierk.* 26:57.

Moir, R. J., M. Somers, and H. Waring.

1956.   Studies on marsupial nutrition. I. Ruminant-like digestion in a herbivorus marsupial (*Setonix brachyurus* Quoy & Gaimard). *Austr. J. Sci. Res., Ser. B, Biol. Sci.* 9:293–304.

Morrison, F. B.

1954.   *Feeds and feeding.* The Morrison Pub. Co., Ithaca, N.Y. 1207 pp.

Morrison, J. A., C. E. Trainer, and P. L. Wright.

1959.   Breeding season in elk as determined by known age embryos. *J. Wildl. Manage.* 23:27–34.

Müller-Schwarze, D.

1971.   Pheromones in black-tailed deer (*Odocoileus hemionus columbianus*). *Animal Behavior* 19:141–52.

————.   1974. Social functions of various scent glands in ungulates and the problems encountered in experimental studies of scent communication. *In* Geist, V. and F. Walther, Eds., *The behaviour of ungulates and its relation to management.* IUCN. Morges, Switzerland. pp. 107–13.

Murie, A.

1935. *Mammals from Guatemala and British Honduras.* Univ. Mich. Mus. Zool. Misc. Publ. No. 26. Ann Arbor.

_____. 1944. *The wolves of Mt. McKinley.* Fauna Series No. 5. U.S. Natl. Park Serv. 238 pp.

Murie, O. J.

1951. *The elk of North America.* The Stackpole Co., Harrisburg, Penn. 376 pp.

Murphy, R. F.

1960. *Headhunters heritage: social and economic change among the Mundurucú Indians.* Univ. Calif. Press. Berkeley and Los Angeles. 202 pp.

Murphy, Y. and R. F. Murphy.

1974. *Women of the forest.* Columbia Univ. Press. New York. 230 pp.

Myers, N.

1980. *Conversion of tropical moist forests.* Natl. Acad. Sci., Wash., D.C. 205 pp.

_____. 1981. The hamburger connection: how Central America's forests become North America's hamburgers. *Ambio* 10:3–8.

Nalbandov, A. V.

1964. *Reproductive physiology.* 2nd Ed. W. H. Freeman, San Francisco and London. 316 pp.

Neal, B. J.

1957. Techniques for trapping and tagging the collared peccary. *J. Wildl. Manage.* 23:11–16.

_____. 1959. A contribution on the life history of the collared peccary in Arizona. *Amer. Midl. Nat.* 61:177–90.

Neal, B. J. and R. D. Kirkpatrick.

1957. Anomalous canine tooth development in an Arizona peccary. *J. Mamm.* 38:420.

Nelson, E. W.

1918. *Wild animals of North America.* Natl. Geo. Soc., Wash., D.C. 227 pp.

Nichol, A. A.

1936. Large game mammals. *In* Arizona and its heritage. *Univ. Ariz. Bull.* 7(3):60–74.

Nietschmann, B.

1971. The substance of subsistence. *In* Lentnek, B., R. L. Carmin, and T. L. Martinson. *Geographic research on Latin America.* Benchmark. 1970. Ball State Univ., Muncie, Ind. pp. 167–81.

_____. 1972. Hunting and fishing focus among the Miskito Indian of eastern Nicaragua. *Human Ecology* 1:41–67.

Nogueira-Neto, P.
　　1973.　*A Criacão de animais indígenas vertebrados.* Edições
　　Tecnapis. São Paulo, Brasíl. 327 pp.
O'Connor, J.
　　1939.　*Game in the desert.* The Derrydale Press, New York.
　　264 pp.
Oh, H. K., T. Sakai, M. B. Jones, and W. M. Longhurst.
　　1967.　Effect of various essential oils isolated from Douglas-fir
　　needles upon sheep and deer rumen microbial activity. *Appl.
　　Microbiol.* 15:777–84.
Oh, H. K., M. B. Jones, and W. M. Longhurst.
　　1968.　Comparison of rumen microbial inhibition resulting from
　　various essential oils isolated from relatively unpalatable plant
　　species. *Appl. Microbiol.* 16:39–44.
Ojeda, R. A. and M. A. Mares.
　　1982.　Conservation of South American mammals: Argentina as
　　paradigm. *In* Mares, M. A. and H. H. Genoways Eds. *Mammalian
　　biology in South America.* Vol. 6. Spec. Pub. Ser. Pymatuning Lab.
　　of Ecol. Univ. Pittsburgh, Pittsburgh.
Olin, G.
　　1959.　*Animals of the American Southwest.* Southwest Monu-
　　ments Assoc. Globe, Ariz. 112 pp.
Olsen, O. W.
　　1974.　*Animal parasites, their life cycles, and ecology.* 3rd Ed.,
　　Univ. Park Press, Baltimore. 562 pp.
Opler, M.
　　1941.　*The Apache life-way, the economics, social and religious
　　institutions of the Chiricahua Indians.* Univ. Chicago Press,
　　Chicago. 500 pp.
Orellana, A. de.
　　1906.　Carta del Padre Antonio de Orellana, sobre el origen de
　　las misiones de Mojos, 18 Octubre, 1687, in Maurtua, 1906a.
　　10:1–24.
Orr, N.
　　1974.　The prickly pear cactus used as a vegetable today. School
　　of Home Economics. Univ. Ariz., Tucson. (Unpublished).
Orton, J.
　　1876.　*The Andes and the Amazon: or across the continent of
　　South America.* Including notes of a second journey across the
　　continent from Para to Lima and Lake Titicaca. 3rd Ed. Harper
　　and Brothers, New York. 645 pp.
Owen-Smith, R.
　　1974.　The social system of the white rhinoceros. *In* Geist, V.
　　and F. Walther, Eds. *The behaviour of ungulates and its relation
　　to management.* IUCN, Morges, Switzerland. pp. 341–51.

Pádua, M. T. J., and A. T. B. Quintão.
    1982.   Parks and biological reserves in the Brazilian Amazon. *Ambio* 11:309–14.
Pearson, H. S.
    1927.   On the skulls of early Tertiary Suidae, together with an account of the otic region in some other Artiodactyla. *Phil. Trans. R. Soc. London,* Vol. 215, Ser. B: 389–462.
Phelps, J. S.
    1971.   Behavioral thermoregulation in the javelina (*Tayassu tajacu*). M. S. Thesis, Univ. Ariz., Tucson. 34 pp.
Pursley, D.
    1976.   Javelina hunt information and population trend. Work Plan 12, Job 1. New Mexico Dept. Game and Fish. 2 pp.
Ralls, K.
    1974.   Scent marking in captive Maxwell's duikers. *In* Geist, V. and F. Walther, Eds. *Behaviour of ungulates and its relation to management.* IUCN. Morges, Switzerland. pp. 114–23.
Raven, P. H.
    1981.   Tropical rain forests: a global responsibility. *Nat. Hist.* 90:28–32.
Ray, C. E., C. S. Denny, and M. Rubin.
    1970.   A peccary, *Platygonus compressus* Lo Conte, from drift of Wisconsin age in northern Pennsylvania. *Amer. J. Sci.* 268:78–94.
Reed, W. W.
    1941.   Climates of the world. In *Climate and man. Yearbook of Agriculture.* U.S. Dept. Agr., Wash., D.C. pp. 665–84.
Restrepo, V.
    1960.   *Viajes de Lionel Wafer al Istmo Del Darién.* (Cuatro meses entre los indios) Traducidos y anotados. Bogota, 1888. No. 14, Panama. Imprenta de "La Academia" — 1960. No. 14 Publicaciones de la revista "Lotenia" + 1 de colofon.
Richards. P. W.
    1975.   Doomsday for the world's tropical rain forests. *Courier* 28:16–24 and 32.
Richardson, G. L.
    1966.   Eye lens weight as an indicator of age in the collared peccary (*Pecari tajacu*). M.S. Thesis, Univ. Ariz., Tucson. 47 pp.
Roberts, G. A.
    1921.   Rinderpest ("Peste bovina") in Brazil. *J. Amer. Vet. Med. Assoc.* 13:177–85.
Robinette, L.
    1958.   Unusual dentition in mule deer. *J. Mamm.* 38:156–57.
Robinette, L. and O. A. Olsen.
    1944.   Studies of productivity of mule deer in central Utah. *Trans. 9th N. Amer. Wildl. Conf.* pp. 156–61.

Röhl, E.
    1959.   *Fauna descriptiva de Venezuela*. Cuarta edición. Corregida
    y aumentada. Nuevas graficas. S.A. Madrid-España.
Roosevelt, T.
    1914.   *Through the Brazilian wilderness*. John Murray, London.
    374 pp.
Roots, A.
    1972.   Fringe-eared oryx digging for tubers in the Tsavo National
    Park (East). *E. Afr. Wildl. J.* 10:155-57.
Roots, C. G.
    1966.   Notes on the breeding of the white-lipped peccaries
    Tayassu albirostus at Dudley Zoo. *Intl. Zoo Yearbook* 6:198-99.
Ross, E. B.
    1978.   Food taboos, diet, and hunting strategy: the adaptation to
    animals in Amazon cultural ecology. *Current Anthropology* 19:1-36.
Rusconi, C.
    1930.   Las especies fosiles Argentinas de pecaries (Tayassuidae)
    y sus relaciones con las del Brasil y Norte America. *An. Mus.
    Nac. Hist. Nos "Bernardino Rivadavia"* 36:121-241. 18 pls.
Russell, F.
    1975.   *The Pima Indians*. Re-edition of 1904-1905 Twenty-Sixth
    Amer. Rept. Bur. Am. Ethnol. Introduction, citation and bibliog-
    raphy by Bernard L. Fontana. Univ. Ariz. Press, Tucson. 479 pp.
Salati, E. and P. B. Vose.
    1983.   Depletion of tropical rain forests. *Ambio* 12:67-71.
Samson, K. S. and B. R. Donaldson.
    1968.   Parasites of the javelina in New Mexico. *Bull. Wildl. Dis.
    Assoc.* 4:131.
Samuel, W. M. and W. A. Low.
    1970.   Parasites of the collared peccary from Texas. *Bull. Wildl.
    Dis. Assoc.* 6:16-23.
Santos, E.
    1945.   Entre O Gambá e O Macaco. 1945. In *Vide e costumes dos
    mamíferos do Brasil*. Desenhos de Marian Colonna. F. Briguiet
    and Cia. Rua do Ouvidor, 109. Rio de Janiero.
Schaller, G. B.
    1967.   *The deer and the tiger: a study of wildlife in India*. Univ.
    Chicago Press, Chicago. 370 pp.
Scheffer, V. B.
    1950.   Growth layers on the teeth of Pinnipedia as an indication
    of age. *Science* 112(2907):309-11.
Schenkel, R.
    1947.   Ausdruck-studien an Wolfen. *Behaviour* 1:81-129.
Scholander, P. F., R. Hock, V. Walters, F. Johnson, and L. Irving.

1950. Heat regulation in some arctic and tropical mammals and birds. *Biol. Bull.* 99:259–71.

Schulz, J. P., R. A. Mittermeir, and H. A. Reichart.
1977. Wildlife in Surinam. *Oryx* 14:133–44.

Schwartz, B. and J. E. Alicata.
1933. Description of two parasitic nematodes from the Texas peccary. (*Parostertagia heterospiculum,* new genus and new species described. *Parabronema* sp. and *Physocephalus sexalatus* recorded.) *Proc. U.S. Natl. Mus.* 82(15):1–6.

Schweinsburg, R. E.
1969. Social behavior of the collared peccary (*Pecari tajacu*) in the Tucson Mountains. Doctoral Dissertation, Univ. Ariz., Tucson. 115 pp.

———. 1971. The home range, movements and herd integrity of the collared peccary in southern Arizona. *J. Wildl. Manage.* 35:455–60.

Schweinsburg, R. E. and L. K. Sowls.
1972. Aggressive behavior and related phenomena in the collared peccary. *Zeit. Tierpsychol.* 30:132–45.

Scott, G.
1964. Rinderpest. *In* Brandley, C. A. and E. L. Jungherr, Eds., *Advances in veterinary science.* Academic Press, New York and London. 9:113–224.

Scott, W. B.
1913. *A history of land mammals in the Western Hemisphere.* The Macmillan Co., New York. 693 pp.

Seeger, A.
1981. *Nature and society in central Brazil: the Suya Indians of Mato Grosso.* Harvard Univ. Press, Cambridge. 278 pp.

Sellers, W. D. and R. H. Hill.
1974. *Arizona climate.* Univ. Ariz. Press, Tucson. 616 pp.

Seton, E. T.
1929. *Lives of game animals.* Volume 3, Part 2. Doubleday, Doran and Co., New York. pp. 720–43.

Shively, C. L.
1979. Digestion trials with the collared peccary *Tayassu tajacu* (L.). M.S. Thesis, Univ. Ariz., Tucson. 44 pp.

Short, L. L.
1975. *Zoogeographic analysis of the South American Chaco avifauna.* Bull. Amer. Mus. Nat. Hist. No. 154, Art. 3:164–352.

Simpson, G. G.
1941. Vernacular names of South American mammals. *J. Mamm.* 22:1–17.

———. 1945. *The principles of classification and a classification of mammals.* Bull. Amer. Mus. Nat. Hist. No. 85. 350 pp.

————. 1946. Bones in the brewery. *Nat. Hist.* 55:262.

————. 1949. A fossil deposit in a cave in St. Louis. *Amer. Mus. Novitates* No. 1408, pp. 1–47.

————. 1950. History of the fauna of Latin America. *Amer. Scient.* 38:361–89.

————. 1980. *Splendid isolation, the curious history of South American mammals.* Yale Univ. Press, New Haven. 266 pp.

Siskind, J.
    1973. *To hunt in the morning.* Oxford Press, New York. 214 pp.

Skinner, M. F.
    1942. *The fauna of Papago Springs Cove, Arizona, and a study of Stockoceros: with three new antilocaprines from Nebraska and Arizona.* Bull. Amer. Mus. Nat. Hist. No. 80, pp. 3–24.

Slaughter, B. H.
    1966. *Platygonus compressus* and associated fauna from the Laubach Cave of Texas. *Amer. Mid. Nat.* 74:475–94.

Smith, N. J. H.
    1976. Spotted cats and the Amazon skin trade. *Oryx* 13:362–71.
————. 1976. Utilization of game along Brazil's Transamazon highway. *Acta Amazonica* 6:455–66.

Smith, W. J.
    1977. *The behavior of communicating: an ethological approach.* Harvard Univ. Press, Cambridge. 545 pp.

Smith, N. S. and L. K. Sowls.
    1975. Fetal development of the collared peccary. *J. Mamm.* 56:619–25.

Smole, W. J.
    1976. *The Yanoama Indians, a cultural geography.* Univ. Texas Press, Austin. 272 pp.

Soares de Sousa, G.
    1587. *Tratado descriptivo do Brasil em 1587.* Brasiliana Serie 5^a Vol. 117.

Sowls, L. K.
    1961a. Gestation period of the collared peccary. *J. Mamm.* 42(3):425–26.

————. 1961b. Hunter check stations for collecting data on the collared peccary (*Pecari tajacu*). *Trans. 26th N. Amer. Wildl. Conf.* pp. 497–505.

————. 1965. Reproduction in the collared peccary, *Tayassu tajacu. J. Reprod. Fertil.* 9:371–72.

————. 1966. Reproduction in the collared peccary (*Tayassu tajacu*). *In* Rowlands, I. W., Ed., *Comparative biology of reproduction in mammals.* Zool. Soc. London. pp. 155–72.

————. 1974. Social behavior of the collared peccary, *Dicotyles tajacu* L. *In* Geist, V. and F. Walther, Eds. *The behaviour of ungulates and its relation to management.* IUCN. Morges, Switzerland. pp. 144–65.

————. 1975. The collared peccary. *Def. of Wildl.* 50(1):67–69.

————. 1978. Collared peccary. *In* Schmidt, J. L., and D. L. Gilbert, Eds. *Big game of North America, ecology and management.* Stackpole, Harrisburg, Penn. pp. 191–205.

————. In Press. *Ecology, behavior and status of the Chacoan peccary (Catagonus wagneri) or taguá in Paraguay.* Nat. Geog. Soc. Res. Rep. 19 pp.

Sowls, L. K., V. R. Smith, R. Jenness, R. E. Sloan, and E. Regehr. 1961. Chemical composition and physical properties of the milk of the collared peccary. *J. Mamm.* 42:245–51.

Sowls, L. K., N. S. Smith, D. W. Holtan, G. E. Moss, and L. Estergreen. 1976. Hormone levels and corpora lutea cell characteristics during gestation in the collared peccary. *Biol. Reprod.* 14:572–78.

Steiner, P. E. and H. L. Ratcliffe. 1968. The hepatic lobules of Suidae, Tayassuidae, and Hippopotamidae. *Anat. Rec.* 160:531–37.

Steward, J. 1948a. Western Tucanoan Tribes. *In* Steward, J. H., Ed. *Handbook of South American Indians.* Smith. Inst. Bur. Amer. Ethn. Bull. 143, pp. 737–48.

————. 1948b. The Witotoan Tribes. *In* Steward, J. H., Ed. *Handbook of South American Indians.* Smith. Inst. Bur. Amer. Ethn. Bull. 143, pp. 749–62.

Steward, J. and A. Métraux. 1948. The Peban Tribes. *In* Steward, J. H., Ed. *Handbook of South American Indians.* Smith. Inst. Bur. Amer. Ethn. Bull. 143, pp. 727–36.

Steward, J. H. and L. C. Faron. 1959. *Native peoples of South America.* McGraw-Hill, New York. 481 pp.

Stewart, J. A. 1964. The anatomy of the alimentary tract of the javelina *Tayassu tajacu.* M.S. Thesis, Univ. Ariz., Tucson. 31 pp.

Struhsaker, T. T. 1967. Auditory communications among vervet monkeys (*Cercopithecus aethiops*). *In* Altman, S. A., Ed. *Social communication among primates.* Univ. Chicago Press, Chicago. pp. 281–324.

Struve, J. 1911. Die perioden der Brunst bei Rinder, Schweinen und Pferden. Fuhlings Landwirtschaft. *Ztg. Jahrgang* 60:832–38.

Sumner, L. 1951. A biological survey of Saguaro National Monument. Unpub. Rept. Natl. Park Serv.

Supplee, V. C. 1981. The dynamics of collared peccary dispersion into available range. M.S. Thesis, Univ. Ariz., Tucson. 51 pp.

Swank, W. G.
    1958.   *The mule deer in Arizona chaparral.* Wildl. Bull. No. 3. Arizona Game and Fish Dept., Phoenix. 109 pp.
Symons, D.
    1978.   *Play and aggression, a study of Rhesus monkeys.* Columbia Univ. Press, New York. 246 pp.
Taylor, W. P. and W. B. Davis.
    1947.   *The mammals of Texas.* Bull. 27, Game, Fish and Oyster Comm., Austin. 79 pp.
Teixeira, H.
    1982.   The Amazon boom. *World Press Review* 29:30–32.
Teles, F. F. F.
    1977.   Nutrient analysis of prickly pear (*Opuntia ficus indica,* Linn). Doctoral Dissertation. Univ. Ariz., Tucson. 157 pp.
Tembrock, G.
    1968.   Communication in select groups: land mammals. *In* Sebeok, T. A., Ed. *Animal communication, techniques of study and results of research.* Indiana Univ. Press, Bloomington. pp. 338–405.
Tener, J. S.
    1965.   *Muskoxen in Canada: a biological and taxonomic review.* Canad. Wildl. Serv. Queen's Printers, Ottawa. 166 pp.
Terborgh, J. and R. A. Kiltie.
    (In Press). *Ecology and behavior of rain forest peccaries in Southwestern Peru.* Natl. Geog. Res. Repts. 19 pp.
Thornber, J. J. and A. E. Vinson.
    1911.   *Native cacti as emergency forage plants.* Univ. Ariz. Agric. Exp. Stat. Bull. 67, Tucson.
Tinbergen, N.
    1952.   Derived activities: Their causation, biological significance, origin and emancipation during evolution. *Quart. Rev. Biol.* 21:1–27.
    ———. 1961. *The herring gull's world: a study of the social behavior of birds.* Basic Books, New York. 255 pp.
Tipton, V. J. and E. Mendez.
    1966.   The fleas (Siphonaptera) of Panama. *In* Wenzel, R. L. and J. Tipton, Eds. *Ectoparasites of Panama.* Field Mus. Nat. Hist., Chicago. pp. 289–386.
Treutlein, T. E.
    1949.   *Pfefferkorn's description of the province of Sonora.* Univ. of New Mexico Press, Albuquerque. 329 pp.
Tyson, E.
    1683.   Anatomy of the Mexico musk hog. *Phil. Trans.* 13:(153): 359–85.
Ullrey, D. E., D. E. Becker, S. W. Terrill, and R. A. Notzold.
    1955.   Dietary levels of pantothenic acid and reproductive performance of female swine. *J. Nutr.* 57:401–15.

United States Department of Agriculture.
    1920. Farmers' Bull. 1072. U.S. Government Printing Office. Wash., D.C.
Van Pelt, A. F.
    1977. A mountain lion kill in southwest Texas. *The South. Nat.* 22:271.
Varona, L. S.
    1973. *Catálogo de los mamíferos vivientes y extinguidos de las Antillas.* Academia de Ciéncias de Cuba, Havana. 139 pp.
Wagley, C.
    1953. *Amazon town: a study of man in the tropics.* The Macmillan Co., New York. 305 pp.
Wagley, C. and E. Galvão.
    1948. The Tapirapé. *In* Steward, J. H., Ed. *Handbook of South American Indians.* Smith. Inst. Bur. Amer. Ethn. Bull. No. 143, pp. 167–78.
Walker, E. P., F. W. S. E. Hamlet, K. L. Lange, M. A. Davis, E. Uible, and P. F. Wright.
    1975. *Mammals of the World.* Johns Hopkins Univ. Press. 3rd Ed. Rev. by J. L. Paradiso. 2 Vols. 1497 pp.
Wallace, R. A.
    1979. *The ecology and evolution of animal behavior.* Goodyear Publ. Co., Santa Monica. 284 pp.
Walther, F.
    1968. *Verhalten der gazellen.* A. Ziemsen Verlag, Wittenberg.
    ————. 1974. Some reflections on expressive behaviour in combats and courtship of certain horned ungulates. *In* Geist, V. and F. Walther, Eds. *The behaviour of ungulates and its relation to management.* IUCN. Morges, Switzerland. pp. 56–98.
Walton, A.
    1960. Copulation and natural insemination. *In* Parkes, A. S., Ed. *Marshall's physiology of reproduction,* Vol. 1, Pt. 2, Longmans, Green, London. pp. 130–60.
Webb, S. D.
    1974. Chronology of Florida Pleistocene mammals. *In* Webb, S. D., Ed. *Pleistocene mammals of Florida.* Univ. Presses of Florida, Gainesville. pp. 5–31.
Webster, H.
    1942. *Taboo, a sociological study.* Stanford Univ. Press. 393 pp.
Weiss, G.
    1974. Campa cosmology. *In* Lyon, P. J., Ed. *Native South Americans, ethnology of the least known continent.* Little, Brown, Boston. pp. 251–66.
Werner, H. J., W. W. Dalquest, and J. H. Roberts.
    1952. Histology of the scent gland of the peccaries. *Anat. Rec.* 113:1:71–77.

Wetzel, R. M.
    1977.   The Chacoan peccary, Catagonus wagneri (Rusconi).
    Bull. Carneg. Mus. Nat. Hist. No. 3. 36 pp.

———.   1981a. The hidden Chacoan peccary. Carneg. Mag. 55:2:
    25–32.

———.   1981b. Comparison of the peccaries (Tayassuidae). Unpub.
    Ms. 9 pp.

Wetzel, R. M. and J. A. Crespo.
    1975.   Existencia de una tercera especie de pecari. (Fam. Tayas-
    suidae, Mammalia). En Argentina: Rev. Mus. Argent. de Ciencia
    Nat. "Bernardiono Rivadavia". Zool. 12:25–26.

Wetzel, R. M. and J. W. Lovett.
    1974.   A collection of mammals from the Chaco of Paraguay.
    Univ. Conn. Occas. Papers, Biol. Sci. Ser., 2:203–16.

Wetzel, R. M., R. E. Dubos, R. L. Martin, and P. Myers.
    1977.   Catagonus, an "extinct" peccary, alive in Paraguay.
    Science 189:379–81.

Whiffen, T.
    1915.   The northwest Amazon. Constable and Co., London. 319 pp.

Wilbert, J.
    1972.   Survivors of El Dorado, four Indian cultures of South
    America. Praeger, New York. 212 pp.

Wislocki, G. B.
    1931.   Notes on the female reproductive tract (ovaries, uterus
    and placenta) of the collared peccary (Pecari angulatus bangsi
    Goldman). J. Mamm. 12:143–49.

Woodburne, M. O.
    1968.   The cranial myology and osteology of Dicotyles tajacu,
    the collared peccary, and its bearing on classification. Memoirs
    of S. Calif. Acad. Sci. 7. 48 pp.

———.   1969a. Systematics, biogeography, and evolution of Cynorca
    and Dyseohyus (Tayassuidae). Bull. Amer. Mus. Nat. Hist. 141:
    2:271–356.

———.   1969b. A late Pleistocene occurrence of the collared peccary,
    Dicotyles tajacu, in Guatemala. J. Mamm. 50:121–25.

Young, S. P. and E. A. Goldman.
    1946.   The puma, mysterious American cat. The Amer. Wildl.
    Inst., Wash., D. C. 358 pp.

Zervanos, S. M.
    1972.   Thermoregulation and water relations of the collared
    peccary (Tayassu tajacu). Doctoral Dissertation. Ariz. State Univ.,
    Tempe. 160 pp.

_____. 1975. Seasonal effects of temperature on the respiratory metabolism of the collared peccary (*Tayassu tajacu*). *Comp. Biochem. Physiol.* 50A:365–71.

Zervanos, S. M. and G. I. Day.
1977.   Water and energy requirements of captive and free-living collared peccaries. *J. Wildl. Manage.* 41:527–32.

Zervanos, S. M. and N. F. Hadley.
1973. Adaptational biology and energy relationships of the collared peccary (*Tayassu tajacu*). *Ecology* 54: 759–74.

Zeuner, F. E.
1963.   *A history of domesticated animals.* Harper and Row, New York. 560 pp.

Zuckerman, S.
1953.   The breeding seasons of mammals in captivity. *Proc. Zoo. Soc. Lon.* 122(4):827–950.

Index

Abronia (sand verbena), 41
Acacia (acacia, catclaw), 32, 41, 82
Accidents, 92–93
Acclimation, 37. See also Metabolic rate; Temperature; Thermoregulation
Acorns, 41–42
Acromia sclerocarpa (palm), 42
Activity patterns: daily, 96–97; drinking, 43, 97–100; feeding, 43–44, 96–99; movements, 111, 149–150; seasonal, 97. See also Behavioral adaptations; Feeding; Shelter seeking; Standing watch; Thermoregulation
Adaptations, behavioral. See Behavioral adaptations
Adaptations, physiological. See Physiological adaptations
Aepyceros melampus (impala), 66
African swine fever. See Diseases and infections
Agave (agave, century plant), 31, 41–42, 73, 89, 98, 116, 197, lechuguilla, 41, 83; palmeri, 32–33, 53
Age determination, methods of: annulations of cementum in lower incisors, 66, 76–78, 80, 172–173; eye lens weight, 76; field observations, 75; game survey counts (hunter kills), 66, 76–81; tooth replacement (eruption) sequence, 66, 76–79; tooth wear patterns, 66, 76–79, 95; trap-release, 76–79

Age structure, 75–82. See also Age determination; Annual recruitment; Herds; Longevity; Reproduction; Survivorship Index

Aggression (aggressive behavior, aggressive meetings), 118–124, 151, 155, 173; biting, 173; butting, 122; charging, 173; chasing, 155; confusion with play, 131; ear flattening, 121; face-to-face "argument", 155; gape, 122; growling, 121; lunge, 122; nuzzling, 123; snarl, 121; sparring position, 121; squabbling, 19, 121–122, 173; tooth-chattering, 122, 135, 173; whirl-around, 173. See also Display; Dominance behavior; Ferocity; Fighting; Submission; Threat actions

Aggressive vocalizations, 112, 116–117, 135, 157, 160; barking, 114; chattering, 116; during feeding, 157; growling, 114, 116; grumbling, 116, 160–161; grunting, 116–117; snorting, 160; tooth-clicking, 116–117, 160; wheezing, 160. See also Alarm vocalizations

Alarm behavior, 133, 135
Alarm posture, 116

237